AF553373

Issues in Higher Education, Literature and English Language Teaching

(*Critical Essays & Research Articles*)

Issues in Higher Education, Literature and English Language Teaching

(*Critical Essays & Research Articles*)

T. C. Joseph
Associate Professor
S. G. M. College Kurkheda,
Gadchiroli (Dist.), Maharashtra

R. G. Munghate
Principal
S. G. M. College Kurkheda,
Gadchiroli (Dist.), Maharashtra
www.sgmunghatecollege.ac.in

Issues in Higher Education, Literature and English Language Teaching

Edition 2023

ISBN 978-93-87537-28-6

Published by:
CRESCENT PUBLISHING CORPORATION
4806/24, Mathur Lane,
Ansari Road, Darya Ganj,
New Delhi - 110 002
Ph.: 011 - 23244131
Mob.: + 91 - 9711991838, 9999021668
E-mail: crescentbook@gmail.com
Website: www.crescentpublishingcorp.weebly.com

Printed at:
Roshan Offset Printers
Delhi

Contents

B.Critical Writings on Literature

C. Facets of English Language Teaching / Learning

D. Articles on General Topics

Preface

This book composed of some 35 articles and research papers, and organized into four parts is born of a strong desire to share with the readers some useful insights into and observations on the rapidly changing higher educational scenario, and the English Language Teaching-Learning Methods. Most of the articles that appear here have been published earlier in conference proceedings or as research papers in journals. All these articles and research papers have been written over a long span of a decade or so. Some critical articles on literature and a few articles of general interest are also included in this collection which too are hoped to enlighten the avid readers on these topics. The reason behind the publishing of these articles as a single volume has been the persistent insistence and demand of our academic friends who wished all these papers to appear in a single volume rather than being scattered in numerous proceedings, periodicals or journals.

The author and the collaborator have been in the field of education for a considerably long period of time and closely watching the dramatic changes taking place in the field of education and teaching-learning methods. Despite some of the articles having been written a decade ago, their relevance has not so far diminished in any way. On reading them, one in all likelihood will feel their contemporary relevance in the same degree as they would at the time they had been written. No claim is made to absolute originality since many of the ideas and suggestions proffered here are likely to be discussed in several educational forums, proceedings, or journals and so the possibility of their having seeped unconsciously into the thought patterns of the writers cannot be denied. Nevertheless, the mode, the presentation, the reactions, and the verbal constructs are mostly original. Several insights are personal and are expected to stimulate further thinking in the readers. It is hoped that this book will provoke thinking, rouse the imagination, whet the intellect and excite the passions of the readers.

We would be delighted if the book serves its purpose and makes the readers sufficiently critical in these times of unprecedented and sometimes unwarranted changes which have made life highly complex and stressed. Rather than dancing attendance on all the whims and fancies of the change-crazy intellectuals and passively conceding to all that happens around by way of torrential changes, one should be wise enough to apply brakes of wisdom and curb the changes to suit the needs of the current and future generations without inflicting great damages on their psychic world. In a mad rush to embrace changes all too eagerly and unquestioningly, we should not connive at cultural erosions and attenuate the loss of values or even the time-tested methods. While coping with change that is inevitable we should be highly prudent in compromising things which we hold close to our hearts. Hence several premonitory warnings and vague fears are articulated here and there in the various critical articles in this book with special reference to education. At the same time, no hesitation is made in making a clarion call to bring about healthy changes wherever they are required to 're-engineer' our educational edifice so that it serves the stakeholders as best as it can, preparing our youth to cope with the contemporary realities and brace up for challenges of the future.

We hope the readers would appreciate the spirit and message of the book and overlook the lapses, if any, which might creep into it either by way of imperfect editing or lack of proper deliberation or hasty generalizations on our part.

Joseph. T. C.
R.G. Munghate

SECTION-A

QUALITY AND OTHER ISSUES IN HIGHER EDUCATION

1

Quality Enhancement: A Drive towards Professionalism

Introduction

Education is traditionally viewed as a deliberate effort to modify the natural impulses, instincts, talents or mental powers of an individual. It also aims at intellectual training, character formation, and the all-round, harmonious development of the personality of an individual. It encompasses the physical, mental, moral, and spiritual training and it strives to transform the individual into an integrated, balanced personality enabling him to live as a healthy member of society. It also emphasizes his socialization and seeks to prepare him for complete living with a vision and purpose. But training based on such general education did not succeed in offering higher standards of living for the vast majority in countries like India. On this score its relevance is currently challenged, and the changed circumstances of the 21st century force to reanimate and rebuild it with necessary curricular changes, quality enhancement, and professional thrust. Quality enhancement is a well-planned-out endeavour and a great drive towards professionalism.

The Need for Quality Enhancement

The mighty edifice of our educational system is being rocked to its very foundation by the recent chain of radical changes. Globalization unleashed violent transformation in the entire educational system. Liberalization and privatization accelerated the pace. Information and

Communication Technology (ICT) usurped into a dignified place in the educational system. Traditional disciplines have been eclipsed by the brilliance of the new-comers. Market economy demanded 'application-orientation, trans-disciplinarity and heterogeneity' in the skills. Vocationalization of education and job-oriented courses were greatly encouraged. Educational system had to prepare students to face internal and international competition. This was the scene soon after 1991. The current situation is not much different. Bertrand Russell's words (*New Hopes for a Changing World,* p.1) echo the current plight: "The present time is one in which the prevailing mood is a feeling of impotent perplexity". The new nerve-racking challenges necessitated 'quality enhancement' in all spheres of educational activity. This alone can properly solve the riddles of the new knowledge-driven society and make education relevant to the current economy.

All the sensitive educationists of our country are now actively involved in re-thinking, re-engineering and re-building the existing educational system so as to fortify it against the violent tides of changes as well as adapting to it. The changes have necessitated converting it to a system that suit the needs of the day and those called for by the market economy. Since the employability of a person hinges largely on the quality and relevance of the education he has received, concerted efforts have of late been made in enhancing the quality of all the parameters of our educational set-up. Preparing a suitable environment to enable the students to have easy access to various professions and careers has been the prime motive behind this drive. Our policy makers and educationists have now realized that education has to be so modified as to prepare the learners to live comfortably as income-earning members of the current skill-based, knowledge-based society. The best way to realize this is through enhancing the quality of the education imparted and the excellence in the respective areas of study.

What is Quality Enhancement?

Quality Enhancement is a comprehensive and holistic concept. It implies a continuous improvement in the value, utility, and efficiency of all the subjects of study and stakeholders of the educational system, and all the aspects of the structure, process and other parameters of our educational set-up. Excellence is the other side of the same coin. Quality enhancement strives to make net addition to the existing quality, value and usefulness through progressive measures and deliberate planning. This encompasses the numerous components of our educational edifice and all those who are associated with it. Quality enhancement increases the employability of the students and leads to personality development as well. It is intended to help them improve their standard of living as well. It is a conscious endeavour to make the best of any educational context. It calls for concerted and sustained efforts. Quality enhancement is the magical formula as well as the linchpin of the new educational paradigm. It is a catalyst that is hoped to transform education. Although this panacea sounds quite marvellous and simple, experience as well as perusal over it has revealed the complexity of the task, for quality will not easily seep into the various areas of the educational system which are highly insular and resistant to change.

Quality Enhancement and the Parameters of the Current Educational System

Quality enhancement is the conscious and continuous process of bringing about the desired and desirable changes in the existing pattern after a proper comparison with the standard practices of the best ones in the same field of activity. It requires co-ordinated and integrated efforts of all the persons and institutions associated with it. Quality enhancement is highly desirable. But its materialization is a Herculean task. Many factors or parameters of our educational system oppose the desirable changes to be brought about for quality enhancement. These factors often act as constraints and limit quality enhancement. They are briefly discussed below:-

1. The Policies of the Government and other Regulatory Bodies

The policies of the government and that of the regulatory bodies like the UGC and NAAC have a great bearing on the educational system and the materialization of quality enhancement. Of late, government has been highly indifferent to the expansion of general education on the ground that it was not job-oriented and that 25% to 30% of the state revenue was annually spent on education which did not actually result in much quality enhancement or development of skills and competencies. Higher education is now viewed as an unaffordable luxury. In order to reduce the burden on the state governments, it has to be fairly shared by the central government as well. Funding of higher education should not be the responsibility of states alone. If funding is equally shared, (because 'education' comes in the Concurrent List), higher education can be considerably fortified both in quantity and quality. Wealthiest nations are those with the highest level of higher education. It is 60% in the USA and Canada, and about 40% in most countries of Europe. But in India it is only 9% between the age group of 17-23. The growth of a good number of colleges in India, especially those in the rural areas, is thwarted by the adverse and hostile policies of the government and the regulatory bodies like the UGC. It has been pointed out that 95% of its resources are distributed among less than 5% of the national higher education institutions. The beneficiaries form only a minority. The vast majority of students are denied the benefits of improved quality education. Hence the existing colleges are to be liberally helped to improve the quality of their education for which much financial help must be offered.

2. The Policies of the Universities and the Nature of the Curriculum

The affiliated colleges depend on the universities for any curricular changes. Curriculum should be so devised by the universities as to be sufficiently flexible, progressive, and adaptable. It should offer choices for as many job-oriented subjects as possible. Any course of study offered in an Arts, Science, or Commerce college should have a job-oriented specialization in addition to the main subject of study. Every student has a right to live with the minimum required standard of living. This is possible only when the course of his study has a job-oriented subject and he acquires the necessary skills in that subject. The recent demand for such integrated courses stresses the quality expected of the curriculum. Compartmentalization between arts, science, or commerce also makes the system rigid and deprives a section. Interdisciplinary researches must be encouraged. As many universities are apathetic to such demands and remain unresponsive to such wise suggestions, recently a good number of colleges are trying for autonomy which would enable them to devise their own career-oriented, quality assuring curriculum embedding in them their vision as well as wisdom. Some have already experimented with the Choice Based Credit System, which allows for greater scoring to the more brilliant and more hardworking students. It is a bold step assuring higher quality in their education since it suits a purpose with high utility.

3. Infrastructure and Campus of the Institution

Quality education presupposes the existence and proper utilization of adequate infrastructural facilities – the college buildings with good class rooms, hostel facilities for far- off students, a considerably large library, a computer centre, science laboratories, language laboratory for English language learning, canteen facilities, etc. The campus must be large enough to accommodate various facilities including playgrounds for diverse games, sports, and other related activities of physical training. All these facilities together contribute greatly to quality education. In the absence of these, all-round development of the students is not possible.

4. Management and Governance

The role played by the management is pivotal in any institution of higher learning. Their policies, the objectives they set, the mode of implementation of various programmes, their vision, educational insight, tactful dealing with the faculty, staff and the Head of the institution, timely and judicious measures to step up quality, their willingness and eagerness to learn from other institutions of excellence, dynamism, readiness to help the academic staff for higher learning including research and skill-development courses, etc., go a long way in enhancing the quality of the institution.

5. Academic Community and their Commitment

The role played by the academic community is very crucial in imparting quality education. Teachers must be men of great learning and be fully dedicated. They should be equipped with the knowledge of advanced teaching technology. The 'matter' (content) of learning as well as the 'manner' (method) of teaching assumes vital significance. There are many scholarly teachers who fail to bring about the desired impact on the students. Only preparation and planning for teaching and the inspiring mode of presenting knowledge and skills will create lasting impressions on the students. A good teacher always establishes the necessary rapport with the students and displays great interest in their well-being and learning experience. He is hardworking and innovative and encourages students to participate in research activities. He should be a voracious reader avid for enriching and expanding the horizon of his knowledge. Otherwise, he will be disconcerted by what Goethe said: "There is nothing worse than a teacher who knows no more than what the students ought to know". Good teachers never die. They always live in the hearts of their students. Quality enhancement requires the availability and presence of such brilliant and hardworking teachers. Refresher, Orientation and Short Term Courses, seminars and conferences/ workshops can mould teachers to some extent as good teachers. They must update themselves with the latest knowledge and use the latest educational technology for better teaching.

6. Students, Parents, and the Local Society

Students occupy the centre stage in the drama of education. The whole educational system is basically meant for them. They are the customers of the educational service rendered at the HIEs. Students with more fertile brains and good self-discipline always have better chances of benefiting more from quality education. Less bright ones, through great effort, can stimulate their brain cells and emerge as quality products. Students should have a receptive and open-mind ready to be modified by the power of knowledge. It is good for them to ponder over S. Radhakrishnan's words: "For man to live means to give existence to the possible". Actualizing possibilities requires will-power and persistent effort. Quality education aims at realizing the full-potential of the individuals and it cannot be fully materialized if students are not co-operative. In the same way, parents also should play their own expected roles as stakeholders of education. They should be alert and sufficiently enlightened to involve in educational matters concerning their children. In rural areas where parents are not properly educated, quality enhancement cannot be easily achieved since they do not participate in 'parent-teachers' meeting' and do not motivate their children, nor do they give them timely corrections or advice on educational matters. The type of society from which students come to colleges also affects quality enhancement. If the society is progressive and modern, students will have better aptitude for learning and research activities. On the other hand, if the local society is conservative and backward, the students are also likely to be poorly motivated and remain apathetic towards studies. In such a background, realization of quality enhancement is no less than an uphill task.

7. Cultural and Socio-Economic Background

Quality enhancement is also affected by the cultural and socio-economic background of the students. Students with a good intellectual background can easily gain knowledge, but those with illiterate and ignorant backgrounds will have to strain every nerve for it, for they generally lack the aptitude for learning and remain alien to the processes of intellectual pursuits. This accounts to some extent for the low performance of students from backward and tribal belts. Attaining quality education in such rural areas is not an easy task. Poverty is yet another encumbrance. Poor children cannot perform as well as is expected of the rich children. Hunger distracts them from their studies. Gandhiji rightly observed: "Food is the music of the hungry." Hence education should be context-bound and culture-specific. There are many jobs which are to be performed only in the rural areas and require skills pertaining to their specific nature. Such subjects have to be incorporated into the curriculum. Extension services offered to rural areas should be increased. Literacy campaign should be emphasized in such areas.

8. Learning Resources (Library, computers, internet facility, laboratory, etc.)

The availability of modern learning resources and their optimal use determines the extent of quality enhancement in any HEI. Library is said to be the 'temple of learning'. A good library blessed with an abundant stock of different types of books, periodicals, web and digital resources is highly instrumental in enhancing the quality of education imparted in an HEI. Students should be encouraged the reading habit, browsing and research. Francis Bacon's words "Reading maketh a full man" are relevant even to this day. Books are treasure troves of knowledge and wisdom and so students must lavishly draw from them. Computers have become an integral part of modern education. Students can avail themselves of the vast ocean of information stored in computers and comes handy through the internet. Internet facility increases easy accessibility to knowledge from all parts of the world. CDs/DVDs of good quality collected from relevant sources will become attractive and efficient learning resources. Science labs and language labs help the students in enhancing quality in scientific and language studies through the relevant items and software. Quality enhancement calls for all these and many more related learning resources to be made easily available and judiciously used.

9. Quality Assessment and Accreditation

Quality assessment and accreditation boost the quality enhancement drive. The role played by the NAAC deserves special praise because it has ushered in an educational renaissance in India. In fact, it is with their assessment, accreditation, and post-accreditation initiatives that the great drive of quality enhancement for professionalism gathered momentum and attained great magnitude. They roused the higher educational institutions from their complacent slumber and opened their eyes to the reality of where they are and where they should reach in order that they assure for themselves survival and relevance. Theirs was a clarion call for quality enhancement and sustenance in all spheres of educational activity. Indirectly it was a great drive towards professionalism - to produce better and more professionals - teachers, managers, journalists, educationists, scientists, lawyers, administrators, etc.

Quality enhancement depends on the proper integration, combined efforts, judicious combinations, and necessary alterations of all the above-mentioned factors.

The Drive towards Professionalism

The term 'drive' implies big effort to achieve something by an institution, company or government. Professionalism stands for great skill and ability, especially those expected of the members of a profession. In short, quality enhancement is a great and conscious effort intended to develop great skill and ability in he students so as to enable them to have easy access to a profession or a job. This drive is a direct response to the demands of the market, globalization, and the consequent changed perception of education. Accordingly, education should not only impart knowledge, and inculcate values, or develop the intellect, but should empower the students to cope with the challenges of the modern world as well. It should enable them to face the economic and social realities, and ultimately help individuals attain higher living standards. Quality enhancement is thus an attempt to make education useful in life by developing quality and skills.

Quality enhancement and the quest for greater academic excellence, by their very nature, lead to professionalism in so far as it is a relentless effort to bring about a series of changes that assure greater and more desirable quality in the education provided, increased skill development, innovativeness, knowledge expansion, creation of greater ability in the beneficiaries, and above all, 'application-orientation'. The repeated insistence on 'trans-disciplinarity' or interdisciplinary research implies a large number of new cross-bred branches of knowledge culminating in greater knowledge explosion capable of answering to the needs of the new knowledge-based society. Students availing themselves of such quality education are expected to be more skilled, possessing greater ability, deeper need-based, diversified knowledge, increased critical faculties, an analytical frame of mind and research aptitude. All these, on closer study, reveal that the orientation of quality enhancement is towards professionalism.

Concluding Remarks

A careful examination of the recent educational reforms, the thrust on quality enhancement, the call to include more job-oriented courses by relevant changes in the curriculum, the stress on the fusion of various disciplines, the increased rate of new knowledge generation, the emphasis on inter-disciplinary research, refresher and orientation courses for teachers to increase their subject knowledge and skills in teaching, the repeated exhortation of the political leaders of the nation to impart quality and skills to students, India's position of being the second in the world for human resources and the same fact being our core competency reveal that quality enhancement is the pragmatic step, the current necessity, and a major drive towards professionalism.

References

1. Ross James, S (1942), *Groundwork of Educational Theory,* London: G. G. Harrap & Company Ltd.
2. Livingston Richard, W (1946), *Some Tasks for Education,* London: Oxford University Press
3. NAAC (2004) *Quality Higher Education and Sustainable Development: NAAC Decennial Lectures (1994-2004),* Bangalore: NAAC.
4. Russell Bertrand (1951) *New Hopes for a Changing World,* London: George Allen & Unwin Ltd.
5. Radhakrishnan, S (1955) *Recovery of Faith,* New York: Harper & Brothers Publishers.
6. Bacon Francis, *Of Studies* (from *Essays*)

2

Social Commitment of Higher Education and the Concept of Mass Education

Introduction

Amidst the clamours of violent changes which are fast re-orienting our educational system, there is heard every now and then the jarring and warning notes of some wary souls who are not fully convinced of the philosophy of such radical and drastic changes in the higher educational set-up. They have not seen sufficient substance in the new educational paradigm based on Information Technology, vocationalization and utility-orientation to justify it replace the old system. The main reason is that the new educational paradigm negates mass education.

It is true that the new type of educational alternative will help many individuals personally to get jobs and improve their standard of living. But then, this type of education is not holistic as the traditional education was. Traditional education, as we practised it till a decade or so ago, aimed at the all-round development of the individual. It was highly value-oriented and arts and humanities had had a dignified place in it to make better beings out of humans. Unlike the professional and vocational courses which were affordable only by the rich the general education in most of the higher educational institutions in India was cheap and affordable. It was easy for the general public and so was aimed at mass education. But the lack of social commitment by the teachers on account of rampant unionization of the teaching community and their lackadaisical nature adversely affected productivity, efficiency and quality. Hence the nation suffered immensely and the government came forward to rescue the general public by ensuring accountability of performance by all those being paid from the public funds and serving in granted colleges. The result was the several restrictive and qualitative measures the government adopted and the curb on mass education, which contributes apparently nothing to increase either productivity or to the Gross Domestic Product (GDP). But this move has far-reaching effects in an over-populated country like India.

The Need for Mass Education

India is the largest democracy in the world. The success of democracy hinges on educated masses. Only a high level of education can mould ideal citizens and thereby a successful democracy. The demand for mass education emerges on account of increasing population. Modern mass media have stirred in people escalating aspirations for a brighter future. People believe that it is possible only through higher education. They view education to be a passport to prosperity. Although at present our education is affected by the wave of inexorable changes sweeping our society, it should not deviate from its diverse goals like individual goal, social goal, knowledge goal, moral goal and vocational goal. The individual goal of education is to contribute to the personality development of the individual and make him/her self-reliant. On the contrary, the social goal is to provide education for socialization, citizenship, social efficiency and social service. The knowledge goal is related to the imparting and acquisition of relevant knowledge. The moral goal is aimed at formation of character. Vocational goal aims at the preparation of individuals for contributing to economic development and national wealth through productive employment. Mass education has all these goals except the vocational goal. As for the presently emerging mode of education, for all its claims, it has merely vocational goal and lacks in other goals. No doubt, it speaks a lot about knowledge and knowledge society. But, what kind of knowledge it favours is obvious – mostly technical and job-oriented. This is not a happy state of affairs void of repercussions.

First, knowledge of liberal arts, social sciences, and humanities are now relegated to the background. One should know that this knowledge is essential to make a good and wise human being. This knowledge is imperative to make good leaders, artists, historians, literary men, administrators, politicians, statesmen, economists, sociologists, anthropologists, psychologists, philosophers, and even good scientists. They all have their great relevance in society. We need, not merely computer operators, technicians and engineers, but poets, novelists, dramatists, essayists, and thinkers. These writers unravel the mysteries of the more complicated inner world of men than the inanimate and sub-human outer world. The modern education which is materialistic purely focuses on the phenomenal world and ignores the more important transcendental world of ideas and spiritual experience which men for thousands of years hugged as the true source of joy and solace. Mere economic aspect or vocational dimension will satisfy only one aspect of the complex human psyche. Unless and until all these aspects are duly taken care of, there will be tremendous inner disturbances for man leading to personality problems and shrinking of the inner man. Increased wealth will not solve these problems. In the mad rush to augment our national wealth and thereby increase the material wellbeing, we should not forfeit the enduring aspects of our mind and soul. If we do so, our society is likely to turn itself to a cesspool of callous, selfish, pleasure-seeking rich people with no penchant for moral and spiritual values or even humanity. The type of education we always need is holistic that takes into account all factors with a sense of proportion. This will make life 'fuller, richer and more meaningful'.

The main objection against mass education based on the traditional education is that it is not job-oriented. It is true indeed. But then, it is this same education that is capable of producing good citizens with civic consciousness, selflessness, concern for society, and the desire to serve society rather than getting a good job, and comfortably settling down to lead a life of ease and pleasure which contributes nothing to societal well-being.

The traditional education may not guarantee jobs to all except probably those who are exceptionally brilliant and talented. But the same education can assure all-round development of the personality with developed thinking power, critical insight, analytical powers, better moral sense and spiritual values with greater focus on the culture of the land and, in our case, the great Indian culture. Since this liberal mass education does not guarantee us the economic benefit of a job, if we are in a hurry to bury it, we shall be losers from all other points of view barring the economic. Being a member of society and having benefited from it, it behoves us to stand for it with a sense of social obligation.

Mass education is needed from another point of view also. We have (in 2006) nearly 300 universities, about 12000 colleges, more than 3.5 lakh teachers, and India has the second largest educational infrastructure in the world. But shockingly enough, only 6% to 7% of the students in the age-group of 18-23 have access to university education. This is really appalling when we compare it with the situation in the developed countries where 50% to 51% are getting university education. Again, only 1.5% pursues research in India whereas 10% to 15% do research in the advanced countries. When 6.5% GNP is the required investment rate on higher education, India spends only 3.5% of GNP. All these point to the need for spending more on mass education and encouraging more and more colleges and universities to be opened to meet this need. At the same time, the government must take stringent measures to make the courses economically useful as well.

India has the second richest human resources of over one billion people i.e., more than 16% of the world's population. Yet, it has failed to achieve high rates of human resource development because it did not make education sufficiently need-based by imparting skills, making investment in health, research and development. Education, no doubt, failed to empower people economically to lead an independent life. With the setting up of NAAC, quality ensuring measures have been stepped up. At the same time, it should not discourage mass education. It should only remedy the evils from which mass education has been ailing. State governments must also extend development grants to all colleges whether or not they are aided. It has been suggested that 50% of the development grants should go for infrastructure creation and maintenance, and the remaining 50% should be used as scholarship for meritorious students under socially and economically disadvantaged groups.

It is high time the rigid, watertight compartment system between arts and science be removed. In its stead, both should be fortified and empowered by job-oriented subjects. This will make an Integrated Course with a basic degree plus a job-oriented subject. The Liberal Arts and Science colleges should be allowed to start such Integrated Courses which would qualify a student with a basic degree along with a specialization in a subject that is highly job-oriented to secure jobs in future. The result will be human resource development of mid-level manpower which is in great demand. This solves the problem of mass education, and India can emerge in the imminent future as the most human resource rich country in the world.

Social Commitment of Higher Education

Being a 'social good' higher education is funded in India by the government. Hence the stakeholders of higher education ought to have public accountability or rather answerability and commitment to the society in general. The stake holders, who are but the students, teachers, parents, management, the government, etc, have their own rights and duties. These stakeholders together must ensure the quality of higher education.

i. Teachers

Teachers/lecturers must be men of vision, dedication, scholarship and hard work. Much more than a mere knowledge supplier, a lecturer now-a-days should be prepared to act as a trainer, facilitator, mender, guide, and counselor to the students. Lecturers are required to develop their competencies continuously to perform the tasks well in the changed times. Even for the survival of the organization such motivated, competent and hardworking teachers are imperative. Moreover, the students and society in general can gain only if the lecturers are competent and braced with the latest knowledge in their respective subjective areas. It necessitates qualitative training to be given to them. This should be a recurrent phenomenon and not a sporadic one. Universities have facilities for Refresher Courses, Orientation Courses, Short Term Courses, etc, to address this issue. Besides, teachers should actively participate in academic workshops, seminars and conferences at various levels. They must be stimulated to reach to the core of their subjects and mainstream issues with genuine interest. This increases their subject knowledge and can benefit the students. The various grants made available to the teaching community by the UGC for Major and Minor Research Projects are intended to spruce up their research aptitude and make contribution to the nation building process. Funds are also available from several research funding agencies. All these empower teachers professionally and in its turn will enable them to fulfill their social commitment. Commitment also demands punctuality, regular presence in the college and proper teaching, and finishing the portion of syllabus well in time, helping and inspiring the students for self study and library work, acting as role models and catalysts for students by being exemplary in behavior and character., academic excellence, sincerity and devotion to the task, with proper interaction with the students, showing readiness to help them at all times in all their problems, etc.

ii. Management

When a higher educational institution comes into being it should have sufficient justification for its existence by way of a *mission* and a *vision* that finally aims at social betterment. Thus, those who own and found such institutions owe society a deep commitment. Their mission and vision should be clearly articulated into long-term and short-term objectives. All their activities should aim at the materialization of these objectives. Their ulterior motives should not betray the expressed purpose. The members of the faculty should be properly consulted in articulating the vision and the mission, and in devising the various strategies for their actualization. Unless the members of the staff develop in them new competencies and skills, the objectives of the institution may not be fully achieved. It is the duty of the management to ensure that these requirements are fulfilled. The managements of educational institutions differ from those of other service institutions like banking, hospitals, insurance, etc. In educational institutions the managements have to tackle the intellectuals. Therefore, it is their duty to impart to them sufficient intellectual training and help them develop new competencies. Although it is the primary duty of the teachers themselves, yet they must be galvanized and goaded by the management so as to avert any possibility of an intellectual slumber by the teachers under the bower of safe and secure jobs. The managements must keep vigilance over the teachers to ensure that the teachers fulfill their commitment to society by way of research, innovation, social service, and other quality enhancing measures.

iii. Parents

Parents also have serious responsibilities as stakeholders of higher education. It is parents who make the educational investment of money on their children in the hope of human resource development and a bright future. Hence, they should not shy away from visiting the colleges occasionally where their children study. It behoves them to attend 'Parents Meetings' in the college. But many parents are ignorant and rely on the teachers to guide their children. This is not an entirely healthy practice. Here too teachers can offer help to the parents in effectively rearing their children. Classes should be arranged for them on child psychology, counselling, family life, sex-education, family planning, child rearing, personality development, etc. Such supportive training and leadership to parents and students by the teachers is part of their social commitment. Teachers can perform this duty for the betterment of society much better than anyone else since they occupy a respectable and influential position in Indian society. This should be a part of the social commitment of higher education.

v. Students

Responsive and receptive students with a keen desire for knowledge and motivated by a definite aim in life will make higher education fruitful. They should, as far as possible, refrain from activism and unnecessary political involvement. Such activities have recently clouded the educational ambience and it presents a dismal academic picture. Such students and the unmotivated ones alike will dampen the spirit of many a good teacher. This will inevitably ensue pedagogical lethargy and discouragement. The presence of brilliant students will necessitate teachers to brush up their knowledge and keep alive their reading and research tendencies. Hence students also must be aware of their social commitment as stakeholders of higher education.

Conclusion

To sum up, social commitment of higher education necessitates quality enhancement in every aspect of education as also an increase in fulfilling responsibilities towards society. For this purpose, mass education should not be discouraged in the name of lack of social commitment or economic usefulness. There are many immeasurable, invisible benefits stemming from mass education by way of an enlightened general public which is essential for the success and survival of a democratic society. As Dr. S. Radhakrishnan aptly remarked, "Man hungers and thirsts not only for bread, but for the bread of eternal life, for truth, beauty, goodness and holiness." So, let the teachers and other stakeholders of higher education be totally committed to society through their effective teaching and socially useful work since their payments come from the public funds which in turn are generated by the taxes paid by the general public - both the poor and the rich.

References

1. Patnaik, Prabhat (2004) *Quality Higher Education and Sustainable Development: The "Organic Intellectual"*, Quality Higher Education and Sustainable Development; NAAC Decennial Lectures (1994-2004). Bangalore: NAAC.
2. Tilak, Jandhyala B. G (1997) Human Capital for Development and the Development of Human Capital in India, "*Anvesak 27*" (1&2) (January- December).
3. Verma, J. S (2004) *Education, Sustainable development and Human Rights Approach*, Quality in Higher Education and Sustainable Development; NAAC Decennial Lectures (1994-2004). Bangalore: NAAC.
4. Perlmutter, H. V (1965) Towards a and Practice of Social Architecture: The Building of Indispensable Institutions. London: Tavistock.
5. Deshmukh, Snehalata (2004) *Quality Higher Education and Sustainable Development: Values and Educational Strategies*, Quality in Higher Education and Sustainable Development; NAAC Decennial Lectures (1994-2004). Bangalore: NAAC.
6. Pillai, Rajasekharan, V. N (2004) *Quality Higher Education and Sustainable Development: Freedom and Social Harmony*, Quality in Higher Education and Sustainable Development; NAAC Decennial Lectures (1994-2004). Bangalore: NAAC.

3

The Role of Students in Improving the Quality of Higher Education in India

Introduction

Students are the most important stakeholders of any educational system. This is particularly true in the case of higher education in which the principal beneficiaries are the students or learners themselves. The educational system is primarily meant for them and centred on them. So educationists point to the need for 'student-centric'/'learner-centric' education as a paradigm shift. Ironically enough, the students have traditionally been playing a less active role than has been expected of them. The changed circumstances can no longer brook this apathy. Based on the new educational paradigm with great thrust on quality enhancement, excellence, professionalism, job-orientation, transdisciplinarity, heterogeneity, equity, accessibility, moral and cultural values, etc., steady efforts are being made to re-engineer our higher educational edifice. Improving and sustaining quality in education has become the major concern today. Materialization of this goal presupposes concerted efforts by every stakeholder, particularly the students.

Being the most important stakeholders, students can no longer shy away from playing their crucial role. They are now exhorted especially by the NAAC to come forward and play their major role in improving the quality of higher education in India. They should no longer be complacent to remain as passive spectators of the educational drama, but rather assume their role boldly as the protagonists. It was with this purpose that the NAAC declared 2006 as the year of 'Students Participation in Quality Assurance' (SPQA), and drafted a 'Students' Charter' to be publicly displayed in every accredited HEI. Besides, the several seminars organized by the selected directors of the UGC-Academic Staff Colleges in collaboration with the NAAC in 2006, enabling students from several universities to participate in the discussion on 'Students' Participation in Quality Enhancement' (SPQE, and the NAAC Foundation Day International Conference on "Student Participation in Quality in Enhancement" organized at Bangalore on 16 & 17 Sept, 2006, have been major steps taken by the NAAC to emphasize the role of students in improving and assuring the quality of higher educational institutions in India. These and the subsequent activities of the NAAC were intended to empower students and infuse in them the necessary quality literacy which enables them play their decisive role in quality enhancement in every HEI in India.

Nature of the Students' Role

Students have a very responsible role to play in providing proper and judicious 'Students Feedback' on teaching-learning and other related activities. The feedback should be objective and given with utmost sincerity so that the institution can resort to appropriate follow-up action on the students' feedback. This can then lead to drastic changes in the teaching-learning activities. Every teacher will realize his comparative strengths and weaknesses and strive to do better by overcoming the lacunas. Naturally, this will result in improved academic outcomes, and the quality of teaching and the students' experience of learning will also be better.

The new provisions enable students to have their representatives in the IQAC. This increases transparency and the democratic spirit. Students can, thus, have their voice heard in the IQAC meetings and make valuable suggestions regarding planning, implementation and evaluation processes of the IQAC leading to an improvement in the over-all quality of the institutional performance.

Even when the students have a right to demand fulfilling the institution's responsibilities towards them as they are clearly written in the NAAC-'Students Charter', they have a simultaneous duty to fulfill in their responsibilities of learning as spelt out in the same Charter. Thus, the students should play their role in both the ways. They should know about the goals and objectives of the institution and realize what kinds of programmes are offered for the materialization of the same. They can expect the institution to offer them a wide range of programmes or courses with adequate flexibility.

The charter enables them to realize that the institution is bound to resort to occasional student feedback on the initiation, review and redesign of programmes, and several such other provisions. On the other hand, the charter insists that students shall help the institution in realizing the goals and objectives, and must have clear knowledge of the programmes, admission policies, rules and regulations of the institution. Students are required to undertake regular and intense study of learning materials and make optimal use of the learning resources, and other support services available in the institution, etc. Thus, the charter highlights their role by way of a series of responsibilities assigned to them. All these reveal that the students are partners in the educational system and have an important role to play.

It is heartening to note that the approach by the NAAC is highly proactive in including students in quality assurance activities recognizing them as the key element in quality assurance in higher education. The approach of the NAAC is 'Total Participation Approach', not just representational. This approach is both eclectic and an improvement over the internationally recognized approaches such as the 'Students Feedback Approach', the 'Students Rights Approach' and the 'Students Co-constructor Approach'. In short, when 'Total Participation Approach' is adopted, all the students have a serious role to play in improving the quality of the institution in which they are studying.

Complexity of the Role of Students in Quality Improvement

Quality is a subjective notion viewed and perceived by individuals from different perspectives conditioned by their own philosophy of life or peculiar psychology. People who are concerned with mere economic progress and mundane gains may view quality as a condition that prepares students with the necessary knowledge and skills to obtain a good job. This surely helps students get good salary, assures economic security adds to physical comforts and probably gives them a high-income status. But the greatest danger is that life is more complex than mere economic and physical aspects. When confronted with non-economic problems such as psychological, moral, spiritual, social problems, etc, these students are likely to be caught unawares and become deeply upset and may even commit suicide, for all their safe economic position.

This means that quality should be a much more comprehensive term with due emphasis on improvement in vital aspects of life and evince a sense of proportion while devising the curriculum which should aim at all-round development of personality as well as a broad outlook on life. Hence, every student in the HEIs should be wise enough to acquire as much knowledge as possible from numerous branches of knowledge - scientific, and humanitarian, physical and spiritual, moral and psychological, analytic and synthetic, thought-oriented and emotion-oriented, artistic and literary, so that every mental, physical, moral, and spiritual need can be fairly satisfied and the trials and tribulations which lurk in the unknown future can be faced boldly with fortitude and living itself becomes both meaningful and exciting.

Students need to be mature both emotionally and volitionally. This maturity will help them react to situations with a sense of balance and proportion and take decisions thoughtfully and judiciously. Any wrong decision taken can ruin a person's life. Volitional maturity helps a person take decisions sensibly and rationally. Emotional maturity helps him/her adjust to diverse situations. Students, who are to enter family life sooner or later, should prepare adequately to adjust with the partner hailing from a different cultural and social background. Hence only adaptability developed through emotional maturity can help a person lead a happy life. Thus, the long-run goal of preparation for life should not be lost sight of.

Every student should play the role of a voracious reader and fill the vessel of his/her mind with as much knowledge as possible and take part in the various activities and programmes arranged by the institution for personality development or for social benefit. They should adequately and simultaneously develop their 'individual self' as well as 'social self' to lead a healthy life befitting a civilized member of the society. College life gives them a golden chance to explore their subtle inner world and the complex external world. They should play the role of ideal students interested in research activities and eager to delve into the world of ideas and enjoy that adventure. Thus, students must make optimum use of the library and the web resources in the quest for greater level of knowledge. Computer literacy has now become an imperative need for both the teacher and the taught to download and put to good use the ocean of exploding knowledge stored in incredible degrees in numerous web-sites on the internet. This will be instrumental in boosting the quality of the stakeholders especially the students, teachers and the management, ultimately benefitting the institution.

Students should study systematically and prevent any 'leakage of time'. Time should not be frittered away in any idle pursuit of pleasures and in quenching libidinous appetites which mark subhuman trivialities. Students should also refrain from drug-abuse, activism, destructive activities, and inordinate involvement in party politics. It is high time they channelized their psychic energies for constructive purposes which prove individually and socially useful. There is a considerable degree of complexity in the role to be played by students towards the realization of quality improvement under the changed circumstances. Internal and international competition makes high demands on each and every student. They must opt for such programmes as would ensure the students jobs in future, on the one hand, and enable them to imbibe such necessary values as would make life meaningful, on the other. These require them to learn quite a good number of skills needed by the working place and at the same time acquire knowledge and emotional intelligence to become healthy members of society. Some of the necessary skills to be acquired are leadership skills, planning skills, logical thinking skills, problem solving skills, self-learning skills, vision-building skills, time-management skills, linguistic skills, decision-making skills, creativity and innovation skills, analytical skills, communication skills, team-work skills, execution skills, adaptability skills, scientific and reasoning skills, etc. But at the same time, students should be rooted in their culture and strive hard to uphold and preserve the richness and greatness of that culture.

In the case of Indian students who have inherited a rich and varied cultural heritage, they must learn about the diverse aspects and greatness of that culture and promote it as true citizens of the country. Otherwise, the fast pervading evil aspects of the western culture of consumerism and materialism and the mere outward glitter of material prosperity will wipe out the core spiritual values we have been nourished by for thousands of years. Spiritual emptiness and moral anarchy will cause crimes and social problems to multiply. Newspapers abound these days in reports of anti-social and anti-human activities. Mass media, especially the TV channels, mobile phones and lurid magazines have been contaminating young minds and unleashing the dark, evil forces of the unplumbed depths of the human psyche, often resulting in fanaticism, terrorism, sex-crimes and other anti-social activities.

Students should make proper use of the counseling facilities available in the HEIs and be imbued with nobler aspirations to make earth a better place for the fellow-beings and for future generations. They should also take help from the Career Guidance Cell to get good placement. To play the role of a good student is to realize all-round quality improvement of the institution and of themselves, besides being partners of the nation-building activities for which they should assume the role of responsible citizens. They should have a thirst for social justice and regard for egalitarian values. They must develop compassion for the misery of the poor and the suffering millions. Securing jobs for themselves and retiring to the comforts of their economic cocoon is unbecoming of them as human and moral beings. They are also expected to preserve the integrity of their selves and walk on the path of truth, if our education is to create a better society and a better morrow.

Conclusion

Globalization, privatization, liberalization and ICT have brought in tremendous changes in our educational system. We are reshaping our educational system to approximate it to global standards and international demands. Quality enhancement is a major step towards it. Students among other stakeholders of education are assigned a key role, a participatory role to play. But true quality improvement is both internal and external. Mere job-orientation is not enough. Students have to be ideal and play the complex role they are supposed to as voracious readers, partners in decision-making, implementation and evaluation, and as participants in all those programmes intended for their personality development, character-building, intellectual training, and finally, for the good name of the institution itself. It would be commendable on their part if they strain every nerve to transcend man-made barriers and mere economic concerns and be conscious of the manifold burning issues of life itself. Such a complex role admirably played will make them true quality students and turn their institutions exemplary with a comprehensive vision and a noble mission. This alone will nourish and benefit Indian society in the long run!

References

1. Kuppuswamy Rao K and Jagannath Patil, (2004) *Best Practices in Student Support and Progression,* Best Practices in Higher Education, Bangalore: National Assessment and Accreditation Council.
2. NAAC (2006), *Internal Quality Assurance Cell Activities,* Bangalore: National Assessment and Accreditation Council.
3. NAAC (2007), *Student Feedback and Participation: Case Presentations, Bangalore: NAAC.*
4. NAAC (2004) *Quality Higher Education and Sustainable Development,* Bangalore: National Assessment and Accreditation Council.

4

Reaccreditation Process as a Retrospective Evaluation Exercise of the Quest for Quality Sustenance and Enhancement

Abstract:

Reaccreditation of HEIs is an occasion for evaluating their concerted effort in the previous five or more years. It gives them a chance to see where they stand on the pedestal of quality, and helps them retrospectively view the degree of sincere labour they have put into the cause of quality enhancement in their institution and think as to what more can be done to attain to a higher status. Reaccreditation presupposes well-planned genuine work and preparation to receive the deserving certificate. A lot can be done in the seven criteria/key areas identified by the NAAC. Both quality enhancement and quality sustenance should go hand in hand to fare upwards on the ladder of institutional growth. Quality Sustenance implies maintaining the high level of quality achieved. For this purpose technological up-gradation and innovative practices, consistent quality enhancing activities are essential. In this paper the author has focused on the various activities to be undertaken by every aspiring institution preparing for reaccreditation to both enhance and sustain quality. Since "Teaching, Learning and Evaluation" is given the highest weightage by the NAAC that aspect is given greater focus in this paper also.

Introduction

Gales of changes have been sweeping the academic institutions, particularly the HEIs, across the length and width of India, ever since the NAAC started accrediting the academic institutions of the country. With the thrust on quality, excellence, equity, access, etc, the NACC gave a new direction and a fillip to the academic institutions so as to enable them to be braced up in the globalized era to face both external and internal competition which is likely to pose a grave threat to their very existence. This clarion call was intended to shake and rouse our educational institutions which were in a deep slumber of apathy and curricular decadence. The institutions realized, though slowly, to their great horror, the lurking dangers of globalization (though not without bright prospects), and their necessity to strive hard to forge ahead with the times, the dire need to re-engineer the whole educational set up, and also to enable students to be employable in the present rapidly changing world with all its stark realities. Soon they prepared themselves for accreditation, and after five years every accredited institution is now to opt for reaccreditation if the certification is to remain valid for another five years. This implies that five years of toil and relentless preparation is to be followed by yet another five years and to be repeated in that order ahead till another directive comes from the NAAC.

The changes that have now come over the colleges and other institutions are quite unbelievable. But there is neither a full stop nor any respite to this intense activity focused on realizing quality enhancement. The high level of quality achieved in too short a period is to be sustained, and that is the most difficult thing about it. For this, unremitting industry is called for. Not only that, fine planning, vision, imagination, periodic revaluation of the policies, sensing the lacunae in the institution and building on the strengths are of utmost significance. These are broadly spread over seven areas corresponding to the seven criteria/ aspects as identified by the NAAC. In a way, every reaccreditation process is a golden chance for the HEIs to make a retrospective evaluation of their quest for quality sustenance and quality enhancement. It gives them also a chance to realize the deeper implications of their efforts and to know where they stand. Their self-estimation may be at variance with that of the assessment made by the NAAC-Peer Team or it may be in close approximation. In either case, whether or not they are contented, they can move ahead with renewed vigour, if the attitude is positive and self-corrective. Both quality enhancement and quality sustenance should go hand in hand. Sustenance of quality requires technology up-gradation and consistency in quality enhancement activities It is a dynamic concept and not a static one. After reaching a certain level of quality it has to be maintained and augmented so as not to retrograde. This paper looks into some of the serious quality issues for a deeper consideration so that they may be given due emphasis in the reaccreditation phase.

Focus on Learner-Centred Education – The Paradigm Shift

The reaccreditation phase should be marked by a shift in educational paradigm, from teacher-centred to learner-centred education. After all, educational institutions should stand for the cause of students. Their all-round personality growth, skills development, character formation, and intellectual training are the bounden duties of the educational institutions. Very often the stake holders of HEIs ignore many of these aspects. Their ulterior motives in starting educational institutions are sometimes mere profit, fame, self-glory, and self aggrandizement. Students and their welfare are to be found nowhere in their priority list. The activities which go on in the institutions run by such people, speak volumes to attest to the veracity of this observation. Quality education aims at preparing students to become socially responsible, responsive, and politically alert. If democracy is to become a success in a country like India the citizens have got to become eternally vigilant, civic-conscious and sensitized. Only quality education only can produce such citizens from the raw materials of ignorant and irresponsive students. If students don't seem to be responding to the classes and facilities offered in an institution, the root cause of that malady must be sociologically or psychologically explored. Numerous traditional, cultural, economic, sociological, psychological, political, and regional causes may be at work to bring about this 'cumulative causation' paralyzing the very purpose of our educational institutions. The growing absenteeism and drop-out rates are all indicative of this malady.

Mechanism for obtaining students' feedback and to take effective actions based on that feedback is necessary. Counselling Cells and Grievance Redressal cells have to be active. If experts are not available in the institution, they must be invited from outside for occasional guidance. The adolescents and adult students face many psychological problems. They are in fact baffled by the vastness and complexities of the world growing within and without. Their psycho-sexual problems and doubts haunt their minds and gnaw at their peace. Their egos now fully swollen do make them truckle to conventions and customs. The resultant restlessness make them unable to sit in the class for long and they prefer to idle away their time outside the classroom for peace of mind. This situation has to be understood by the educational practitioners. They should not insult them nor bore them. On the contrary, they should light-heartedly and humorously make learning a delightful experience. They should interact with them and share their own youthful experiences with empathy to reassure them and make them realize there is nothing wrong with them. This will boost their self-confidence. Also the NSS activities should be so devised as to make leaders out of them. Service will help them escape from the grips of their egos and they feel greatly relieved. Again, they begin to become socially acceptable members of society. When they are loved by society they begin to feel their existence has a meaning and naturally become self-contented. Education should actualize this. Moreover, training them to have various life skills and job skills will ensure economic security through guaranteed jobs.

In learner-centred education, students are made to involve in several activities. They are helped to become self-learners. The teacher's role is that of a counsellor, guide, needs analyst and friend. Gone are the days of the dogmatic, dictatorial teachers who tormented the students through their dull lectures and peremptory instructions. This redefinition of the teacher's role makes teaching-learning activity technology-assisted and tasks-based. Long and tedious lectures are no more welcomed and students go to the computers and browse the internet for detailed information of their topics to be studied. Numerous are the web-sites offering additional materials to students for further study. The various packages available, the utilization of the well-equipped computer assisted language laboratory, the use of CD ROMs, DVDs, etc., in addition to the books and periodicals available in the library make learning less teacher-dependant and more of self-regulated one. An advanced student should thus be guided by the teacher to develop his metacognition—the way he self-regulates his studies. What is more, now there is another trend slowly being ushered in. The centre of educational activity is currently not the teacher, nor the student, but learning itself. But co-operative effort from the teacher and the student leads to real learning. HEIs should create the suitable facilities and environment for this leaning to take place by redirecting the teachers and reorienting the learners. Identifying learner needs and acing accordingly is of paramount import in the changed circumstances of the day if learners are to benefit. Introduction of job-oriented certificate courses, diploma courses, computer classes, and encouraging folk arts and folk music will help students display their special skills. Courses in Spoken English, Communicative English, and Functional English will help the aspiring learners. In addition to vocationalization of education, transdisciplinarity is also highly stressed nowadays. Management Studies, Administration, Computer Applications, newly emerging hybrid sciences like bio-technology, bio-chemistry, etc at post graduate levels will prove highly job-oriented. Above all, giving inspiration to undergraduate students to have depth in their chosen subjects is of immense value in that their pursuit of post graduate studies will be easier and interesting. No doubt, teacher has a missionary role here to play in guiding and inspiring the students.

Evaluation must also be modified based on the curricular changes brought about from time to time. Objective and oral questions as well as solving original problems which require much thinking skill have to be included for a better examination system. The evaluation patterns have to be free from all sorts of malpractices if students have to take to serious studies. Otherwise, the whole pattern will be self-defeating with students having good marks on paper and no quality substance in their minds. Such students will be misfits for jobs; if at all they get jobs they will only spoil the next generation, through their own loose moral activities. Malpractices adopted in order to have short-term benefits will have long-term 'backwash effects' on society. So it is suicidal and must be got rid of at the earliest viewed from moral and cultural perspectives.

Other Key Areas of Quality Sustenance and Enhancement

a) Library and Learning Resources

A well-furnished library with a considerably large collection of books (the collection depending on the needs of the students and befitting the locality of the institution) periodicals, CDs, DVDs, with internet facility preferably with NRC will help students make their learning process easier and interesting. Library is "a temple of learning". It is not merely a treasure house of knowledge but one that is capable of changing the destinies of people if properly made use of. Library research should be made a part of the normal syllabus so that students will take to research activities with greater ease and love at a later stage. Library has to be digitalized in course of time. Book Bank Scheme and Inter-library Borrowing must be initiated and sustained properly. Books should be well categorized, with sub-categories and placed in perfect order. Books should bear Accession Numbers so that books can be easily accessed by students and research scholars. Students should not be permitted to keep the books back in the racks or shelves but the librarian or his assistant should do it lest misplacing should take place. Students should be allowed to select the books they like and sit and read in the allotted place for reading. The library should benefit the students at any cost. Librarian should be a voracious reader and a bibliophile himself so that he has the due reverence for books to preserve them well. Periodicals have to be preserved for future research in back-volumes. Libraries should be kept clean and neat with several ventilators for fresh air to circulate properly. In addition to the regular bookshelves/cupboards, they should have their own notice boards, periodical-stands, racks, tables, chairs, desks, computers, printers, reprography, catalogues and power-backing systems. It should be sufficiently lighted. Every year an adequate number of new arrivals by way of books and periodicals is necessary to replenish the library. The carpet are of the library should be in proportion to the size of the college. There should be perfect silence in the library for undisturbed intellectual pursuits. In many libraries there is neither order nor any system. This will adversely affect their accreditation.

b) Infrastructural Expansion

Since quality education requires all those facilities which would ensure easy and effective learning process, good infrastructural facilities are necessary if not essential. For in the absence of quality staff, students cannot hope to get much from the imposing buildings and impressive classrooms. There are instances where even in the absence of mighty infrastructural facilities students had acquired astonishing levels of scholarship and amazing degrees of intellectual developments. We can remember our ancient '*gurukul*' system of high quality education in India and the minimal facilities which produced some of the greatest scholars and thinkers of all time in ancient Greece, namely, Socrates, Plato and Aristotle. Hence we can safely infer that given other essential conditions, infrastructural facilities can contribute greatly to enhance quality. Strong, spacious and beautiful buildings with attractive and well-furnished classrooms that are bedecked with teaching aids, comfortable seating arrangements, fans, air-conditioners etc can make students feel comfortable and make them divest themselves of distractions. The advanced countries have such institutions galore. But we have a dearth of them and in the competitive world of today it behoves us to make available such facilities to our students too in order that they will not be lured away from us through such facilities provided by others. If the institution has a large number of students, they do require large buildings; if they have a huge collection of books, they need large library buildings. Further, they need good playgrounds and sports fields. Institutions waiting to be accredited must make provisions for hostel facilities for students, sports buildings, infirmaries, vehicle parking, and residence for the staff, drinking water facilities, toilets, water coolers, canteens, students centres, indoor courts, science labs, language labs, students' resting rooms, gymnasia, video conferencing halls, store-rooms, stationery stores, easy mobility and other facilities for the physically challenged etc, so that students' welfare and conveniences can be increased considerably.

c) Research, Consultancy and Extension

In the research field much can be done if the faculty members focus on M. Phil, PhD, and Post Doctoral Studies, not from career advancement view point alone, but from the research culture, from the thirst for more knowledge, from the impulse of creativity, from sheer curiosity and academic disinterestedness. Many standard colleges have PhD and M. Phil Sections in several departments of the institution. It should become a habit for teachers to write books and publish them, get articles published in magazines and periodicals of regional, national and international level circulation having ISSN/ ISBN numbers. Further, research papers in journals, and full papers published in proceedings of national, and international level seminars/conferences, etc are of great value. Participation and paper presentation in conferences also go a long way in this effort. Articles in news papers, chapters written for books, fully self-authored books, Minor and Major Research Projects etc, reveal the research culture of the staff. The more such activities the college engages in and encourages, the better is going to be the quality indication. Moreover, extension activities such as being the chief guest at functions, being the resource person for various classes or programmes, or anchoring the programmes, etc are also expected of teachers. Consultancy services can be offered by faculty members of science, technology, commerce, management, administration, computer science streams, but arts streams do not have much scope in this area. N.S.S activities have to be well-planned and seriously conducted. These activities surely help the students to become service-minded, patriotic, self-confident, selfless, and mould themselves as the future leaders of the nation.

d) Student Support and Progression

Proper documentation of students who left the institution, or were drop-outs, went for higher studies, got employed, etc should be done over years to reveal student support and progression on the part of the institution. An active Alumni Association, their feedback, valuable suggestions, sharing of experience, participation in the activities of the college, moral and financial support, etc are of invaluable assistance to the development of the college. Former students in fact are in a better position to point out what the society expects of the institution and what the latest changes are in the employment market, and so what the college should do for the present and future generations.

e) Governance and Leadership

Though quality teachers are the boon of the college, yet proper utilization, guidance and harnessing of the talent depends on the management. Good management discerns the talent of the teachers and uses them optimally for not only teaching activities but also for all those activities which contribute to the good name and development of the college. Leadership should come from the management in quality related activities. All the future plans of the college should be properly envisioned, a prospective plan should be drafted and faithfully implemented, periodically revised and revalued. Good governance makes the institution grow enviously. Governance should be done with transparency and through democratic processes of discussion and dialogues rather than on autocratic lines. Synergy is better than one-sided decisions. Cordial relationship with the staff, timely appreciation of good work done by the staff and corrective steps taken are all indicative of good governance.

f) Innovative Practices

The search for efficiency and quality enhancement should lead to identifying the lacunae and discovering the strengths. In both cases modifications and welcoming changes should be brought about. These lead to innovative practices. The very question: "What can be done to get rid of this problem/ overcome this weakness?" will lead to surprising solutions and unexpected discoveries. Or "In what way more can be built on the strengths and make them more efficient and competitive?" will help new ways and means to increase quality and efficiency. Innovative practices and best practices should be identified and properly recorded for both accreditation and reaccreditation. Such practices can be followed in any of the thrust areas identified by the NAAC.

Conclusion

Reaccreditation Process is quite strenuous and taxing but amply rewarding. It is an occasion to revalue the achievements and identify the constraints of the five years' period after the previous accreditation. But one feels greatly satisfied at the laudable level of achievements made if and when such a retrospective evaluation is done. It also gives a chance to enlist the numerous useful activities that can be done in future. Also one comes to know where one stands after five years of quest for quality enhancement. Sustenance of quality calls for technology up-gradation and introduction of more useful plans consistently. There should be no room, nor time, for complacency!

References

1. Pillai, Latha B. R. Manjunath, and Wahidul Hasan (Editors) (2006) *Community Engagement – Case Presentations*, Bangalore: NAAC.
2. NAAC, *Great Institutions of Higher Learning- Accredited Colleges in India* (Vol. I) (2005), Bangalore: NAAC.
3. Pradhan Ashok, Antony Stella, and Jagannath Patil (Reporters) (2004), *State-wise Analysis of Accreditation Reports – Maharashtra,* Bangalore: NAAC.
4. Pathan, S. N. (2005), *Quality Improvement Programme in Higher Education through NAAC,* Bhopal: Intellectual Book Bureau.
5. Singh. S. P (Ed.) (2001), *Profiles of Affiliated Colleges,* Amritsar: Guru Nanak Dev University.

5

Role of Governance, Leadership and Management in Quality Enhancement in Higher Educational Institutions

Introduction

Quality enhancement is the outcome of a deliberately initiated process sustained over a long period of time. It is also a continuous process requiring careful planning, proper execution and timely evaluation. Quality enhancement implies that certain benchmarks are identified, definite and achievable goals are set and steady efforts are made in that direction bringing about positive and desirable changes. But who will initiate such a process? Who are responsible for quality enhancement? In a way, all the stakeholders of higher education are. But, on closer examination, it becomes clear that it is the management that is most responsible for the proper governance and efficient leadership that ultimately brings about the quality enhancement. For, under a passive and nonchalant management that cares for only its own financial benefits, fame (often unscrupulously maneuvered), and wielding of power over its employees, other stakeholders, however brilliant they may be, might not put in their best to harbinger greater quality. Hence the managements of higher education (if not all, the vast majority) badly needs a second birth, a psychological birth, with better attitudes, proper value systems, noble objectives, sufficient awareness about the latest changes in the educational arena, and sublime visions to elevate our educational system to exalted heights. The role of the management, their leadership and governance, is crucial in bringing about an educational revolution in India along the lines envisioned by the UGC and the NAAC. This paper makes an attempt to explore some of the implications of the topic in question.

Role of Governance of Higher Educational Institutions

Higher Educational institutions are governed either by the bodies appointed by the government or those constituted by the private management. In either case educational goals can be attained only if governance is along the right lines. How should educational institutions be governed is a long debated topic. Governance, in democratic countries like India, should be based on democratic principles like equality, freedom, fraternity, transparency, discussion, persuasion, human dignity, etc. Democratic process is not one-sided nor is it dictatorial. It is all inclusive. This implies that educational institutions should resort to such governance as will involve all the stakeholders in its various processes and activities. Decisions should not be taken unilaterally by the top management and imposed on the rest of the faculty or staff. Decisions should be taken after proper deliberations with the faculty and staff, and, if necessary, with other stakeholders like the students, parents and the representatives of the local society. The reason is that all the stakeholders have a voice, a say in the matter, and the right to get the benefit of proper education and the management has the duty to ensure the provision of the same.

Education is not a charity done by the management, as many frequently claim. Parents and students pay for it by way of fees; the governments pay for it lavishly by way of salary and non-salary grants and even scholarships and freeships. Such amounts come from the taxes paid by the people at large. Hence the management has a social accountability to anything they do in the field of education. That is why they should not take decisions at their sweet will or based on their whims and fancies and then impose on those below. All their decisions in educational matters need not be right or good for the society. Sometimes they are merely to serve their expediency. That the management runs the institutions does not entitle them to tyrannize over the employees. What they can do is to run the institution based on the democratic principles mentioned above. Exhortation, persuasion and discussions should be their weapons in governance. It should not be one of revenge and retaliation as it occasionally happens here and there.

They should not resort to secretive policies and hide things from the faculty and the staff. On the other hand, transparency should be the policy and the stakeholders have to be apprised of all that happens in the institution. The reason is that government is funding the institution and so the stakeholders have a right to know how the institution is run. They should come out of their feudalistic mentality and embrace the modern democratic spirit. They should update themselves with the latest knowledge pertaining to the changes taking place in the educational arena. Or else, they will lag behind in this competitive world of today and will be the losers in the game, even as others forge ahead at an unimaginable speed. The faculty and the staff have to be treated with an egalitarian mentality. The talents of the faculty and the staff should be optimally used by the management for the proper running of the institution and in imparting the best quality education. Their talents should be utilized in taking mature and wise decisions. When the management is on the right track, teachers can be asked to be hardworking, sincere, and devoted for providing the best education possible within the constraints. Nay, they should ensure it through eternal vigilance, right policies and timely decisions.

Significance of Leadership in HEIs

Educational leadership is given by the UGC and NAAC or such bodies of higher education and also by the management - both private and government. In all these cases, only proper leadership can take education on to elevated planes and meet the myriad of challenges of the day and that of the students. Whoever gives the leadership should always bear in mind the true meaning of education. The education that merely prepares the youth to live in the modern world is not education, in the true sense. Under the western and especially the American influence our educational system is so modified nowadays as to be a replica of the western system. We should not for a moment forget that education should so fashion the youth that they become true human beings with compassion, love of mankind, desire for service, selflessness, dedication to the cause of the nation by refraining from malpractices such as corruption, favouritism, nepotism, exploitation of the poor to enrich themselves, and so on. Education should liberate the individual from all such subhuman trivialities. S. Radhakrishnan wisely exhorted, "We must rise from the animal to the human and from the human to the divine levels". This transcendence in our existence should be worked out through education which is the 'dynamic side of philosophy'. Further, the aim of education is not bringing about sudden material prosperity. This prosperity bereft of the development of the human side will only turn us into epicureans and neo-barbarians given to the pursuit of wealth and sensual pleasures. We have already seen this phenomenon taking place in India where the new the members of the generation with the new educational training are reluctant to take care of their parents, care a hang for the poor and the deprived in society, and are on the look out for quick money by hook or by crook, despite unprecedented material progress. So, what we need is the harmonious development of all the good aspects of an individual such as his psychic potentialities, his spiritual core, his physical side, and his artistic and cultural sides. Indian education should help preserve the Indian culture – I mean to say the noblest side of our cultural heritage. Our educational leadership should consider this very seriously.

Richard Livingston, (sometime President of the Corpus Christie College, Oxford), rightly remarked: "One of the important tasks of education is to break the stronghold of the 'present' on the human minds". Aren't we too much preoccupied with the present and its problems ignoring the vast past and the immense knowledge of the past? Livingston further pointed out that intellectual training, character formation, love and appreciation for the noblest and best in human civilization, preparing the youth to live in the modern world, bringing out the best in every individual, creation of a thirst for moral values, appreciation of the best achievements of the past, creation of a broad outlook, pursuit of truth etc, are some of the important tasks before education. The curriculum should comprise all these. The current education as modified recently is repelling the students from humanities and arts subjects. What is more! Students have greatly shunned even the pure science subjects. The consequences will be dreadful. Research activities of pure science will shrink, naturally; running away from humanities and Social Sciences is running away from life itself, from the collective wisdom of the past and the noble artistic pursuits of yore. Mere employability is no guarantee for the birth of good human beings. Those in higher positions of leadership should be scholars of the first-rate to avert all possible calamities for the future generation of India and to us, too. Numerous are the factors to be considered in education, not just one or two. Speaking of the great institutions of higher learning in his introductory remark, Prof. V. S. Prasad, the former Director of NAAC, observes: "The institutions presented here have distinguished themselves as performing colleges for learner development; enhancement of social access to higher education; nation building through extension programmes for community development; advancement of research; and promotion of collaboration with national and overseas agencies. They have been agents to reach a large body of youth in the country who are shaped in the most impressionable age to develop sensitivity to quality in intellectual attainment; to assume roles as responsible citizens and leaders to determine the destiny of the country; and acquire a cultural identity and values, which bridge tradition and modernity." (Prasad, p.2, 2005)

Coming to leadership by the managements of the higher educational institutions in the private sector, it is to be underscored that they have a crucial to play. They should ensure that quality education, in the true sense of the term, is provided to the students. They should be pioneers of desirable changes in the educational institutions. Their vision and the objectives of their societies should be translated into reality through well-planned activities and programmes. They should have an action plan that is to be implemented within a time-frame. The management should be the inspiring leaders to the other stake holders in different directions of quality hitherto unexplored. Their enthusiasm should be so infectious as to inspire others to catch up with them. But very often this does not happen. They themselves are neither good leaders of quality enhancement nor are they ideals to be emulated. Leadership should be in academic, extra-curricular and co-curricular matters as well as in social responsibilities. Others naturally are bound to follow their leadership. But this does not, more often than not, happen. Hence management should relinquish their single window perspective of mere economic benefit from the institution and become real altruists in the matter of proper leadership as it is a matter of social indebtedness. If quality is to seep in they should identify the areas of quality enhancement and give proper guidance and leadership in those directions.

The Key Role to be played by the Management

If the changes expected by the NAAC and the UGC should take place in HEIs, neither the teachers nor the Principals can bring them about in isolation. What the other stakeholders need is the wholehearted co-operation and moral support from the management. If the management is an enlightened body keeping abreast of the times, then the work of the co-ordinator and other IQAC members is very easy. Otherwise, it is very difficult to go ahead with the plan of the accreditation or reaccreditation work. Lot many contradictions will mar the process. Co-ordinators will have sleepless nights. The main problem is that generally managements have not yet understood the central role the IQAC has to play in any college. They just consider it as any other cells and marginalize its role. This weakens the purpose of the IQAC under which everything has to gravitate in an institution. "To make quality assurance mechanism an integral part of the education system and at the same time to attain academic excellence, it is expected that the Higher Education Institutions establish the IQAC." (*Internal Quality Assurance Cell Activities*, p.3) The mere attempt of the management to just form a name's sake IQAC and showing everything in paper will not bring about the democratic decentralized process of administration and quality enhancement as NAAC envisions. The main reason for this situation is that management as well as the principal fear that they lose their power if IQAC norms are followed. But here also the principal has nothing to lose since he himself is the Chairperson of the IQAC. But this remains a riddle and coordinators struggle between the faculty and the principal. This is the situation prevailing in many an institution. Hence the first step the management has to do is to establish a really functioning IQAC with all the members as insisted by the NAAC and call frequent meetings and function as per the rules laid down by the NAAC. This will automatically help the institutions march along the path of progress. The next step is to do the accreditation/ reaccreditation process in time with the synergy of all the stakeholders. The reason is that "The process of accreditation is just one step, but a significant one in the march towards quality - a point of institutional introspection (the self-study report) and external evaluation (the peer team visit and report). The NAAC realizes that to fulfill its mandate of assuring the quality of higher education in India, it has to go beyond the mere conduct of the process of accreditation." (NAAC...2004, p. i)

The management must ensure that the best faculty members are appointed in the institution. The merit of the candidates should precede pecuniary considerations. Otherwise, mediocre hands will occupy responsible positions and baulk every effort at progress. Commercialization of education is the bane of the day. Money rules the roost. Donations of the rich candidates jeer at the merits of the poor. This aggravates the situation and makes a mockery of education. The society consequently suffers. People lose faith in moral values and heave a helpless sigh of frustration. Therefore, the management must sense the pulse of the general public and become ready to change lest they should bring upon themselves the ire of the general public.

The management should see to it that students are given quality education at any cost. Since it is education that empowers the youth it should go for real quality and genuine result and not the fabricated fancy results achieved through malpractices in the examinations. Giving tacit consent to students to copy answers during the exams tantamount to a theft – a kind of intellectual theft. This helps the management to project their institutions as ones with good academic performance. But this glossy outward picture will crumble to dust when the general public and the students eventually become the losers after being educated from such institutions. How can students with such manipulated merit certificates perform well in the interviews? They turn losers, unless they overcome the hurdles with donations which once again only the rich can afford. Hence under no circumstances, the management should compromise quality with quantity and malpractices.

Good managements always keep vigil over the educational processes going on in their institutions. They should ensure that classes are properly taken, exams are duly and properly conducted, answer papers are duly checked, actions are taken on feedbacks, modern teaching technology is adopted, teachers update themselves and actively involve in research activities, etc. Apathetic and diffident teachers or other indolent members of the staff are to be warned of punitive action and goaded into action for the benefit of the students. Every member has to put in the labour for the payment he receives. Otherwise it is a sheer waste of public wealth and the society will retrogress. Construction of good infrastructure, making available good libraries, modern gymnasia, spacious playgrounds, provisions for commodious reading rooms and cozy rest rooms, canteens, halls, co-operative stores, and such facilities is the duty of the managements.

They should frequently plan, implement and evaluate, through agencies like the IQACs, the future course of events of the institution and bring about timely changes to adapt themselves with the needs of the times. They should make 'needs-analysis' and effect necessary changes in the curricular areas to help the students prepare themselves for their future. It is basically the management that should ensure that benchmarking takes place periodically. "In order to be applied to education, benchmarking may be seen as an ongoing systematic means for determining the best practices of the best-in-class institutions and using the information as basis for goals, strategies and implementation. More simply best practices benchmarking for quality enhancement would be 'finding and implementing the best practices which would lead to significant improvement in the quality of educational provisions'." (*Best Practices...*, p.3). Managements, in short, ensure that their students are productive members of society and that they fare well in life through the education they receive from their institutions. This done, everything is O. K.

Conclusion

Quality enhancement is a positive and desirable change in the direction of excellence. It is the outcome of conscious effort by the various stakeholders. The conscious effort is properly directed by the wisdom of efficient governance, excellent leadership and imaginative management with a vision and mission. It is the duty of the management to bring about the synergy of other stakeholders to achieve progress of the institution and ensure a bright future for the students. Dedication of the management, faculty, the staff and co-operation by the students can bring about quality enhancement. But unless concerted efforts are put in, everything will remain a fluid idea and education a farce, a white elephant that drains the wealth of the nation!

References

1. NAAC, *Best Practice Series: Internal Quality Assurance Cell Activities,* Bangalore: 2006.
2. Prasad, V. S., *Great Institutions of Higher Learning, Accredited Colleges in India* (Vol.1, 2002-2004), NAAC, Bangalore: 2005.
3. Stella Antony & V. S Prasad, *Best Practices in Higher Education,* NAAC, Bangalore: 2004.
4. Prasad, V. S *State-wise Analysis of Accreditation Reports – Maharashtra,* Foreword, NAAC, Bangalore: 2004.
5. Livingston Richard, *Some Tasks for Education,* London: Oxford University Press, 1978.
6. Radhakrishnan, S, *Spirit of Religion,* New Delhi: Jaika Publishers, 1980.

6

Absenteeism among College Students: Some Causative Factors

Absenteeism among college students has now emerged as a tricky proposition assuming gigantic proportions at an alarming rate. The magnitude of this problem can no longer be treated as an isolated phenomenon confined to a particular geographical area alone. Rather, it is an ominous, pandemic canker capable of wilting and withering the mighty tree of higher education. Before it plunges the whole educational system into the quagmire of an impasse, we should see to it that this problem is sufficiently tamed. It entails a close scrutiny of the various factors that engender this problem and devising some strategies to counter it. The subtle nature of absenteeism can be probed well through an examination of the exogenous and endogenous factors involved in it. No doubt, absenteeism is a "cumulative causation" brought about by the interaction of these two sets of factors.

(A) Exogenous Factors:

These originate from outside the students. These are partly responsible for making the one time full-class rooms now near empty. It is not because of the fall in admissions but due to the absenteeism of students. It is as though some mysterious forces are now luring away our students. Numerous are the exogenous factors which repel students from classrooms. I would like to deal with the more important ones briefly:-

1 **Monotonous and Ill-informed Curricular Transaction**: Students in colleges are very often disgusted with the prosaic and stereotyped mode of curricular transaction or rather the dull mode of teaching the prescribed syllabus. Teachers very often teach in a mechanical way bereft of any vivacity. Many are neither enthusiastic about their teaching nor sincere. Again, geed many teachers do not have the required level of knowledge. They fail to impress the students and capture their attention. The result is that most students bunk the classes and move furtively after things more fascinating. Here the teachers are to blame for the problem.

2 **Time-worn Teaching Methodology:** Most teachers follow the traditional lecture method-no doubt, an excellent method if teachers have oratorical skills, wonderful verbal mastery and laudable subject knowledge. But it is the most boring and timeworn method if teachers lack the above qualities. Witnessing teachers fumbling after words and stammering in the absence of sufficient subject knowledge is a deplorable experience. Such a situation is an insult to the imagination and artistic sensibility of the students. Their intellectual curiosity also will remain unquenched. Students, in such situation, would opt to remain outside the classroom. The old methodology is undemocratic since it treats students like passive, dump listeners. But, this teacher-centered teaching has to be replaced by student-centred teaching which allow for free interaction with teacher and hence democratic in method. Co-operative learning/ participatory learning/ group learning is proving to be better.

3 **Lack of Job- Orientation of the Academic Programmes Offered**: Pure science subject and subjects of the arts stream lack career orientation. Students who complete these courses do not generally have any employability unless further higher studies are pursued with

missionary zeal and manage in scoring reality high marks. Most students who are but mediocre get upset with this notion and so choose to idle away their time outside the classes and view degrees only as status symbols in society.

4 **Unenlightened Teachers:** As Goethe said: "There is nothing worse than a teacher who knows no more than what the students ought to know" Students expect the teachers to have considerable depth in the subjects being taught. When this expectation is not fulfilled, they bid adieu to the classrooms, numerous are the teachers who have sneaked into the sublime field of teaching unfair means and possess no genuine quality, of required skills. Constant reading and continuous upgrading of knowledge is an integral part of teaching profession. Teacher's when lack wit and wisdom, are not accepted by the students. But they turn out to be mere laughing-stocks, from whom they do prefer to stay away.

5 **Globalization and Related Factors**: Globalization has set in an unprecedented period of accelerated change, which has a telling effect on the students. "A dynamic society" as Jawaharlal Nehru aptly remarked, "produces tension in the individual as well as in society". Changes are taking place at an unprecedented rate in all walks of life. Students are absolutely baffled by these changes. They begin to doubt whether their painful effort at learning well fetch them any fruitful job in future. This doubt drains away their interest in studies and prompts them to indulge in pleasures outside the classrooms. Hence their frequent absence from classrooms.

6 **The Role Played by Mass Media and ICT**: Students are tremendously influenced by the mass media such as newspapers, magazines and periodicals, the film, T.V, mobile phones, computer and the internet. Films and film stars have a marked influence on their

character, way of thinking and behavior patterns, so also those programmes which appear on the T.V. screens. The various unhealthy but interesting programmes, very often pandering to the low testes and stimulating sexual feeling, available through cable and satellite television do enchant the students much more than anything else in the classrooms and campuses to hold them back. I. C. T., with its internet and websites does play a crucial role to replace the teacher and spur the students to flee from classes. Many students find solace in the songs and talks, messages and photos in mobile phones.

7 **Cultural and Family Background of Students**: These have a lot to so with their aptitude for studies. Students from some cultures seem to be more interested in studies than those from others. Family background is another important exogenous factor. Students with educated and intellectual backgrounds are inclined to study hard and enjoy deep cerebrations. Those from uneducated and rural backgrounds generally evince less interest in studies. These students tend to remain absent frequently. Besides, students from broken families are less inclined to studies than those from healthy families. The former are deeply disturbed and unable to focus on studies whereas the latter with their serene minds can easily take to deep studies.

8 **Drug-Abuse, Alcoholism, Romantic Love, Pleasure-seeking Nature, etc**: Many students who fall easy victims to the trap of the drug mafia. Once they taste drugs, it is very difficult to bring them back to normalcy and they will find it hard to sit in the classes. There are also numerous students who bunk classes and find pleasure in alcoholism. Again, the youth is a period of romantic love and partner hunting. Much attention is occupied by these activities as well as other pleasure seeking activities such as partying, visiting nightclubs, etc. All these activities pull the college students back from classes.

9 **Availability of Numerous Guides on Texts, and Tuition Classes**: Markets are flooded with study materials and guides. Students have easy access to them and they rely on them heavily. This reduces teacher dependence in the classrooms. Before the exams they mug up whatever is written in the guides and pass the exams. Hence students feel that they can save the time listening to the dull lectures of teachers. The saved time simply means absence from classes. Mushrooming tuition centres also attract students through result-oriented coaching classes, which they probably value more than the regular classes in colleges

10 **Agricultural Activities**: Students in the rural areas have to take part in agricultural operations to help their families. Hence during the cropping and harvesting seasons they refrain from attending classes.

11 **Poverty, Unemployment and Family Burdens**: These also act as adverse factors leading to absenteeism among students.

12 **Absenteeism among Teachers**: This acts as dampener to aspiring students. Students who expect good and regular classes feel frustrated if teachers themselves go frequently on leave.

13 **Involvement of Students in Party Politics**: This often is a major reason in many universities for absenteeism of students. These students dance attendance on the whims and hidden agendas of the political leaders. Therefore they miss many classes.

14 **Cyber-cafes and Internet Browsing:** These entrap many students into sensational websites to which they soon get addicted. The cases of several students who visit such cafes and delight in pornographic websites or even watching blue films have been reported in several newspapers.

15 **Excess Pocket Money being Gifted by the *Nouve Riche* Parents:** Excess pocket money in the hands of students tempt them to have recourse to many a forbidden pleasure. This becomes habitual after a while and they bunk classes or become truants. The upstart parents are to blame for pumping so much money into the pockets of their children just to show- off and vie with other rich students.

16 **Loss of Moral and Spiritual Values**: Materialism, consumerism, etc, are mesmerizing many a student to follow a way of life in tune with their caprice. Consequently, students care a hang for the time tested moral and spiritual values and lead a bohemian life of unbridled pleasures.

17 **Fashion Mania and Passionate Age**: Fashion crazy young students also pay more attention to their clothes and appearances than their studies of even attending classes. The passionate period of youth also carry them away.

(B) Endogenous Factors

The second major set of causes of absenteeism can be traced to endogenous factors (i, e. those originating from the mind of students themselves). The inner world of the students themselves is of equal significance as the outside world. Some such major factors leading to absenteeism are as follows.

1) **The Pangs of Adolescence and the Throes of Youth**: The adolescence is near its end when students join college. This period is one of serious psychological implications for the students. They are really baffled by the fast growing inner world and stunned by the expanding horizons of the outside world. It is a painful period of confusion. When they join colleges they have the hangover of this period having just crossed and begin to feel the travails of the new period of youth ushering in. These cause a lot of tension and inner

conflicts resulting in restlessness which urges them to escape the dreariness of regular classes.

2) **Psychological Needs:** Youth is a period when students long for fulfilling the harrowing psychological needs such as (i) the need to love and to be loved (ii) the need for acceptance and recognition (iii) the need for attention (iv) the need for new experience (v) the need for adventure (vi) the need to satisfy aesthetic and artistic urges (vii) the need for self-actualization, etc. They are always on the lookout for satisfying these needs. If right channels are not available or accessible they will turn to the wrong ones, knowingly or unknowingly. For them fulfilling these needs are no less important than mere academic pursuits. They resist excess discipline, which is repugnant to their turbulent inner nature. Therefore, these violent urges from within often compel them to be absentees in colleges and seek fulfillment outside or elsewhere.

3) **Thirst for Knowledge**: Youth do have powerful thirst for knowledge, but often when lecturers do not prove to have enough knowledge, or when impart knowledge in a dull manner, these highly aspiring young folk, feel disillusioned and turn hesitant to be guided by the half- educated charlatans. Some turn to libraries, some to guides, and some others to coaching classes. The result is absence from classes.

4) **Susceptibility to Romantic Love**: A period when the love and attention of the opposite sex matters more than anything else, falling in love and enjoying the thrills of love experience prove to be more exhilarating than the boredom within the four walls of the class room.

5) **Libidinal Appetites or Strong Sexual Urges**: It is a period when the students are tucked about by the violent sexual emotions. These biological urges and psychological forces frequently torment their minds,

and the expression of these, further, complicates the issue. Therefore, they have to self-manage all these diverse, disturbing facts of life. Occasional disappearances from classrooms could be attributed to sex related activities such as romantic love, philandering and just friendship with the opposite sex as an outlet for these violent passions.

6) **Ambition, High Expectations from Teachers Disillusionment, etc**: The fire of ambition generally kindles youth. They long to reach high positions in life. They also expect much from lecturers and educational institutions when their expectations are not fulfilled and ambition is thwarted, they will be frustrated. The resultant disillusionment discourages them to attend classes regularly.

7) **Prejudices and Preconceived Notions:** The youth enter educational institutions with several prejudices about the subjects, teachers and institution itself. These affect their future dealings and studies. These distort reality leading to disappointment. Hence they often remain absent in classes. The other important psychological factors or rather endogenous factors leading to absenteeism among college students are lack of good mood to attend the classes caused by guilt-feelings, inferiority complex restlessness, and emotional problems caused by strained relationships, tension, strains, stress, fatigue, feelings of insecurity and uncertainty, lack of self-confidence, self doubt, stage-fright, confusion, lack of rational development, loneliness, lack of volitional and emotional maturity, etc. All these factors that rob the students of favourable a mental condition to sit in the class for long. No wonder the inner storm hurl them out.

Conclusion & Recommendations

If teachers understand the students well and become friendly with them, it is a long step to attract them to classes.

Much more than a friend, philosopher and guide, the teacher must be a brother, sister, father or a mother to these students, though such roles are recently pointed out to be risky for the teachers. If teachers are prudent and vigilant any good role can be played within safe limits. Teacher's love will win them back to classes. Teachers need to have psychological insight and genuine love for students. Further, the classes have to be extremely interesting and informative. Learning experience should be pleasant and rewarding. No students will then bunk classes. Counseling session should guide the students well and guard them against possible drug abuse or alcoholism. Infrastructure facilities, good and attractive campuses, modern and effective teaching methodologies, plenty of cultural and entertainment programmes, co-curricular and extra activities, personality development programmes, judicious use of multimedia package for teaching learning experience, interactive classes, co-operative learning, use of discussion method, brain storming sessions, debates, seminars, assignments, etc, will also enhance learning experience and attract the students to classes. Moreover, plenty of career-oriented certificate and diploma courses should be introduced to ensure students' employability. The backgrounds of students have to be studied through personal interactions. Students' feedback should be sought occasionally to improve curricular transaction. Hostel, canteen facilities, etc, need to be arranged. Awareness programmes have to be conducted on several important matters. The inclusion of practical exams along with theory paper for all faculties will force students to stay back in classes. The use of mobile phones inside the campus should be prohibited. Long-term objectives of education have to be stressed. Moral and spiritual values must be inculcated through value education. All these steps will prove beneficial in countering absenteeism.

References

1. Kuppuswamy, B (2007). *Advanced Educational Psychology*, New Delhi: Sterling Publishers Private Limited.

2. Weiten, Wayne and Margaret A. Lloyd (2007). *Psychology Applied to Modern Life: Adjustment in the 21st Century,* New Delhi: Cengage Learning India Private Limited.
3. Finley, Guy (1998) *Freedom From Negative Thoughts,* Delhi: Pusthak Mahal
4. Hurlock, Elizabeth B (1981), *Developmental Psychology: A Life-Span Approach,* New Delhi: Tata McGraw-Hill education Private Limited.
5. Goleman, Daniel (1998), *Working with Emotional Intelligence,* London: Bloomsbury Publishing Plc.
6. Murphy, Joseph (1997) *The Power of your Subconscious Mind,* New Delhi: Replika Press Pvt. Ltd.

7

A Post Accreditation Review of Accredited Institutions for Sustaining the Quality Education

Spurred by globalization, privatization and liberalization the Indian education scenario has given the greatest thrust on 'quality' as the single most important factor to enable our educational system to withstand the internal and international competition. Quality, excellence and utility are identified to be the hallmarks of any good educational system for its survival against the forces of globalization which are governed by market forces of demand and supply. Rightly did the NAAC stress these hallmarks to be essential for educational advancement. In a country like India with a huge human resource potential only high quality higher education can actualize the potential, and convert the vast population into a "core competency" for India as Hon. A. P.J. Abdul Kalam pointed out recently. Such conversion will make India one of the richest nations in the world in terms of human resources, with a rich reservoir of scientists, engineers, technicians, and other professionals.

What does Quality Imply?

'Quality' is a highly subjective term. But in H.E.Is quality nowadays implies equipping the students with all the required values, skills, and professional requirements in order to enable them to secure the jobs which will assure them a comfortable and decent life with a reasonable standard of living. Quality assures job competency and personality development. It furnishes the students with up-to-date information and sufficient knowledge in the different fields of study. It is not mere acquisition of knowledge, but acquiring more professional skills and job competency.

Quality is betterment in all areas of activity. It is a holistic concept. It is a positive improvement in all areas of educational activity as far as higher education is concerned. In a complex phenomenon like education, and especially higher education quality implies desirable changes in the infrastructure, management and administration, teaching and nonteaching staff, teaching, learning and evaluation activities, extension and research activities, curricular and extracurricular aspects, student support and progression, etc.

The desirable changes are such that they aim at steady improvement and focus on excellence and utility. Everything is expected to rise to the internationally accepted standards and even excel them. This necessitates incessant progressive activities in all parameters of higher education, and all stake holders should be mentally and physically braced up for the strenuous efforts expected of them. Educational system has to be modernized with judicious use of Information Technology. It must retain and renovate all that is traditionally held to be valuable and useful. Realization of quality requires identifying the benchmarks for best practices which the NAAC has done quite admirably and the process has, of late, gained momentum. These benchmarks or standards serve as yardsticks for all to emulate and implement. Those slow to act will have to pay a high price in the competitive world, and lethargy will inevitably invite one's doom, in the globalized situation. Concerted efforts, quick decisions and immediate implementation will accelerate the pace of progress and lead to marvelous achievement. Those with sharp innovating brains, initiative, and industrious nature stand to gain and those with apathetic attitude and status quo maintaining approach will be losers.

Post Accreditation Review of Accredited Institution for Sustaining the Quality Education

The vast majority of accredited institutions had taken the call by NAAC for accreditation and assessment quite seriously and rose from their slumber and worked day and night, and brought drastic changes in all aspects of the institutions they run. They also realized that in the changed circumstances our H. E. Is should adapt themselves to the current situation. This enabled them to follow the guidelines given by the NAAC and forge ahead in that direction. Most of them keep themselves busy sustaining the rate of improvement they have brought about, or rather the level of quality, they have achieved. For better grading in accreditation they have to document whatever good work they have done in infrastructural growth, teaching learning activities, or academic performance, or management and administration.

The Higher Educational Institutions (HEIs) now proffer a very interesting scenario as each institution is busy to excel the neighboring ones. They are keen on bringing about several new inventive and desirable changes in all areas of activity. This has made the academicians and managers think continuously about one aspect or the other for betterment in terms of quality. This manifests itself in the modernization, expansion and modification of the buildings, campus, library facilities, computer centers, hostel facilities, residence for teachers, better sports equipments and their installation, etc. Many institutions have now several activities in their agenda which make the academic year fully busy and time is hardly wasted. Several conferences, seminars, workshops, debates, symposia, quiz contests, talks, N.S.S.& N.C.C. camp, celebration of festivals and inauguration of associations such as literary associations and nature clubs, study tours, picnics, women's study centre activities, population study cells, celebration of important days, remedial teaching, best practices etc. keep the staff and management totally preoccupied in addition to the regular work done. Many colleges keep on introducing job oriented courses to increase the course utility. All these activities aim at making education complex, meaningful activity imparting to the stake holders a greater level of experience, better utility and thereby higher quality. Initial objections and licentious murmurs against accreditation is subsiding and the majority are marching ahead for post accreditation, having met the fate with resignation. All-round accelerated, progressive actions with a view to attaining higher quality level in education make our H.E.Is now internationally competent, although the number is not as yet very large.

Challenges and Constraints

There are many H.E.Is which got accredited fairly well. But for the quality level they acquired at the time of accreditation, they had to finance themselves and remained in the hope of securing grant from the U.G.C. soon. After accreditation, even after long period, many of them have not received grants for their development. Continued self-financing is a heavy burden for many of them and almost impossible for a few. In preparing the annual report of IQAC, they have to mention the new developmental activities undertaken or completed. But if there are no grants forthcoming, what will these institutions do to sustain the educational quality they had attained during the accreditation? It has become both a challenge for and a constraint of their quality sustaining effort. Hence there should be no delay in sanctioning and making the grants reach the institutions.

Another major problem faced during post accreditation period is the rural back ground in which many colleges are situated. A large number of colleges in the rural background have no internet facility available. Again, inter-library borrowing, book banking, etc. have no relevance in these areas where reading habit itself if very low. When the existing library facilities are hardly utilized, what is the use of borrowing books from other libraries, or introducing even book bank scheme? The bigger libraries in bigger college also do not gain much by borrowing from the smaller libraries of smaller rural colleges. Hence they are not interested in getting linked to rural colleges. College-industry linkage is a good idea. But there are hardly any industries near rural areas where these colleges can establish their linkage. When such conditions are nearly impossible to fulfill the post accreditation is likely to cause adverse results for the colleges. This, again, is a cause of apprehension for rural colleges in so far as quality requirements are not fully satisfied. Generating income from external sources is not easy in rural backgrounds, nor is it easy from internal sources since student themselves and the alumni are also poor. Research and related activities also do not interest the staff in village background since their work does not have much practical bearing nor the augmented knowledge necessary or welcome among the rural students.

In order to enhance and maintain quality, more and more job-oriented courses have to be introduced. But the government and universities will not finance them. Hence the management will find them unaffordable after a while. This will impose a limit to the introduction of more courses. Hence quality enhancement and sustenance becomes, in course of time, a titanic task for many an economically unsound management. Thus the challenges and constraints before these colleges in the genuine task for sustaining quality in the post accredited period are numerous.

A Few Feasible Solutions for Quality Sustenance

Although many schemes for quality sustenance and enhancement call for release of generous funds which are not easily forthcoming, there are a few schemes which are the outcome of mere intellectual and physical labour for which no considerable financial expense is required. But this intellectual and physical labour must come from the staff, the management and the students. Energetic teachers can afford more teaching hours for students before or after the regular hours of teaching. It can come by way of serious remedial teaching or mere extra hours of teaching. This will improve the results and the students will benefit. But teachers should have the willingness and energetic nature to do that. Teaching then becomes more of a service than mere paid wor...' In the intellectual area again comes the desire of teachers for more and more learning and research. The result will be more doctoral, post-doctoral theses and projects. This will not only benefit them, but the institution and the students benefit from it as well. One of the most important factors is the attitudinal change of the management, staff and students. Here also teachers can do more than both the other parties. Good teachers through their work, exhortation and discussion with the students can create changes of attitude in the student community which will make them hardworking with definite aims in life. Students have to be properly guided on moral and intellectual lines, no to ignore the spiritual values. It is the teachers who can do it better through their interaction with the students than the management. Again, innovative ideas should come from resourceful teachers for the development of the institution, and the management should have the receptivity and pragmatic sense to translate them into actions for quality augmentation and sustenance. As Goethe said "There is nothing worse than a teacher who knows no more than what the students ought to know." Hence teachers must move with the demands of the times and should not turn apathetic or remain nonchalant to vigorous activity for quality enhancement and sustenance; so also the management should be alert and sensible.

References

1. Prasad, V. S., *Great Institutions of Higher Learning, Accredited Colleges in India* (Vol.1, 2002-2004), NAAC, Bangalore: 2005.
2. Pradhan Ashok, Antony Stella, and Jagannath Patil (Reporters) (2004), *State-wise Analysis of Accreditation Reports – Maharashtra,* Bangalore: NAAC.
3. Kochhar, S. K (2006), Guidance and Counselling in Colleges and Universities, New Delhi: Sterling Publishers Pvt. Ltd.
4. Adair, John (2009), Effective Motivation: How to Get the Results from Everyone, London: Pan Macmillan Books Ltd.
5. *Manual for Self-Study- Affiliated Colleges,* (2006) Bangalore: NAAC.
6. NAAC, Bangalore: 2006, *Internal Quality Assurance Cell Activities.*

8

Quality Assurance of Higher Education Institutions (HEIs)

Abstract

Quality assurance in HEIs is generally realized through the external quality assurance bodies (like the government, MHRD, UGC, and so on, as is the case in India) and the intra-institutional quality assurance bodies like the IQAC. HEIs like the colleges and institutes can assure greater quality by ensuring that the best candidates are chosen for the faculty and the staff, proper training is given to them, effective teaching methods are adopted and timely and continuous evaluations are done for the students. Classrooms should be ICT enabled and the number of students in each class should be small. Plenty of program-options should be given to the students. 'Learner autonomy' and the development of 'meta-cognition' must be the hallmarks of advanced students. Several 'cells'/'centers' are to be established for proper implementation of the various schemes and plans. Library and learning resources (knowledge resource centre) should be of high quality and adequate. Excellent infrastructural facilities are to be provided. Research facilities should be sufficient and a 'Research Guidance Cell' should be constituted to help research work. Management and governance should be active and democratic. Powers should be decentralized. The institution should support the students in all possible ways. 'Benchmarks' should be identified and 'best' and 'innovative' practices should be evolved as unique features of the institution. A 'SWOT' analysis should be done and an 'action plan' be made accordingly. A very active IQAC should be a sine qua non for any quality aspiring institution to plan, evaluate, implement and organize various activities in the institution. The 'peer team report' of the external assessment agency should also be properly implemented. The paper delves into the diverse aspects of quality assurance in HEIs.]

(Joseph. T. C & R. G. Munghate, SGM College, Kurkheda)

Introduction

Ensuring greater levels of quality in higher education institutions (HEIs) is an urgent need of the hour, but it is a stupendous task requiring serious attention. It is commendable that the HEIs in the advanced countries have achieved a much higher level of quality than their counterparts in the Less Developed Countries (LDCs). Of course, many LDCs have a few sporadic institutions of global repute which appear like oases in a desert. But, the overall quality profile of HEIs in LDCs is far from satisfactory. Whether it is their lack of perception of what quality actually is or a failure of the assurance systems is a debatable issue. Further, financial constraints, lack of will-power on the part of the authorities including the governments could be isolated as the stumbling blocks. 'Quality' could be equated with 'excellence' in all the parameters of educational institutions conforming to national and international standards. If 'quality' is the best and first-rate of all the desirable aspects of education, then its enhancement and sustenance should be the focal point of all policies related to education. "Quality is often considered to be a standard or norm with which to compare two similar things in order to assess the worth of the thing compared. It is a benchmark arrived at after reckoning the best features of the things compared...Quality is context and need-specific....Quality in higher education is a holistic concept."[1] Quality assurance bodies like the Internal Quality Assurance Cell and other institutional cells/centers/committees have a greater role to play in promoting and sustaining quality than the external quality assurance bodies , for instance, like the MHRD, MHRDC, UGC, NAAC, AICTE, University, etc., that play an important role in India.

How can Intra-Institutional Quality be assured in HEIs?

Intra-Institutional quality assurance of higher education can be realized only through genuine efforts with systematic, deliberate, strategic and continuous planning, proper implementation and frequent evaluations and rectifications.

The areas for desirable changes have to be located, the weaknesses and strengths should be judiciously identified, and the opportunities for improvement should be explored. In order to ensure quality, various 'cells' or 'centers' must be established. The functioning of these 'cells' should be effectively monitored and frequently checked by the IQAC and the Head of the institution. Every area of quality improvement should be wisely identified for corrective measures whether or not they are related to teaching-learning-evaluation or infrastructure, or research or library, student support or whatever. It is the duty of the government or universities, or the private management to ensure that the 'quality assurance systems' function vigorously and effectively. Whenever and wherever laxity is noticed, interference from these external authorities by way of policy changes, occasional inspection, verification and corrective steps will go a long way in assuring quality. But the true quality assurance should come from within. All the stakeholders and particularly the teachers, students and the management should develop a culture of constant and steady striving to uplift the standard of the institution in the various parameters of higher education. The application of the concept of TQM is also a good way of ensuring quality in HEIs. There is no room for complacency in modern HEIs as far as quality status is concerned, since there is always stiff competition arising from various sources. Quality reflects in the qualifications obtained from the HEIs. "Quality assurance is fundamental to qualifications. Trust and transparency in qualifications are a requisite for the comparability and recognition of qualifications at the national and international levels."[2]

The Areas and Processes of Quality Assurance in HEIs

From the very advertisement of the vacant teaching or non-teaching posts and the appointment of faculty and staff members, to their upward mobility in their profession, attention is to be paid to every minute detail by the authorities concerned. Only transparent, merit-based and equitable admission of students should be resorted to. An informative 'prospectus' and an 'annual calendar' help the students immensely. As for the faculty and the staff it is to be ensured that adequate advertisement is made in the local and national dailies or periodicals and also on the institutional web site so that brilliant candidates from all over the country can take part in the interview and the best of the lot can be selected. The power of selecting the candidates should be entirely vested with the committee of experts. Here 'private management' should not meddle with the matter for any pecuniary benefits other than voicing their right to have quality-candidates. Contrariwise, the members of the committee should be 'real' experts and not those 'mere' experts appointed through favoritism or nepotism or any such mal-practices. The university should play a very crucial role in offering the best panel of experts so that their selection of the candidates will be flawless. All the degrees and documents of the candidates must be from standard and reputed institutions/universities and should be carefully verified. Another option for ensuring quality at this level is to choose faculty candidates through a 'written test' conducted by the Public Service Commission of the country, and then subject them to a screening 'oral test' to check their communication and teaching skills as also personality traits. Those passing this practical test can be held to be the best candidates. If more candidates are selected 'a reserve pool' can also be made available to be appointed in future. Once this done, the next focus should be to update the teachers with the modern teaching methodologies and changing paradigm shifts – from 'teacher-oriented' to 'learner-centered' and from there to 'learning-oriented'. 'Blended-learning' at this level is an ideal option to fuse the 'online' with the 'face to face' teaching-learning experience. "Although blended learning design and implementation may be context-dependent, an institution-wide systematic consideration and strategic planning of blended learning may be necessary for all HEIs to bring about transformations in teaching and learning practices."[3] Similarly, the members of the staff should also be updated for honing their skills.

The next step in quality assurance is to ensure that real learning takes place in the classrooms which modifies the behavior of the learners so that they become productive members of the modern world and turn suitable for gainful employment. "Attitudes, abilities, knowledge and skills may be taken as four different pillars on which the higher education stands for empowering the youth for excellence."[4] Good learning elevates the learners to higher levels of 'critical' and 'independent' thinking powers. Real learning should be such that the candidates are properly guided to lead a 'meaningful life' and to be able to 'face the challenges of everyday of life'. Hence mere 'employability' is not enough but knowledge of values and diverse aspects of life duly imbibed to have a comprehensive view of life. This prepares them to be citizens of the world with a broader outlook and a better sensibility. This braces them for harmonious co-existence with the people of varied religions, cultures, races, languages and so on. Quality education leads to 'developed intellect' and 'noble character'. The syllabi should be comprehensive and need-based. Here the roles of the Board of Studies and Academic Councils are crucial. The eligibility criteria of these bodies should be foolproof. If this is guaranteed, the curricular aspects will be well-taken care of, and only their transactions should be made effective in the institutions. To measure this, the learning outcomes can be checked, and if academic results are excellent, and if students have become properly developed personalities with high levels of self confidence, courage, preparedness to face real social situations, and have acquired good communication and soft-skills, then, one can be sure of a high level of quality achieved by them. Introduction of various 'career-oriented certificate/diploma courses' in the HEIs will be a blessing for students of humanities and social sciences. Various 'clubs' like the debate club, elocution club, and fine arts club, and literary or subject 'associations' can help improve co-curricular activities of the students. Both the 'content' of syllabus and 'teaching method' are critical. 'Continuous' and proper evaluation and timely 'feedback' to the learners are also necessary to encourage and facilitate the learning process. No malpractices like copying the answers should be allowed to ensure the learning outcome quality. CCTVs should be installed in examination halls.

Learners must eventually be transformed into 'autonomous learners' with developed 'meta-cognition' so that they could 'self-regulate their studies' and develop highly 'effective learning strategies'. 'Teacher-dependency' should be minimized and learners must be encouraged to pursue independently their knowledge-acquisition activity either by reading books and periodicals, or by gleaning information from the internet. Reading critically and analyzing carefully and then storing the final product or assimilating it is true learning. Guidance should be given in this regard by giving the students 'tasks' and 'assignments' and organizing occasional 'student seminars'. This goads them to read and browse for information. Excellent reading habits should be cultivated in the learners to develop 'learner autonomy' so that they become 'life-long learners'. Further, adequate lab, on-field, and internship experiences enhance the quality of the different types of learners depending on their fields of study. Well-equipped labs, well-developed language laboratories and a large library/knowledge resource centre with a good collection of book-volumes, periodicals, reference books, encyclopedias, soft copies, digital items, online books, the latest volumes of books, etc., are needed for quality learning as 'student support systems'. The better the library, the better is the learning facility. It should be finely ventilated, with comfortable seating arrangements, reprography and printers, and with research-rich materials. 'Interlibrary-Loan' and 'Book Bank Scheme' facilities also benefit a good number of learners. Learning resources should be optimally utilized. Periods should be set aside for library work to cultivate the reading habit. A 'Library Advisory Committee' should be appointed and it should operate actively. Its suggestions and observations should be perused over seriously.

Infrastructure of the HEIs should be good enough to pursue advanced learning in a comfortable and convenient manner. Imposing and majestic structures have a psychological advantage of stimulating awe and wonder in the learners' minds about higher education, and this prompts them to take study seriously. But, apart from this, adequate facilities to suit the needs of the students like IT-enabled, a/c classrooms, diverse teaching-learning aids including power point facility, or such similar high-tech facilities, internet-connectivity, interactive boards, the use of MOODLE (Modified Object-Oriented Dynamic Learning Environment) or MOOC, etc., plenty of computers/lap-tops, a swimming pool, a vast and well-beautified campus with gardens and greenery, botanical gardens, good drinking-water, vehicle parking, canteen, horse-riding facility, gymnasia, a vast playground for all sorts of games, athletic tracks and fields, indoor stadium, theatres, state-of-the-art conference halls, banking, stationery, co-operative stores, hostel facilities, solid waste management facilities, CCTVs, only a limited number of students in each classroom, and so on., are all a part of the standard HEIs. In all these areas innovations and state-of-the-art modifications are to be effected for quality enhancement.

An ideal HEI is one that encourages good research work. It is not in the 'quantity' of research work, but in its 'quality' there lies the real worth. 'Quality' in HEIs should not be equated with mere research. "While research productivity is critically important to quality higher education, any narrow conceptions of quality do not represent the range of knowledge, skills and competencies required of faculty today."[5] Excellent researches contribute to nation-building and human progress. As a quality assurance measure, 'Research Guidance Cells' must be established in the universities and HEIs. This can not only promote research but cultivate the research culture as well. The teaching community needs to be trained well in research methodology and process. The research problems of a novice research scholar should be addressed by the 'Research Guidance

Cells' of the university by way of organizing courses in 'Research Methodology' and other issues related to research. Knowledge of the internationally reputed and recognized journals and book publishers should be made quite handy for the researchers. Knowledge of patents, citation index, impact factor, availability of funds, and so on should also be imparted to them. Considerable incentives should be given to the researchers. The higher education institutions should make all infrastructural facilities to the researchers and make easily available all the required research materials. Research should not become an unaffordable luxury to the brilliant and economically challenged scholars.

The duty of HEIs is not over after conducting the classes and awarding the students qualifying degrees. During the stay of the students in the HEIs or during their participation in the programs offered, it is to be ensured that students are well-taken care of by providing them with all sorts of 'support mechanisms' for their overall personality development and skills acquisitions. HEIs should closely watch the 'progression' of their students to higher education and gainful employment. In other words, facilities for post graduate studies, research pursuits at doctoral and post-doctoral levels should be offered with high quality centers and faculty. Further, making available to students diverse and useful programs to choose from is also a part of ensuring quality in 'student support and progression'. Students can also participate in quality assurance of the institution as is evidenced by the project proposal of NAAC on 'Student Participation in Quality Improvement' submitted to Asia Pacific Quality Network (APQN). NAAC has worked admirably on the international project group on 'Student Participation in Quality Assurance.'[6] Students should not only be empowered to get jobs in future but also inspired to play creative and productive roles in society and in the nation building process. Their societal engagement really matters.

Those running the HEIs should be imbued with a sense of mission and commitment. They should further have a noble vision for a better future of the society at large and a definite plan. Both 'short term' and 'perspective' plans have to be drafted and sincerely executed besides a 'Master Plan' of the institution. For all these the role played by the management and the type of governance undertaken are of paramount significance. A 'College Development Committee' is to be appointed, and it should function effectively and mandatorily. Quality assurance requires that the management be alert, energetic and imbued with enthusiasm. It is also essential that the policy adopted for governance is based on transparency, efficiency and decentralization. "Good quality assurance is transparent and builds capacity as it operates, and for this to be enabled good strategic leadership is necessary."[7] Efficient governance of the institution should be averse to 'centralization of power' in the hands of an individual or a few. Providing 'departmental autonomy' is essential in HEIs for 'decentralization of power'. The various heads of the departments should be vested with enough power to run their departments efficiently. The democratic spirit of 'discussion' and the resultant synergy contributes to quality enhancement. Good management makes the stakeholders 'accountable to the public', or follows the principle of 'social accountability' or commitment. Efficient management ensures that the best faculty and staff join the institution, and also their abilities are optimally used for the benefit of the institution and the stakeholders. The administration or governance should also make sure that all activities are fully 'computerized' and 'automated'. Everything has to be 'well-documented'. 'Collaborations' with several HEIs, reputed institutions and companies, 'signing of MOUs' with them and 'interface with the industries' are all necessary for the betterment of the institution and also the students. "Industry involvement in all stages of the qualification process and quality assurance process is critical for strengthening the fitness for the purpose of qualifications and the validation of and confidence in the outcomes."[8]

HEIs need 'benchmarking' and also identifying of a good number of 'best practices'. Since 'benchmarking' implies setting standards against which things may be compared, the quality aspiring institutions should be on the lookout for models of excellence from various top quality institutions for emulation. NAAC in India, for instance, offers 'criterion statements' to be used as 'best practices benchmarks'. "Under ideal conditions, the practices we can expect an ideal institution to adopt are identified as *criterion statements*. They serve as best practices benchmarks."[9] Besides, 'innovative practices' can generate certain practices in the institution out of which some may be chosen to highlight the unique practices of the institution which make it distinct. In addition, a proper consideration of an objectively made 'SWOT analysis' gives plenty of insights to improve the quality profile of the institution. Every bit of important information related to the institution must be show-cased on the institutional web-site, which itself needs to be periodically updated.

The Role of the Internal Quality Assurance Cell

For all the overall planning, evaluation and implementation of the numerous schemes and programs of the institution, the IQAC is singularly responsible. 'In the words of NAAC, "The IQAC has to ensure continuous improvement in all the operational aspects of an institution and also assure its stakeholders of the accountability of the institution for its own quality."[10] It serves as an 'umbrella cell' under which there can be so many' sub-cells' for effective functioning. Its chairperson, the Head of the institution, and the IQAC co-coordinator are the key persons of the cell. The members chosen from various walks of life and representing the student, parent and professional communities also play important roles in assuring quality in the institution. The cell helps the institution to prepare itself properly to face its assessment and accreditation. Frequent meetings, discussions, judicious planning, proper implementation and occasional evaluation, adequate documentation, development of a strong digital data base, organization of workshops and seminars on quality related themes, helping the internalization and institutionalization of quality, and finally the timely adoption of effective corrective steps are the important functions of the IQAC, which assures the enhancement and sustenance of quality in an institution. One of the important agents for quality assurance in India, for example, is the 'peer team' sent by the NAAC for on-site evaluation of quality and validation of the SSR. It makes valuable recommendations in the 'peer team report' (PTR) soon after their site-visit. This, in its turn, must be implemented faithfully for scaling greater heights in quality. But the 'capacity' of assessors should be built properly for the authentic assessment of HEIs. 'Feed-backs' must be taken from all the stakeholders regarding the quality of teaching, teachers and the institutional support. Further, various types of 'audits' can also stimulate greater quality. 'Academic', 'administrative' and 'environmental' audits are more important than others. 'Academic audit' is essential for quality enhancement in an educational institution. It "reviews the processes or procedures that faculty members use to provide quality education in their departments/ schools."[11]

Conclusion

Quality assurance is a subtle and complex process. It can be brought about only by the cumulative work and proper co-ordination of the external quality assurance bodies and the internal or intra-institutional bodies. All the parameters and criteria of higher education should be duly considered and the IQAC should plan, evaluate, implement the feasible action plan and the sub-cells under it should work in unison to quench the institutional thirst for quality enhancement and in realizing the institutional vision and objectives. The Head of the institution and the coordinator should always be vigilant and enthusiastic for materializing high quality-related aspirations. The teaching-learning-evaluation activity, curriculum, infrastructure, library, management, research, student support, best practices - all should be fulfilling the quality norms and catering to the student needs, not to mention the needs of the industry.

References

1. Francis Soundararaj, 2004, Education, Sustainable Development and Educational Management. *Quality in Higher Education and Sustainable Development - NAAC Decennial Lectures.* Bangalore: National Assessment and Accreditation Council, pp.23-24.
2. UNESCO, 2017, *Towards Quality Assurance of Technical and Vocational Education and Training,* p. vii
3. UNESCO, 2017, *Blended Learning for Quality Higher Education: Selected Case Studies on Implementation from Asia-Pacific,* p. xviii
4. A. Kumar, 2017, Incubation and Innovation in Higher Education: Issues and Approaches, *University News (Special Issue): A Weekly Journal of Higher Education,* Vol. 55, No.48, November 27-December 03, 2017.
5. UNESCO, 2017, *Recalibrating Careers in Academia: Professional Advancement Policies and Practices in Asia-Pacific,* Foreword, p.vii
6. NAAC, Bangalore, 2007, *Student Feedback and Participation: Case Presentations,* p.2.
7. UNESCO, 2017, *Towards Quality Assurance of Technical and Vocational Education and Training,* p.46
8. UNESCO, 2017, *Guidelines for the Quality Assurance of TVET Qualifications in the Asia-Pacific Region,* p.6
9. NAAC, Bangalore: 2006, *Internal Quality Assurance Cell Activities,* p. 2.
10. Prasad V S and Antony Stella, 2004, Best Practices Benchmarking for Quality Enhancement in Higher Education, *Best Practices in Higher Education: Report of the National Conference Organized by NAAC,* p.4.
11. Ganesh Anant Hedge, 2017, Academic Audit: Pathways for Quality and Sustenance. *University News: A Weekly Journal of Higher Education,* Vol.55, No.15, April 10-16, 2017.

9

Recent Shifts in Educational Paradigms and their Pedagogical Implications

Abstract

Of late, a series of paradigm shifts occurred in the Indian educational arena. These have brought with them several attendant issues of grave concern for the teaching community and the learners alike. Coping with the unprecedented changes and bracing up to face challenges through 'life-long learning' process have been the most pedagogical imperatives to survive in a world of cut-throat competition. The learners also had to take up the cudgels in favour of the shifting paradigms to move with the times and make themselves employable. 'Capacity building' became a desperate need of the hour. But unlike the techno-savvy new generation, the pedagogic community had more agonizing woes lying in the womb of time to address on account of the demands of the times. This paper attempts a brief survey of the shifting educational paradigms and their pedagogical implications.

Introduction

The past two and a half decades witnessed staggering change in every sphere of life in the country. Such an unprecedented pace of change has been precipitated by our signing the GATT in 1990 and GATS in 1991, which ushered in the era of Liberalization, Privatization, and Globalization. The fabulously explosive growth and deployment of Information and Communication Technology (ICT) contributed to the surging pace of the change. India, along with most countries of the world, underwent incredible transformation. There was hardly any segment of society that remained untouched and unruffled by these changes. As in the other areas, in the field of education too, there occurred radical changes. A 'restructuring', and 'reengineering' of the whole educational edifice became the dire need of the times. Several paradigm shifts were necessitated by the changed circumstances. Conventional or traditional 'teacher-centric pedagogy' was challenged, and there was a fervent hue and cry for a paradigm-shift from the teacher-centric mode of education to a 'learner-centric' mode, and later to its variants.

1. Teacher-Centric pedagogy

It was dubbed as 'dictatorial' and lacked freedom of expression. The teacher was always in the centre of attention during curricular transaction. The learners were at the receiving-end, at the periphery of the teaching-learning process. It was more of 'one-sided communication' than a bilateral, dyadic one. Under it the students or learners were said to have suffered great losses as they had to remain like mute spectators to the pedantic monologue going on within the classroom. The students were hardly ever allowed to disagree with the teacher or think critically. All differing voices were stifled and questioning tendencies nipped in the bud. If at all anyone dared to challenge the authority of the teacher or raise doubts about the authenticity of his/her teaching, their critical questions were subdued and suppressed by the exasperated teacher in a hostile manner. Many a time he/she would be the victim of the teacher's wrath. The atmosphere was one that induced fear. Fear made 'clear thinking' almost impossible for most students. The teacher generally assumed the position of an unquestionable authority on the subject being taught. The learners had to accept and absorb all that the teachers taught them. This system lacked liberty which is necessary for free, independent, and clear thinking. Students felt that they were like dumb prisoners within the four walls of the classroom. This system did not foster the creative and critical faculties of the learners. It was more of 'talk' than of learning 'activities' or tasks. Effective teaching aids were wanting. The syllabi taught were not generally career-oriented. 'Vocationalization' and 'transdisciplinarity', and 'application-orientation' were distant dreams.[1] The method was described as 'the chalk and talk method'.

2. Learner-Centric Instruction

This new paradigm shift necessitated a change in 'methodology' which came to be called 'learner-centred' approach. It brought the learner from the periphery to the centre of the teaching-learning process. It made a great difference to curricular transaction. Consequently, the students became the centre of attention. He is the 'consumer' or 'customer' of the educational service. He is at the 'centre' with all the rights of the 'consumer' of education to 'demand' for a quality 'supply' of education which is like any other 'product'. The new method is of course democratic, for it was based on dialogue, discussion, and interaction. Students are given full freedom to express themselves. They are encouraged to involve in several activities or tasks. Learning is to be effected not merely by hearing but by participating, doing, observing, collaborating, and in technology-mediated ways. The democratic methods of dialogues, group discussions, debates, seminars, brain-storming sessions, etc are to be liberally used for active student involvement. These boost their critical thinking power and stimulate their creativity. Conventional teaching aids are relegated to the background and are fast replaced by the computer and the internet, power-point presentations, the interactive boards, the green boards, etc., for diversified, more effective and quicker audio-visual effects. Various soft-wares and web-sites are now available to make learning more interesting and student-friendly. New innovative teaching techniques like the use of the 'multi-media packages' have been resorted to. Various ICT resources particularly from the computer like the graphs, sounds, diagrams, images, colours, animations, effects, etc., are judiciously used for a more fruitful learning process. 'Innovations' are to be attempted at by teachers to render teaching-learning process interesting. Numerous modern approaches and methods have been widely suggested and fairly used to make learner-centred approach a reality. Some of these are: Communicative approach, collaborative approach, co-operative approach, community language learning, task-based learning, computer assisted learning, neuro-linguistic programming, the silent method, suggestopedia / desuggestopedia, etc.

The 'role of the teacher' was the first to be redefined under the 'paradigm shift' from the peremptory and pedantic to that of a philosopher, friend, guide, mentor, counsellor and facilitator. Thus the role of the teacher is reversely shifted but broadened as well. The focus is now the learner and not the teacher. Further, the government, through the *RTE Act - 2009*, has eliminated corporal punishment restricting the right of the teacher to punish the students, pushing him/ her thus further on to the periphery. Thus, the teachers were deprived of much of their conventional privileges. The teacher is thus thrown on his own inner resources to endure the 'naughty' or 'intractable' students, and rectify them through exhortations and persuasive means rather than by violent means. The changed circumstances have thus made teaching profession a 'risky' one for the impulsive and vindictive teachers but an excitingly challenging one to the mentally strong and mature ones who take up educational tasks with a missionary spirit imbued with commitment, love, compassion and a sense of service. It is an imperative need of the day that teachers change themselves - their psychological moulds - and be braced up with considerable adaptability. Attitudinal, methodological and academic changes must occur to fit in with the shift in the paradigm. They have now to constantly 'learn, unlearn, and relearn' many things against their own wishes. Capacity building of teachers is a sine qua non for effective teaching in the changed times. There is a definite range of personal competence that makes a difference to the quality and effectiveness of teaching like sound subject knowledge, communication skills, ability to relate to individual students, self-management skills, organizational skills, classroom management skills, problem-solving skills, a range of teaching methods, teamwork skills, and research skills. In the Indian context most of these competencies are not adequately addressed in the curriculum of teacher education.[2]

As for pedagogical knowledge, the teacher training curriculum needs to encompass a clear focus on understanding of learning and teaching, including concepts of how children progress in the subject, how they acquire key concepts, and importantly an understanding of misconceptions and how they arise. Teacher education curricula in India need to be reformed to develop this range of competencies. The teacher education curriculum needs to develop teachers' abilities to help students learn how 'to learn and to unlearn and to re-learn'. This is what is said in the *National Curriculum Framework for Teacher Education* (2006). This situation has disheartened many and prompted them turn a back to the teaching profession altogether. Many are now repelled by the disappearance of the comfort zone from the teaching profession as against the torpid state by which the educational arena had been stagnated till a couple of decades ago and been instrumental to economic deceleration.

3. Learning-Centred Approach

Of late, educationists insist on the paradigm shift from learner-centred to a 'learning-centred' approach. They point out that 'learning' should take place leading to clear 'learning outcomes'. It is neither the teacher nor the learner who is really important in the process of education but actual 'learning'. Whatever be the method it is to be ensured that knowledge seeps into the learners' minds bringing about learning. For this to effectively take place 'blended learning' has been highly recommended as an innovative method. 'Blended Learning' is a 'process of blending the face-to-face resources with the online resources'. Here the traditional and the modern mingle properly. The best of the both traditional and modern are judiciously mixed for maximum benefit of the students. The UNICEF has fervently advocated this as a highly beneficial method. They point out that 'Blended-learning' is an ideal option to fuse the 'online' with the 'face to face' teaching-learning experience. "Although blended learning-design and implementation may be context-dependent, an institution-wide systematic consideration and strategic planning of blended learning may be necessary for all HEIs to bring about transformations in teaching and learning practices"[3] Similarly, the members of the staff should also be updated for better performance.

4. Constructivism

There is a yet another paradigm shift towards an effective mode of Learning highly praised today – the 'Constructivism' Approach. This is contributory and complementary to the 'learning-centred' approach. "It is a paradigm shift from the earlier behavioural orientation.' Constructivist teaching and learning recognizes that knowledge is created in the mind of the learner and thus, effective teaching approaches delve into the learner's mind through active learning, learner-generated inquiry, authentic experiences, collaborative investigation and discussions and reflection and structuring learning around primary concepts... Constructivism is not a method... It is rather a theory about knowledge and learning that alters teachers' perception of their instructional roles and their learners' goals. Learning is viewed as 'a process of knowledge construction' and *not* of 'knowledge recording or absorption'. Multiple instructional strategies are to be employed to involve the students in the learning process. Teachers are to help learners relate the new content to the knowledge that they already have and also help them process and apply the new knowledge. Before students can solve problems, they must examine the new content in relation to what they already know and build the new knowledge structure.... These 'patterns of prior knowledge' on which students build new knowledge are called 'schemas'. These 'schemas' provide a context for new information and help students understand the content better using instructional strategies that move learners, from giving information learnt by rote, to 'reaching deeper understanding through their own questioning, exploration and working co-operatively with peers'"[4]. Merely involving students in activities such as discussions, question answering etc, does not automatically guarantee successful knowledge construction but 'the quality of their learning strategies' are seen to be critical factors in successful learning outcomes. 'Individuals construct meaning through experiences'. Constructivist-based instructional programmes emphasize the use of reading and writing strategies in a social context that allowed peer collaboration to solve problems. Constructivist teacher's view of learning expects their students to be able to explain, find evidence and examples, generalize, and apply in a new way. Authentic tasks or assignments that have a bearing on real life are given to students to challenge the students solve such problems. It is found that constructivist approach is also highly effective in imparting 'Life Skills' to students. Some of the major "'Life Skills', according to WHO, are: critical thinking, creative thinking, decision making, problem solving, interpersonal relations, effective communication, coping with feelings, coping with stress, self-awareness, and empathy...'Life skills education' is a structured programme of needs and outcomes based participatory learning that aims at increasing positive and adaptive behavior by assisting individuals to develop and practice psycho-social skills that minimize risk factors and maximize protective factors. UNESCO (2003) study reveals that 'Life Skills education programmes are theory and evidence-based, learner-focused, delivered by competent facilitators, and appropriately evaluated to ensure continuous improvement of documented results.'"[5]

5. Need-Based Education

Another paradigm shift is seen in the educational content or the various subjects or topics to be taught to the students and so to be reflected in the curricula or syllabi accordingly. Mere traditional subjects are not enough to prepare the youth to live in the present world of intense competition and market orientation. The subjects and topics of various programmes should be such that they should match the needs of the market and the industry, the service sector, and the knowledge sector of the economy. Accordingly when new and need-based subjects are chosen to be included in the syllabi or the various courses available, the teachers and the faculty should be such that they have necessary expertise in handling these subjects. Such subjects have a lot of job-orientation, managerial and administrative value or IT orientation. Hence, vocationalization of education is taking place at a quick pace. Many hybrid subjects, as a result of much research and transdisciplinarity or interdisciplinary approach are on high demand. Utility is at the core of most of these subjects unlike many traditional subjects which had more intellectual relevance, knowledge-value, and aesthetic appeal. Thus, teachers or instructors have got to be 'life-long learners' to update themselves and survive in these periods of much 'obsolescence' of traditional or modern knowledge due to rapid technological changes taking place making many things out-dated in no time. Innovations after innovations turn things outdated in no time. The changes happening to 'mobiles sets' or 'TV sets' are typical examples such phenomenon leading to terrible wastage when old models are replaced by newer ones. Many inventions also disappear like the radio sets or stereo sets or tape recorders which had had a wonderful time once but now no more demanded. Under such circumstances, teachers have to keep abreast of times by participating in conferences and seminars, orientation programmes and refresher courses or useful short term courses. They should turn techno-savvy and be fond of learning new things to adjust with new generation and their likings. 'Capacity building' for teachers is an imperative need because of the changed circumstances.

6. Skill and Entrepreneurship-Based Education

There is a paradigm shift towards skill development and entrepreneurship. It is pointed that there is a serious mismatch between knowledge base and skill sets of graduates and the industry needs. "Very often our youth are found unemployable by industry due to the lack of suitable skills. This is a major challenge. Connecting people to jobs and creating a job-ready generation is now being undertaken in the Mission Mode through 'Skill India'" says Rohit Nandan (Secretary, Ministry of Skill Development and Entrepreneurship, Government of India, New Delhi). He further points out that based on a skill-gap study conducted recently in view of the emerging trends in Indian economy, it has been anticipated that nearly 12.8 crore new jobs are to be created in India during the next 5-6 years. The major areas of growth would be in construction, retail, logistics, beauty and wellness, hospitality, Telecom, healthcare, Food Processing, Security, Electronics, IT, and IT enabled services, Furniture and Fittings, Ports and Maritime, and Aviation.[6] "The youth has just to ensure that they acquire the right competencies. Educational institutions have to combine 'excellence in education with relevance to contemporary needs'. We are now living in an age where employers are looking for hands on competencies rather than just academic knowledge. Educational institutions have to align themselves to this thought process and expose their students to the new world of skills to make them job-ready and employable. New opportunities are opening up for Indians all over the world. Our IT and Health professionals have made a tremendous impact globally. Today India is the youngest country in the world with 54% of its population below the age of 25. It is expected that by the year 2020, the average age of Indians would be just 29 while that of the USA, Europe, China and Japan would be over 40. It is also expected that the work force in the West is going to decline by 14% in the next decade while that of India would register a substantial rise. Thus, India has an opportunity to become the *Skill Bank* for the world.' Our students should be professionally competent and productive so that they will be demanded. The Government of India has established 16 India International Skill Centres all over the country with courses benchmarked to global standards. The government has 'also started the process of establishing new generation internationally competitive Indian Institute of Skills'. So 'meaningful fusion of formal education and skilling is an urgent need of the day'. 'A new phenomenon is revolutionizing the Indian economic scenario. It is the emergence of daring and successful entrepreneurs. All over the world, progress is driven by innovations and challenges. In India the structure of society and the fear of failure had inhibited the spirit of entrepreneurship. All this is changing fast. Today we have achievers in the form of the Bansal brothers of *Flipkart,* Ritesh Agarwal of *OYO Rooms,* Bhavesh Agarwal of *OLA,* Vijay Shekhar Sharma of *Paytm* and Kunal Behl of *Snapdeal*. These young men are the Tatas and Birlas of today.' So a spirit of entrepreneurship should be instilled in the students to transform the future of India and make it a global economic power, one with the advanced countries, bereft of poverty, squalor and disease. 'Mr. Dhirubhai Ambani is a typical entrepreneur who represents the spirit of new India'. In his own words, 'The success of the new entrepreneur will be the key to India's transformation to the new millennium". 'Entrepreneurs do not seek jobs; they give jobs. They create wealth and hence lead to the development of the economy and society.'"[7] Mere 'hard skills'/professional skills are not enough to live in a world where human interpersonal relationships do matter. Hence, special *'soft skills'* or interpersonal competencies or human skills are necessary. The most important 'soft skills' are: 'Listening Skills, Communication skills, Team Building Skills, Leadership Skills, Problem solving Skills, Time Management Skills, Negotiation Skills, Conflict Management Skills, Skill of Assertiveness), Counselling Skills, Presentation Skills, Mentoring Skills and Feedback Skills'.[8]

7. ICT-Enabled Present Education

Finally, a mention has to be made to the increasing significance of ICT in the field of education. The role played by ICT is ever expanding. It has given boost to a number of facilities in the field of education. It now gives opportunity for Distance Learning, Online Learning, Virtual Classrooms, *MOOC* (Massive Online Open Courses), MOODLE (Modified Object Oriented Dynamic Learning Environment), Video-Audio Conferencing, E-Learning, Digital Library Learning, etc. All these have revolutionized the field of education and changes after changes surge like waves. We are now required to swim with these currents! The online resources made available by the MHRD through the ambitious project of *National Digital Library* provides the following sites with a huge repertoire of resources for scholars and students:- Digital Library of India (DLI): (More than 5,00000 global classical books), Librivox: (More than 2,00000 audio books), SNLR Digitalization of works by R. Tagore, INFLIBNET (1,00000+ thesis and synopsis reports authored by Indian researchers), KRUSHI KOSH: (50,000 agricultural books, journals, articles and reports), NCERT: (Hindi& English books on different subjects for students from primary to 12th standard), NPTEL: (10,000 MHRD-Sponsored video lectures in engineering domain).[9]

Conclusion

It is clear from the foregoing analysis that the rapidly changing educational paradigms have serious implications for the teacher and the taught. The teachers have to change with the times and bring about necessary changes in their methodologies and approaches. They have to play multiple and changed roles efficiently. They have further to update themselves and become 'life-long learners'. Much dedication, sacrifice and hard work is expected of the teachers in the changed circumstances when they cannot resort to corporal punishment but at the same time have to ensure that learning outcomes are good enough. The same is the case with learners too. They have to acquire the necessary subject knowledge from various sources under the guidance of the teachers, develop their skills, and acquire the expected expertise to fulfill the market needs to be job-worthy. They have at the same time to ensure that they acquire sufficient soft skills, imbibe value systems, and the qualities required for being good citizens of the country and efficient members of society at large.

References

1. Francis Soundararaj (2004). Education, Sustainable Development and Educational Management. *Quality in Higher Education and Sustainable Development – NAAC Decennial Lectures.* Bangalore: National Assessment and Accreditation Council, p.23-24
2. Johnsi Priya J (2017). Need for Capacity Building of Teachers for quality Education, *University News: A Weekly Journal of Higher Education,* Vol.55, No.04, January 23-29, 2017, p.08.
3. UNESCO (2017). *Blended Learning for Quality Higher Education: Selected Case Studies on Implementation from Asia-Pacific,* p. xviii.
4. Hardik D Mehta (2017). Constructivism Approach: A Paradigm Shift Towards More Effective Mode of Learning, *University News,* Vol.55, No.20, May 15-21, 2017, p.5
5. Vandana Yadav and Ram Mohan Kesharwani (2017). Imparting Life Skills Education through Constructivist Approach, *University News,* Vol.55, No.20, May 15-21, 2017, p.7
6. Rohit Nandan (2017). Paradigm Shift towards Skill Development and Entrepreneurship, *University News,* Vol.55, No.07, February 13-19, 2017, p.33.
7. *Ibid,* p.44.
8. Bharathi T, Hariprasad M, (Ed. V. Prakasam) (2013). Personality Development & Communicative English. (Hyderabad, New Delhi): Neelkamal Publications Pvt. Ltd, p.3.
9. Abdul Latheef N (2017). National Digital Library: An Overview, *University News,* Vol.55, No.20, May, 15-21, 2017, pp.11-12.

SECTION-B

CRITICAL WRITINGS ON LITERATURE

1

Post Independence Indian English Poetry: A Brief Survey

Post-Independence Indian English poetic scene is marked by an unprecedented and sudden spurt of sprightly creative activity galvanized by the dawn of freedom. Nevertheless, the post-independence era was not bereft of challenges of its own. A perplexing array of problems persistently haunted the psyche of the new poets. Initially, the poets had been struggling to come to terms with the bizarre Indian situation and the direction to be taken by Indian English poetry. The Indian English poetry written prior to independence was mostly swayed by the British and American poetry and remained greatly apish and subservient to the western poetry. The poetry of the period was steeped in western influences. It lacked its own identity, authenticity and individuality. Our writers looked to the west for all sorts of artistic models. The reason was that they did not have any exquisite Indian English poetic models before them to draw inspiration from or emulate. They were like toddlers struggling to stand on their own feet. But the dawn of independence witnessed a sea-change in poetic attitude and our poets began audacious efforts at creating genuine poetry that smacks of Indian culture, making use of a poetic idiom and form of our own unlike the borrowed western poetic trappings which were largely used by the pre-independence poets.

There were oodles of issues the Indian English poets had to address such as the glaring problem of a suitable poetic idiom of our own, the question of 'Indianness', of language, modernity, bilingualism, the appeal of exile, etc. Yet the creative genius of a good number of

Poets like Nissim Ezekiel, Kamala Das, Jayanta Mahapatra, Parthasarathy, A. K. Ramanujan, Shiv K. Kumar, O.P. Bhatnagar, etc., quite succeeded in shaking off these problems from the mane of their creative impulses. Each of these poets found their own channels to traverse through the mountainous terrain of dilemmas and issues and stumbling blocks which had been encumbering the Indian English poetic talent. As a result, the Indian English poetry gradually grew largely mature and self-reliant.

A large number of new poets are now enriching the Indian English poetry through sparklingly original contributions and based on disarming frankness. They write poems of highly evocative power, interspersed with a good degree of obscurity which marks modern and post-modern poetry.

Irony as the Dominant Mode of Indian English Poetry

Irony which ha constituted a new poetics has found a dignified place in the poetry of a good number of Indian English poets like Nissim Ezekiel, Kamala Das, Jayanta Mahapatra and O. P. Bhatnagar. These and many other major poets adopted irony as a dominant mode in their poetry for several reasons. They knew that irony has the in-built power to divest poetic expression of unnecessary sentimentality and to write in an objective manner. According to Bhatnagar, irony deepens insight into situations and expands the dimensions of reflection. The stress on irony came from New Critics of America. There is superb irony and subdued mockery in Nissim Ezekiel's 'Night of the Scorpion'. When the mother is stung by a scorpion the rationalist and skeptical father tries "every curse and blessing, powder, mixture, herb and hybrid", as the peasants swarm into console her, offering advice of strongly ritualistic and faith-healing kind.

Kamala Das in her poem, 'The Old Playhouse' is highly ironic about the treatment meted out to her by her husband.

Her ironic perception of reality is expressed through condensed, original images:

"You taught to break saccharine into your tea
and
To offer at the right moment the vitamins
Cowering
Beneath your monstrous ego, I ate the magic loaf
and
Became a dwarf. I lost my will and reason to
all your
Questions I mumbled incoherent replies."

A. K. Ramanujan's *'Small-Scale Reflections on a Great House'* is very rich in irony:

"...where cows
get pregnant in the broad daylight
of the street under the elder's supervision"

Shiv K. Kumar's conclusion of the poem, *'Kall'* is charged with grim irony:

"If the way to create
Is the way to kill
I have hoarded enough blood
In my throat
For all the hyenas to suck from"

Mamta Kalia resorts to irony as a powerful weapon of social criticism in her poem, *'Hell'*:

"Give up all hope
Ye that enter the kingdom of
Government service...."

In the poem *'Striptease'* Bhatnagar flays the hypocritical attitude of our society and ironically observes:

"We may buy tickets in black-market
To see women raped in films
But our ideals honour women and values more
Than our morals cast"

In the same way, Keki N. Daruwalla, R. Parthasarathy and most other Indian poets use irony as an effective tool to depict the Indian society with all its paradoxes, subtle aberrations, and contradictions.

A Few Notable Poets and their Contributions

It is no exaggeration to state that **Nissim Ezekiel** is to Indian English poetry what T. S. Eliot is to modern English poetry. His contribution to post-independence Indian English poetry is really immense. He wrote poetry in a new style and showed to Indian readers that it is not merely the subject matter, but the craftsmanship is also of serious concern in poetry. He disliked vague poeticism and created a different music to give poetry a greater informality, to bring it closer to the spoken language. He stressed the importance of contemporary idiom. His chief source of inspiration was 'his inner life'. To him writing poetry was a kind of coping with the tension between his inner life and the outer life.

His poetry being introspective, he often expressed self-doubt and self-criticism. Nevertheless, he was fascinated by his relationship with other people, love, sex, and the individual in society. He actively responded to the cultural background of India as well as his immediate social environment. In this way, a wide variety of themes and subjects found their poetic handling and artistic transmutation by Ezekiel.

His poetic treatment is cool, detached, and objective. A matter of fact tone informs his poetry. Resorting to a conversational tone and applying the colloquial speech rhythm, he recreated Indian characters and situations and enriched Indian English idiom. The great effect of his poetry springs mainly from the language of irony and paradox that he effectively applied. His poetic art gave a bold and uninhibited expression to sex and sensual life and freed Indian English poetry from the Victorian prudery, inhibition and repression of man's natural impulses.

His poems, 'Hymns in Darkness', 'Motives', 'At Party', 'At the Hotel', 'Nudes', etc, are such audaciously experimental poems. Ezekiel is a very competent poet from the technical point of view also. He writes in regular iambic meter, blank verse, as well as in free verse. In making of the Indian idiom, he made use of a number of Hindi words like *'goonda', 'guru', 'ashram', 'mantras'*, etc. Again, the Indian use of present continuous tense in place of the British simple present also found ample place in his poetry although he uses it with a touch of satire and tinge of mockery.

The post-independence poetry finds a vociferous female voice with a powerful protest against the male-dominated Indian society in the poetry of **Kamala Das**. Her poetry not only enriched the Indian English idiom but also gave voice to the sexually suppressed and repressed Indian women. She did not hesitate to assert her female ego and to openly admit her sexual urges quite as natural as those of males. She grapples with ideas and abstractions, images f man and woman on several planes, the complex of emotions centering round human activities such as love, sex, companionship, and problems related to her own art.

She questions the seamy side of Indian culture wherein women are male-dominated and much wronged. Her imaginative world derives its power to involve the reader from its rich mimetic content while its enduring quality comes from the verbal imagery drawn from many sources. In her poetry one detects a certainty of touch that seems to reflect a confidence in the direction and purpose of her writing as well as integrity of images of India, style, and subject-matter. Sincerity of utterance is most noticeable in her poems which revolt against the forces that stifle her individuality. She cares for the concrete experiences of people living in the modern world of her own times. One can easily find clarity of thought, intensity of feeling, refinement and subtlety of expression in her poetry. The poet in her could not brook the coercive pressures of our conformist traditional culture. Obviously, the anger and sorrow, the restlessness and bewilderment experienced by the Indian women are of great significance for her.

Like Nissim Ezekiel she also uses poems to explain her background and justify her choice of English as the vehicle of poetic expression. Her feminine sensibility finds its finest and fullest expression in her love poems. She views love from a woman's point of view. It is in her love poems that she creates a new Indian English idiom hitherto unknown in English poetic diction. Her volumes of poetry like 'Summer in Calcutta' (1965), the 'Descendants' (1967), 'The Old Playhouse' and Other Poems' (1973), 'Collected Poems' (vol.1) (1984), etc, gave a direction and substance to the post-independence Indian English Poetry.

Jayanta Mahapatra and A. K. Ramanujan are the other two towering personalities in post-independence Indian English poetry. The poetry of Jayanta Mahapatra is both highly praised and sharply criticized as is the case of any notable writer. In poems like the 'Relationship' some critics find a failure to communicate because the poet is writing with an ulterior motive of impressing the reader outside India. But the poem 'Relationship' has ambivalence and richness that evoke mixed reactions. It is generally agreed that Jayanta Mahapatra is one of the most difficult and obscure of all Indian English poets. Mahapatra's poetry appears difficult because of the nature of experience that is sought to be conveyed.

Keki N. Daruwalla highlights the contemplative nature of Mahapatra's poetry when he says: "His is a poetry of the isolated, rather than the alienated self, a poetry in which energy is not expended in the narrative but in contemplation." It is the kind of imagery used in his poetry that contributes to the obscurity of his poetry. There is in his poetry, a synergetic image making in which the waking world and the world of dreams blend. He also explores the intricacies of human relationship. An awareness of tradition, various references to myths and folk legends, and the Orissa landscape play a major part in shaping his poems. Carefully, by drawing specific details, his poetry attempts to understand the subtleties of man in the web of complex relationships. For him love appears to be a release in the complicated 'mess' of the individual. Mahapatra has, no doubt, contributed his own share to create a new rhythm in contemporary poetry in English.

A. K. Ramanujan, though settled in the U.S.A, writes genuine Indian English poetry since he carries within him the Indian tradition and Indian experience of a considerable period of his life. Some critics find in his poetry the syndrome of expatriation-alienation-obsession with the past. Quite a few critics speak of Ramanujan's rootedness in his Hindu experience, of his 'Indian sensibility sharpened and conditioned by a western education, and of his deep and un-fractured Indian spirit. William Walsh calls him 'the most gifted' Indian poet. Ramanujan's volumes, 'The Striders' (1966), 'Relations' (1971), 'Selected Poems' (1976), and 'Second Sight' (1986) are contributions which really enrich Indian English poetry of the post-independence era. His poetry exemplifies how an Indian English poet can derive strength from going back to his roots, back to his childhood memories and experiences of life in India.

In his poetry one may discern a western-trained intellect looking at things oriental, with a detached interest. Family is the still centre of Ramanujan's poetry. In his well-known poem, 'Small Scale Reflections on a Great House' everything 'lost long ago' revives in the speaker's memory and with a touch f nostalgia and pathos. There is an undertone of irony in his poem. The title itself is ironical. Ramanujan wants to put all his experiences and visions into the texture of his poetry. The country of his birth haunts his mind without end. Hindu consciousness is pivotal to his thinking and it colours his vision of life. His thematic range is limited to and is centred round the family relations, insects, and Tamil and Kannada tradition.

His poetry lacks both moral and spiritual vision. His strength lies in craftsmanship of language and imagery. His language is precise and he has forged 'an oblique, elliptical style of his own'. His poems bear meticulously imaginative titles. An image in his poetry is often an adventure leading the reader into unsuspected avenues of experience. His imagery is noted for its concreteness and power. C. Paul Verghese asserts that Ramanujan's images are "highly concentrated in their effect".

Other notable poets who have helped the growth and independence of Indian English poetry are Parthasarathy, Arun Kolatkar, Keki N. Daruwalla, Shiv K. Kumar, O. P. Bhatnagar, Dom Moraes, Dilip Chitre, Eunice de Souza, Adil Jussawalla, Gieve Patel, Vilas Sarang, Saleem Peeradina, A. K. Mehrotra, Manohar Shetty, Santan Rodrigues, Darius Cooper, G. S. Sharat Chandra, Vikram Seth, P. Pal, etc.

Among thses some need special mention for their remarkable contribution to Indian English Poetry to make it attain to the level of maturity now we take pride in.

R. Parthasarathy's first poetic instinct is not towards expression but reticence. There is an air of fastidiousness about his poetry. His mind is focused resolutely on honing and refining his language, trying to achieve the maximum of economy, with consideration and reconsideration carried to the extreme. It is as a craftsman that Parthasarathy impresses us the most. The management of line-length pauses and overflow, the deft placement of short, one-line sentences, and the sophistication of syntax – these are worth studying. Emotion is caught in a few well-chosen images etched carefully. What delights and surprises the most is the constant play of metaphor which is the hallmark of his poetry. Although he can handle irony fairly well, he is impressive neither in general statement nor in satire.

K. N. Daruwalla stands out amongst Indian English poets for his ability to bring to poetry a range of experience generally outside the ambit of poets. His profession as a police officer has clearly helped him in this. He puts his experience of active life to good use in several poems like 'Curfew in a Riot-Torn City', 'Poems from the Tarai', 'Routine', 'Curfew 2', etc. He portrays in his poetry the contemporary Indian socio-political world. The portrayal is with heavy strokes, laden with savage irony. His mode is that of narration and description. His is poetry of incident and event. He discovers his poetic talent in his exploration of his native landscape. The use of the landscape leads to an illumination of the mindscape.

For Arun Kolatkar, poetry is almost an incantatory rhythm expressing in sharp perceptions of the world the poet apprehends. The religious strain is brilliantly juxtaposed with a modern materialistic consciousness and as a result, one finds sharp concrete images coalescing and creating a new design. Arun Kolatkar may make a mockery of the religious 'dogma'. But by making it look ridiculous, he is also aware of the voyage of the fragmented person, looking back to his life-springs. If we examine the poetry of Kolatkar like the 'Boat Ride' and a sequence of poems '*from* Jejury', we will be struck by the complex images. Two dominant concerns are visible in his poetry. The one is secular, ironic, and at times a taunting voice. The other is a religious strain which is trivialized and appears like a farce. Between these two, the poet tries to achieve 'hypnotic stillness', a quality of poise. The images are finely etched and they give a peep into the consciousness of 'modern' individual.

The contributions by the other poets mentioned just above are also really commendable. But within the purview of a brief study like this, they all cannot be expatiated on in considerable length to do them justice or to take into account the details of their valuable contribution in making Indian English rich, varied and more mature.

Conclusion

After independence Indian English poetry made rapid and significant strides towards the attainment of maturity.

Nevertheless, we are yet to travel a little more to emerge as a force to be reckoned with in world poetry. We need the 'inner dynamics' to be independent enough to fight literary battles of our own, based on different movements that can work out an aesthetic. It requires the dynamic play of forces and counter-forces based on a lively tradition of literary disputes, arguments, debates and controversies.

References

1. Das, Bijay Kumar (1982). *Modern Indo-English Poetry*. Bareilly: Prakash Book Depot.
2. Department of English, University of Delhi (1999). *Modern Indian Literature: Poems and Short Stories*, New Delhi: Oxford University Press.
3. Kurup, P. K. J. (1996. *Contemporary Indian Poetry in English*. New Delhi: Atlantic Publishers and Distributors.
4. Naikar, Dasavaraj (ed.) (2003). *Indian English Literature*. New Delhi: Atlantic Publishers and Distributors.
5. Dwivedi, A. N. (2006). *Kamala Das and Her Poetry*. New Delhi: Atlantic Publishers and Distributors.
6. Sarangi, Jaydeep (ed.), (2007). *Explorations in Indian English poetry*, New Delhi: Author Press Publishers.
7. Pandey, Bijendra (ed.), (2001), *Indian Poetry in English*, New Delhi: Atlantic Publishers and Distributors.

2

Scott Fitzgerald's Treatment of Environmental Degradation in *The Great Gatsby*

An eco-critical approach to Francis Scott Fitzgerald's masterpiece, *The Great Gatsby,* reveals that it has several passages disclosing his grave solicitude over the degradation of nature and its potential threat to man's survival on this planet. He was intent on proving that environmental degradation takes place through man's own avaricious exploitation of nature. No doubt, nature has all that is needed to sustain and nurture man but she does not have the plenitude to cater to his greed. In his greed for superabundance and accelerated economic progress man over-exploits, disfigures, mutilates, pollutes and degrades nature. Consequently our planet is gradually becoming an uncongenial habitation for man and all other living beings. Nature herself seems to react sharply and wreaking revenge on man through typhoons, cyclones, tsunamis, earth quakes, floods, droughts etc, whose frequency is alarming.

The exploitation of nature and its ensuing maladies have been foreseen by the artistic and prophetic vision of Fitzgerald as early as the first quarter of the twentieth century when environmental issues had not drawn such serious attention as it does today. The finest artistic expression of this vision was to be found in his best novel *The Great Gatsby*. The description of the 'valley of the ashes' in this novel reminds one of the words of the great Indian philosopher, Dr. S. Radhakrishnan: "Science with its new prospect of a possible liquidation of the world by man's own wanton interference in Nature reminds us of the warning that the wages of sin is death". (*Recovery of Faith*, p.1). Radhakrishnan equates this "wanton interference in Nature" to a "sin", and one that would inevitably lead to death and destruction, and quite rightly, too. He has definitely alluded to the Biblical warning: "The wages of sin is death", which people have generally ignored in the modern world. A death-like situation prevails in the "valley of ashes", barren of any healthy signs of life. Further, the description of the 'valley of ashes' is similar to that in T.S Eliot's '*Waste Land*'. It is rich in allusive and symbolic significance, too. This artistic portrayal is done for producing the desired effect so that the impact of that horrid picture looms large in the minds of the readers and makes them realize how lethal environmental degradation is.

When we explore Fitzgerald's treatment of environmental degradation, it would be worth-while to catch a glimpse of that dismal, portentous picture of environmental degradation taking place near New York with all its apparent glitter. The uncongenial surroundings in the 'valley of ashes' is but the habitation of the scum of the urban society—the poor, hapless labourers—the exploited section of society, the underdog, the fruit of whose toil not only enriches the urban affluent class but also is instrumental in perpetuating the struggle for survival of these unfortunate victims of capitalistic exploitation. In this way, the theme of exploitation of the labour class is also an integral part of this environmental degradation. The well-drawn and shocking picture of the "valley of ashes" is verbally painted in the opening of Chapter 2 (p.18) of the novel:

"About half way between West Egg and New York the motor road hastily joins the rail-road and runs beside it for a quarter of a mile, so as to shrink away from a certain desolate area of land. This is a valley of ashes—a fantastic farm where ashes grow like wheat into ridges and hills and grotesque gardens; where ashes take the forms of houses and chimneys and rising smoke and, finally, with a transcendent effort, of ash grey men who move dimly and already crumbling through the powdery air. Occasionally a line of grey cars crawls along an invisible track, gives out a ghastly creak and comes to rest, and immediately the ash grey men swarm up with leaden spades and stir up an impenetrable cloud, which screens their obscure operations from your sight. (*The Great Gatsby,* p. 18)

Fitzgerald's philosophy of cynicism and skepticism is also evident in the passage. He finds fault with the society of his day and in that way he is a cynic. Even when he revelled in the outward glitter of that society, he was aware of its shocking, seamy side beneath that gloss. Through a realistic portrayal he hopes to awaken the readers' awareness. In this way, he is skeptical of its much-hyped glory, but rather seem to be convinced of the hollowness of the American Dream. Invariably born of this philosophy is his great concern which he dynamically portrays before the readers. There is something nightmarish about the pictures of society and Nature drawn in the above passage. West Egg and New York, highly prosperous and glamorous, are guilty of turning once virginal land into a desolate one, and once fertile valley into 'ashes' through the process of industrialization. Formerly beautiful landscape is now ugly and polluted and full of ashes. It now looks like 'a fantastic farm'. Here 'ashes grow like wheat into ridges and hills and grotesque gardens'. The words are expressive of the degree of pollution brought about. They suggest the harm and degradation that has happened to Nature where earlier, probably, wheat used to grow, but now ashes take the 'fantastic' shapes and have covered the houses, and chimneys and turn people 'ash-grey men'. These ash-covered men are almost 'crumbling through the powdery air'. Besides, there is the rising smoke from the chimneys of factories that adds to the pollution. One can imagine realistically high doses of dust being inhaled by the 'ash-grey men' or the ash-covered labourers there when they stir-up an impenetrable cloud of ash while probably filling the bags or baskets with coal for the factories nearby (since the phrase 'leaden spades' suggests the 'operation' with coal).

Undoubtedly, the environmental pollution is a health hazard and tolls eventually the knell of man. These labourers who work there when constantly breathe in the ash particles are likely to develop lung problems like asthma, bronchitis and the more dangerous problems like cancer. One can imagine that such a contaminated area cannot afford to have anything unpolluted—air, water or even food. When the skin is being continually covered with such ash and dust, skin problems are very likely to develop, too. In short, all sorts of diseases may be engendered by such an uncongenial, polluted atmosphere. The plight of these wretched labourers stands in striking contrast to the comforts of the wealthy that live either in the prosperous New York or the rich West Egg. Wealth and super-abundance and the squandering of money in the cities, and the want, penury, and the wretched condition in the industrial, polluted area are exquisitely suggested in the above passage and are implied contrasts. Fitzgerald's skepticism is further reflected in the next paragraph where a deeper look at this polluted world and the callous, unfeeling, hoarding society in the cities is symbolized in 'the eyes of Doctor T. J. Eckleburg':

> "But above the *grey land* and the *spasms of bleak dust* which drift endlessly over it, you perceive, after a moment, the eyes of Dr. T. J. Eckleburg. The eyes of Dr. T. J. Eckleburg are blue and gigantic; their retinas are one yard high. They look out of no face, but, instead, from a pair of enormous yellow spectacles which pass over a non-existent nose. Evidently some wild wag of an oculist set them there to fatten his practice in the borough of Queens, and then sank down himself into eternal blindness, or forgot them and moved away. But his eyes dimmed a little by many paintless days, under the sun and rain, brood on over the *.solemn dumping ground*". *(The Great Gatsby,* p. 18*)*

Here also we get a shuddering picture of the badly ravaged Nature which is plundered by man to quench his lust for wealth or money. We also realize how terribly Nature is degraded to a 'ghastly' place as hinted at in the expression: 'above the grey land and spasms of bleak dust'. But the more remarkable thing is the eyes of Dr. T. J. Eckleburg, obviously an advertisement for an optician. But the passage throws light on the advertising-hoarding featuring these eyes. The optician who set it there no longer cared about it, but rushed back "to fatten his practice in the borough of Queens, and sank down himself into eternal blindness". (ibid. p .10) The words 'fatten' 'sank down' and 'blindness' suggest his greed for money, love of indolence and luxury, and carelessness respectively. This, once again, speaks volumes of the ugliness that lies behind the glossy face of American society and deepens the contrast with the poor, unhealthy, people in the highly polluted 'valley of ashes'. The eyes of Dr. T. J. Eckleburg used symbolically by the novelist aims at viewing the scene more clearly and grasping the ominous picture in all its frightening reality so as to discern properly the truth behind the surfaces, behind the appearance, and by extension the truth about modern America. The 'living hell' which Fitzgerald admirably portrays here helps us understand the truth that if society has managed to achieve economic progress, it is only at the 'cost' of Nature, and environmental degradation is a necessary concomitant of the so-called progress and modern civilization which can flourish only on maximum utilization of natural resources.

Towards the end of the novel also among other passages there is a fine and unforgettable passage which hints at the way Americans caused the tree- cover to vanish in their quest for rapid urbanization: "And as the moon rose higher the inessential houses began to melt away until gradually I became aware of the old island here that flowered once for Dutch sailors' eyes—a fresh, green breast of the new world. Its vanished trees, the trees that had made way for Gatsby's house, had once pandered in whispers to the last and greatest of all human dreams; for a transitory enchanted moment man must have held his breath in the presence of this continent, compelled into an aesthetic contemplation, he neither understood nor desired, face to face for the last time in history with something commensurate with his capacity for wonder." (*The Great Gatsby*, pp. 144-45) The above passage reminds one of the time when America was discovered by Columbus. It was then a vast stretch of virgin land full of trees and beautiful vegetation that would induce people to take to bewitched reflections and ecstatic but aesthetic thoughts. But the current reality is sombre with the innumerable houses and buildings which have replaced the trees causing great ecological problems. The charming, salubrious pastoral world is now replaced by the urban conglomeration with its concrete jungle of buildings. But life devoid of trees and other prerequisites though equated with the modern life is indeed a life beset with the perils of atmospheric pollution and ecological imbalance. In short, Fitzgerald has effected a fine artistic criticism of this unhealthy trend in his superb novel, *The Great Gatsby* and torn apart the mask of modern life and exposed to the readers the real cost man has to pay for his so-called progress and what is more, the *myth* of progress!

References

1. Dr. S. Radhakrishnan, *Recovery of Faith* (New Delhi: Jaika Books, 1981) p.1.
2. F. Scott Fitzgerald. *The Great Gatsby*, (Indian Edition, New Delhi: Kalyani Publishers, 2000), p.18
3. ibid. p.18.
4. ibid. p.10
5. ibid. pp. 144-145.
6. John Peck and Martin Coyl, *Practical Criticism: How to Write a Critical Appreciation* (New York: Palgrave Publishers, 1995) pp.160-163

3

Issues and Intricacies of Translation *Vis-à-vis* Comparative Literature

Joseph. T. C. & R. G. Munghate

Abstract

Translation is a subtle process involving numerous intricacies and vexing issues. This is particularly true when translation is taken in relation to Comparative Literature. Since Comparative Literature is highly dependent on translation, a close examination of the various issues pertaining to translation has to be done. Translation has been defined by many in different ways. But translation is much more than what all these definitions mean since it involves a process of analysis, interpretation and creation that lead to replacement of one set of linguistic resources and values for another set. This necessarily leads to the loss of some meaning of the original despite the retention of the original core. Thus, the act of translation comprises within it an act of adjustment as well as a compromise. Translation is both a transforming and creative process. It requires adequate expertise on the part of the translator to translate well. Deep knowledge of both the languages - the source language (SL) and the target language (TL) - is a prerequisite for good translation. This in itself is a serious issue because the mastery of the linguistic aspects of another language is really difficult. Further, there are non-linguistic factors such as the milieu, the socio-cultural factors and the spirit of the time whose knowledge is essential for good translation since they go deep into the making of the text. Further, dialectical idioms and mythological references make matters worse. It is all a daunting task for the translator to tackle them well. Besides, the subjective aspects of the translator himself, such his sensibility, his knowledge and education, his tastes, his bias and prejudices, his

S. G. M College, Kurkheda

attitudes, his ideologies, etc., are all matter, which affects translation in a positive or negative manner. These and many more pose serious issues in translation. The paper examines in detail the diverse issues and intricacies of translation particularly in relation to Comparative Literature. Along with it, the origin and evolution of Comparative Literature and the relation of translation to Comparative Literature have been examined briefly in relation to the context.

Introduction

Translation is a process that, on closer examination, reveals much greater complexities and intricacies than it has generally been held to inhere. It is beset with several issues that defy easy solutions. This is particularly so in relation to Comparative Literature. If Comparative Literature has now emerged as a signal discipline, it is mainly because of translation. Both 'Translation Studies' and 'Comparative Literature' have been assuming greater significance over time and been playing more serious roles over the years and especially in the post globalized era. Since it is 'translation' that enriches and sustains comparative literature, the issues related to translation deserve serious attention. For this purpose, an examination of the nature, issues and intricacies of translation in relation to comparative literature and a study its relationship with the latter, is a prerequisite.

Issues and Intricacies of Translation

Despite the initial neglect it encountered and the inferior status it was earlier accorded, translation has been drawing greater attention and enjoying a much better status over the years. Translation is necessitated by the need for better communication in a world fragmented by thousands of languages and numerous cultures. The effort of the people of different cultures and religions to come closer for commercial, political, social, literary, spiritual or communicative purposes has been at the core of translation activities. Translation can be defined in simple words as both 'a substitution and transference of meaning from one language to another'. It is, in other words, transference of meaning from the source language (SL) to the target language (TL). Dr. Samuel Johnson viewed it as a process that involves "a change into another language retaining the sense". Taking a linguistic stance, J. C. Catford defines translation as "the replacement of textual material in one language (SL) by equivalent material in another language (TL)". There are numerous definitions of this sort. But, basically they all imply more or less the same. Some hold it as an 'art', some others as a 'craft' and yet many view it as a 'science'. But translation is much more than all these since it involves a process of analysis, interpretation and creation that lead to replacement of one set of linguistic resources and values for another set. This necessarily leads to the loss of some meaning of the original despite the retention of the original core. Thus, the act of translation comprises within it an act of adjustment as well as a compromise.

It has been said that 'translation is an operation performed on two languages - the source language (SL) and the target language (TL). When translation is done with the aim of transference of meaning, it is perfectly suitable in non-literary translation. But when it comes to translation of literature the matter gets highly complicated since exact equivalents of the SL cannot be found in the TL. The indeterminacy of the text makes matters worse since the reader's response gives it a colour and construct. The metaphorical language of literature vexes the translator who is unsure whether he should use literal or metaphorical meaning. Again, translation and its quality depends considerably on the translator's knowledge of both the languages (SL&TL), mastery of various linguistic aspects, the sensibility , the feel for words, perspective levels, range of experiences, etc. The greater the possession of such parameters, the better will be the translation, and vice versa. The translator should possess the true spirit, or rather, the inwardness and the inscape of both the languages and the culture of the SL and its people. "His task becomes particularly difficult when the source text is dense in socio-cultural context, using dialect and is steeped in mythological references or folk beliefs". (Shiv Kumar, p.41) One cannot say for sure whether a 'spirit-channelling' by the translator or a rendering based purely on 'rational faculties' is the better of the two. These are all serious issues which arise in relation to translation. It is generally agreed that in case of translation of literary works much more than a 'word-for-word translation' a 'free translation' to capture the true spirit and sense of the work is better. This process is highly creative.

According to Douglas Robinson, translators channel the words and ideas of their source authors. He further argues that "translators channel a wide variety of other voices, using "Other" in the broadest sense possible to include everything vaguely indicated by Henry Reed's claim that 'Everyday, in countless ways you and I are channels of spirit, of ideas, and of resources that come from beyond our conscious personalities'. Whatever seems to come to us from the outside, or from the realm of our conscious awareness or control is 'Other' – when as for Jacques Lacan and other twentieth theorists of Otherness, it speaks to us from "inside our heads."... Lacan wants to draw clear distinctions among the various types of otherness: the "objects" we choose, including love objects (other people and things as invested by and with our needs); idealized forms of our ego, or our "self" as ego-ideal, modeled on parents and other authority figures; and large social-consciousness, forces such as nations, genders, races, classes, age groups, professions, political and economic systems, scholarly disciplines, metaphysical translations, and so on. All of these Others come from outside but speak to us from the inside; and without sticking to Lacan's typologies of Otherness..., I want to explore the ways in which translators channel, and especially how translators become and remain and present themselves as translators by channeling, all these Others, all these becoming-internalized forces, all these voices outside-and-inside our heads." (Douglas, 10-11)

Origin & Evolution of Comparative Literature

Comparative Literature which derives its very being, its staple from translation, has emerged of late as an important discipline. But, it is of fairly recent origin. It originated in the 19th century as a result of a series of French anthologies published in 1816 under the title *Cours de Litterature Comparee.* In *Comparative Literature and Literary Theory* (p.171), Ulrich Weissterin expresses the view that either Jean Jacques Ampere or Abel Francois Villemain "must be regarded as the true father of a systematically conceived Comparative Literature in France – or anywhere for that matter." The decades 1820s and 1830s witnessed the growing currency in the use of the term 'Comparative Literature' in France. The same phenomenon happened in Germany in 1854 when Moriz Carriere used the German term 'Vergleichende Literaturgeschichtre' in a book. The credit for using this term first in English goes to Matthew Arnold who popularized it through his lectures in 1848 and 1857.

The greatest advantage of Comparative Literature is that it makes possible a meaningful comparative study of the notable literary works of a particular language with those in other countries by notable writers of the same genre and same period. It is not merely the stylistic aspects and subject matter or technical excellences but the implied national and cultural aspects can also be unearthed in this act. Comparative study is the foolproof method for judging the artistic merit of literary works. This enables the readers to judge the comparative stature of the famous writers and the merits and limitations of their works.

Comparative Literature also offers the national and regional writers in different languages a good chance to be properly evaluated provides a wider audience or a larger set of readers to ensure them a better possibility of achieving popularity. Those that are worth hearing do get a chance to be heard. Even from regional languages masterpieces are likely to spring forth, and writers of real genius possibly appear with broader vision and deeper insights than those at the national or world level. Only translation of these works, and that too really sincere translation can capture the beauty, merit and spirit of these works and thereby enable them to be compared and contrasted with those great ones in other languages, regional, national, or international.

"Comparative Literature seems to have emerged as an antidote to nationalism even though its roots went deep into national cultures", observes Susan Bassnett. But in India it is closely associated with the rise of Indian nationalism. India is a land of numerous well-developed languages with rich literatures of their own, although not yet properly noticed by the world in general on account of the late birth of Comparative Literature. Now that Comparative Literature is receiving wider popularity and translation is gaining momentum, these languages and literary works have a great chance before them to prove their mettle. Many Indians are convinced that same works in our language s such as Bengali, Marathi, Tamil, Kannada, Malayalam, Hindi, Urdu, etc., can be as good as some of the world classics, if not better. But only painstaking translation can bring out their excellences. Again, Comparative Literature allows for an open approach. Through major world languages like English, if great literary works of all notable languages are made available to the world readers, consensus can be formed about the relative greatness or merits of these products of human minds and cultures. It is also agreed that Comparative Literature is a study of intertextuality. But it is translation that brings to the fore intertextuality and paves the way for better evaluation.

It is through the rendering in our own regional languages that most of us have had access to our great Indian epics - *Ramayana* and *Mahabharata* and not through Sanskrit in which they were originally written. Similarly, standard translations of these works in English by really expert bilingual scholars of Sanskrit and English, imbued with the passion to disseminate the noblest and the best, and armed with the essential qualifications of ideal translators, can give them wider popularity and still better appreciation everywhere in the world. In the same way, many other countries also can have their highly cherished works translated in English and offer the readers throughout the world a chance to relish them and resort to a revaluation of the already established reputations.

Translation vis-à-vis Comparative Literature

If translation is done by really perceptive, imaginative, and highly sensitive translators, the very act of translation can be highly creative and can turn out even a better work than the original one. But this is indeed rare on account of the numerous linguistic, stylistic, semiotic, cultural, and subjective factors that make translation a herculean task. Cultural variations also pose real challenges for the translator. "From the point of view of the reader the success of an English translation largely depends upon its ability to approximate the experience of reading the source text, without subjecting the language of the translated version, to avoidable strain." (Shiv Kumar, p. 37) To those who insist on the faithful version of the original, the deconstructionists gave a fitting reply by pointing out that even the 'original' is also a work of translation of the thoughts and ideas and hence there is no vital difference between the original and the translated version. Even the feminist translation theorists have also questioned the supremacy of the original over its translated version. Prominent among such feminist translator theorists are Susan Bassnett, Barbara Johnson, Barbara Godard, Sherry Simon and Annie Brisset. They used the metaphors of 'infidelity' and 'Cultural Complicity'. Fidelity in translation, as in marriage, connoted the sexualization of translation terminology. In the post 1980 period translator has been accorded a rank equal to that of the original writer by such critics and translators as Lambert, Van Gorp, Theo Hermans, Walter Benjamin, Jacques Derrida, Haraldo, Augusto de Campos, Helene Cixous and a few others.

The 'Cannibalistic' concept of translation as propounded by translators in Brazil and Canada such as Haroldo and

Augusto de Campos wants to eliminate the boundary between the source and target texts. This concept may be understood in the sense of a liberating form and freeing the translation from the original but not as another form of possessing the original. In the words of Gentzler, "Translation is seen as an empowering act, an act of affirmative play that is very close to the Benjamin/Derrida position, which sees translation as a life force that ensures a literary text's survival." In the post-structuralism era, translation is viewed as 'a process of textual manipulation' in which 'the concept of plurality replaces dogmas of faithfulness to a source text.' In the 1990s there occurred in translation a shift in emphasis from semiotic model to intercultural activity. The main architects behind this change were Jose Lambert and Clem Robyns. Translation soon began to be treated as identical with culture. Another view, under Feminist influence, takes translation to be 'a compound act of reading and writing.'

Translation, on the whole, has helped the development of culture the world over, and has brought out the correlation between literature and culture in multi-lingual and multi-cultural societies. Consequently, translation is instrumental in promoting the cause of Comparative Literature. This prompted Bassnett to remark: "We should look upon translation studies as the principal discipline from now on with Comparative Literature as a valued but subsidiary subject area". Translation has now emerged as a discipline on a par with literary and critical theories. It is largely viewed as a process of rewriting of the original without causing the original any harm. It is also thought of as a transformation of the original. It is a bridge between two languages as well. The post-colonial era has witnessed translation as a fast growing activity in India as perhaps elsewhere. We now keep translating from the Indian languages into the languages of the world, especially into the English language. Consequently, there has now come into being a vast chunk of literature called "Indian Literature in English Translation". This has greatly facilitated

Comparative Literature Studies, too. No doubt, both Translation and Comparative Studies have a bright future ahead.

Conclusion

Translation is a complex process with innumerable intricacies which make it quite enigmatic. It involves a process of analysis, interpretation and creation that lead to the replacement of one set of linguistic resources and values for another set. It is an inter-textual activity in which manipulation, empowering and transformation simultaneously take place but nevertheless it ensures the survival of texts. Even when it feeds on the original it captures the spirit and form, within its own constraints, and contributes to cultural edification. Despite its slithery, sloppy start, it steadily advanced and has now established itself as a discipline. With the passage of time the complex nature of translation and diverse issues involved have been closely examined and carefully perused. Comparative Literature has gained most from translation and depends on it for its very sustenance and survival. The great classic works of the world are available to us only through translation. Great regional writers can look forward to an international audience and greater acclaim through translation alone. But translators have to acquire the essential qualifications to be ideal translators. This would lead to fine translations which could be on a par with the originals. Ill-equipped translators would do injustice to the original works by distorting the form and content. Hence translators have to be bi-lingual or multi-lingual experts with adequate knowledge of the moment and milieu especially the cultural context of the texts translated. Their insights into the complexities involved and adequate preparations would ensure a hard task well-accomplished. This will galvanize the field of Comparative Literature.

References

1. Robinson, Douglas. *Who translates?* Albany, State University of New York, 2001.
2. Das, Bijay Kumar. *A Handbook of Translation Studies*. New Delhi: Atlantic Publishers and Distributors. 2005.
3. Catford, J. C., *A Linguistic Theory of Translation,* London: OUP, 1969.
4. Bassnett - Mc Guire Sussan. *Translation Studies,* London: Rutledge, 1991.
5. Smith, A. H., ed. *Aspects of Translation*. London: Seeker and Warburg, 1958.
6. Mini Krishnan, *Translation of Indian Text into English*. The Journal of English Language Teaching (India) vol.45/3, 2007.
7. Parvathi Vasudev. *Translation as an art*. The Journal of English Language Teaching (India) vol.140/3. 2004.
8. Shiv Kumar, P. *Towards a Translation Protocol in the Postcolonial India*. Post colonial Theory and Literature. (eds.) P. Mallikarjuna Rao, Rajeshwar Mittapalli and K. Damodar Rao). New Delhi: Atlantic Publishers and Distributors. 2003.
9. Mishra, Uday Kumar. *Second Language Learning and Translating: a Perspective*. The Journal of English Language Teaching (India) vol.44/5, 2006.

4

Impact of the Indian Aesthetic Theory of '*Rasa*' on Eliot's Theory of Poetry

Abstract

T. S. Eliot, one of the towering figures of twentieth century criticism, and one reputed for his theory of poetry enunciated in his critical essay *Tradition and the Individual Talent,* seems, on deeper study, to have been highly influenced by the Indian Theory of Rasa. A comparative study of both the theories reveals that Eliot has drawn vastly from the Theory of Rasa. Since he has never admitted its impact on his mind, or his having drawn from it, it is highly possible that he has formulated his theory under its unconscious influence. Nevertheless, one cannot just ignore the numerous parallels between both the theories as mere coincidences. The paper examines a series of close similarities between both the theories and establishes the impact of the Indian aesthetic theory on Eliot's formulation of his own theory of poetry.

Key Words: Aesthetic, *Rasa, vibhava, anubhava, vyabhicari bhava, nishpati,* art emotion, passing feelings, permanent emotions, *sthayibhava*s, emotio-motive complexes.

Introduction:

An inter-textual study between Eliot's theory of poetry (as it is enunciated in his *Tradition and the Individual Talent*) and the Indian aesthetic theory of *Rasa* clearly reveals that both the theories have several things in common. Further, the close similarities between them point to the possibility that Eliot might have been considerably influenced by the theory of Rasa whose 'echoes' permeate his well-known critical essay *'Tradition and the Individual Talent.* An attempt is made here to expose Eliot's conscious or unconscious indebtedness (which he has not explicitly admitted anywhere) to the Indian theory of Rasa for the formulation of his own much-hyped theory of poetry. The paper cites the numerous parallels that run between both the theories and calls in question Eliot's intellectual integrity and his reputation for originality.

In order to bring to light these close similarities, it is imperative to have a rudimentary knowledge of the basics of the Theory of *Rasa* itself. It was none other than Bharat, the first known oriental theorist, who made the first signal definition of Rasa Theory as applied to the study of drama and its enjoyment. He formulated the theory in his famous *'Rasa Sutra'* in *'Natya Sastra'* and stated: *'Vibhavanubhavavyabhicarisamyogatrasanishpati'* It means that "the art emotion (aesthetic emotion), comes to be expressed through the conjunction of its causes and effects, and the ancillary feelings (passing feelings) that accompany the emotion", (*Natyasastra* VI, p. 31).

In other words, the causes of art emotion are what generate it and make it known. These causes are termed *'Vibhãva'* and viewed in two different aspects: the object of emotion (*ãlambana*) which may be a person, thing, scene or thought that brings into being the emotion in an individual; and secondly, the circumstantial factors constituting the situation that excites the emotion (*Uddipana*). The effects of the emotion (*anubhava*) are behavioural responses by the individual undergoing the emotions, namely, his words, actions and gestures. The ancillary (passing) emotions (*Vyabhiari* or *Sancara)* are transient or momentary in nature. However, they are associated with the basic, and so reinforce it into an enduring one. Emotions, objects and expressions are not bound to one another in any fixed or invariable relation. Therefore, it is not possible for any one of the same to represent alone the desired emotion. Hence, it is necessary that there should be an appropriate connection (*samyoga*) of all the factors in order to evoke emotive meaning of the poetic discourse.

Bharata enumerates 41 *bhavas* of which eight are the basic or durable ones (*sthayi bhavas*) and the rest, 33, are transient or ancillary feelings. The latter are said to be incapable of existing by themselves and become meaningful only when they are associated with one or more basic emotions. On the other hand, the basic emotions rarely appear in their pure form and usually assimilates the ancillary ones with which they have affinity. Hence, Bharata observes: "*Rasa* manifestation is effected through the conjunction of different *bhavas*". Even in short lyrics where one or two emotional strains may be developed unlike what is done in longer compositions, the unexpressed factor relevant to the emotive situation are derived by the reader through the process of implication. In the longer compositions however, different basic emotions may be combined to create an emotio-motive-complex in which one of the basic emotions is the major and dominant and the others are minor and subsidiary, the principle governing all such combinations of basic emotions is achievement of aesthetic unity, however disparate these constituent emotions may be. Thus, when the disparate emotions are treated as subordinate and together contribute to the development of the dominant one, the poetic discourse communicates an integral but complex emotive meaning.

Later theorists opposed Bharata on several issues and pointed out that poetic creation thus effected need not create *rasa* unless the reader himself possessed the required sensibility for proper enjoyment of the artist's work. So a generally accepted conclusion states that the realization of rasa is possible only when the ideal reader (*sahrudaya/rasika*) interacts with the properly written literary work. In Abhinav Gupta's opinion, only such an interaction results in *rasa* and it is a transcendental experience for the reader who captures the art emotion through aesthetic sensibility. This art emotion is neither personal emotion nor the emotion presented in the art form. Rather, it is the result of getting at the art emotion and letting it interact with his/her own experiences, impressions and knowledge. Thus, *rasa* is an illuminating inner experience (*alaukika*), a throbbing spiritual exhilaration.

This 'art emotion' (*rasa*) is purged of all pathological associations of the personal emotions. It is pure and universal. Here, it is on a par with mystic and religious experience.

Now, when we examine Eliot's theory of poetry as enunciated in his '*Tradition and the Individual Talent*' and read it in the light of the *rasa* theory, surprisingly enough, we find that many of his utterances on the nature of poetry are echoes of the *rasa* theory itself and we have sufficient reason to suspect him of having been tremendously influenced by it at the time when he wrote his theory. This must have happened consciously or unconsciously. In *Tradition and the Individual Talent*, while explaining the poetic process going on in the mind of the poet, using the analogy of a jar containing oxygen and sulphur dioxide Eliot says, "The action which takes place when a bit of finely filiated platinum is introduced into a chamber containing oxygen and sulphur dioxide" he hints that "the mind of the mature poet differs from that of the immature one.....by being a more finely perfected medium in which special or very varied feelings are at liberty to enter into new combinations." (*Tradition and the Individual Talent)*

Here the phrase 'special feelings' resembles the 'dominant emotion' in rasa theory and the 'very varied feelings' are akin to the 'subsidiary emotions' in regard to longer compositions. Eliot further elaborates the analogy: "When two gases previously mentioned are mixed in the presence of a filament of platinum, they form sulphurous acid. This combination takes place only if the platinum shred is present: nevertheless, the newly formed acid contains no traces of platinum and the platinum itself is apparently unaffected: has remained inert, neutral and unchanged. The mind of the poet is the shred of platinum. It may partly or exclusively operate upon the man himself but the more perfect the artist, the more completely separate in him will be the man who suffers and the mind which creates, the more perfectly will the mind digest and transmute the passions which are its materials". (*Tradition...*)

Eliot uses 'passions' (experiences) to mean 'emotions' and 'feelings' which remind us of the '*sthayi bavas*' or permanent emotions and '*vyabhicari bhavas*' (transient feelings) of the Rasa Theory. Moreover, "transmutation" of these emotions is insisted on by him in poetry and so is the case with the Theory of Rasa. Eliot goes on to say: "The experience, you will notice, the elements which enter the presence of the transforming catalyst, are of two kinds: emotions and feelings." Once again, we sense the 'basic emotion' and 'passing feelings' - concepts of rasa - echoing in T. S. Eliot's writings.

There is absolute similarity between Rasa theory and Eliot's theory when he further states: "The effect of a work of art upon the person who enjoys it is an experience different in kind from any experience not of art". It means the experience of the sensible, ideal reader or of any votary of an art is that of the art emotion incorporated in the artistic work through his interaction with it. Rasa theory also holds the same although Abhinav Gupta's interpretation slightly varies. Anyway, art emotion is underlined indirectly. The resonance of the Rasa theory is again heard in another part of the essay when Eliot clarifies: "It may be formed of one emotion or may be a combination of several emotions, and various feelings inhering for the writer in particular words or phrases or images, may be added to compose the final result. Or great poetry may be made without the direct use of any emotions, whatever composed out of feelings solely". (*Tradition......*)

The phrase "a combination of several emotions" immediately brings to our minds the longer compositions mentioned in the Rasa Theory which allow the combination of several basic emotions to produce an emotio-motive-complex in which one emotion is 'dominant' and the rest 'subsidiary'. Again, the phrase 'various feelings' points to the '*Vyabhicari bhavas*' or transient emotions of rasa theory.

Eliot's insistence on 'intensity of the artistic process, the pressure under which the fusion takes place' is very notable.

It is similar to the Indian insistence on proper transmutation of emotions and feelings to turn them into art emotions. Moreover, Eliot's statement: "The difference between the art and the event is absolute" seems to be an echo of the Indian stance that the basic or permanent emotions and the art emotion (rasa) are entirely different. Eliot clarifies his point by giving an example: "The ode of Keats contains a number of feelings which have nothing to do with the nightingale, but which the nightingale, partly perhaps because of its attractive name and partly because of its reputation served to bring together". (*Tradition....*)

Here nightingale becomes the '*Alambhana Vibhava*' or the object of the emotion, mentioned in the theory of rasa. Eliot further clarifies his point on the difference between personal emotion and art emotion: "Impressions and experiences which are important for the man may take no place in the poetry and those which become important in the poetry may play quite a negligible part in the man, the personality". (*Tradition...*) By 'experience' Eliot implies 'emotions and/or feelings'. Surprisingly, Eliot gradually comes to use the phrase 'art emotion' which is the equivalent of 'rasa' in Indian theory. Consciously or unconsciously he had been working with the same ingredients and postulates and finally arrives at the same conclusion as in rasa theory, when again he uses similar words and phrases such as 'structural' (dominant?) emotion and 'floating feelings' (*vyabhicari / sancari bhavas?*). He insists on their combination ('samyogat'?), too. To use his own words, "This is, so to speak, the structural emotion provided by drama. But the whole effect, the dominant tone is due to the fact that a number of *floating feelings*, having an affinity to his emotion by no means superficially evident, have *combined* with it to give us a new art emotion." (Italics, mine). (*Tradition...*)

Conclusion

In conclusion, it can be inferred that the theory of Rasa had exerted a tremendous influence on Eliot. A sensitive reader can find numerous 'traces' of the theory of Rasa in Eliot's theory of poetry which he has enunciated in his essay, *'Tradition and the Individual Talent.'* From the foregoing analysis it is highly possible that he was greatly swayed by the theory of *rasa* whose close parallel runs throughout his theory by way of frequently scattered innuendoes. These can be safely spotted as the 'traces' of the Rasa theory. That he had read the Indian classical works, points to the greater possibility of his having been profoundly influenced by the Indian Theory of Rasa. Therefore, it is none too easy to dismiss these close similarities as quite 'accidental coincidences' in view of his great erudition and the tendency to draw liberally from various cultures of different climes and times and assimilate the fine nuances of their ethos!

References

1. Swami, Rama & V. S. Sethuraman (Eds.), (1986) *The English Critical Tradition - An Anthology of English Literary Criticism* - Vol-2, (Madras) Macmillan India Limited.
2. Eliot, T. S, *'Tradition and the Individual Talent'* (published in *The English Critical Tradition: an Anthology of English Literary Criticism* - Vol-2, (Madras) Macmillan India Limited, (1986)).
3. Sethuraman, V. S. (ed). *'Indian Aesthetics'* (1993).
4. *'Language and Meaning in Indian Poetics'* by Haladhar Pande (Published in *Indian Journal of English Studies* published by All India English Teachers Association, 2007)

5

Artistic Transmutation of Fitzgerald's Philosophy of Life and Social Criticism

Abstract

Francis Scott Fitzgerald, like any other brilliant writer, had encoded in his writings his philosophy of life at different periods of his literary career. He had also great social concern for the decadent tendencies of the American culture and society. But he used the literary medium - mainly fiction - to give an artistic utterance to his philosophy and social concern. In so doing he resorted to proper transmutation of his resources without overtly becoming didactic. For this purpose he made proper use of the vast array of literary devices and techniques. This paper explores how dexterously Fitzgerald transmuted his raw materials including his vision, his philosophy of life and the concern he had for the American society, which was but the dynamic side of his philosophy with all its shifting stances.

Key Words: Transmutation, philosophy, social criticism, imagery, realistic imagination, emotive rendering, aesthetic perception, aesthetic distance, connoisseurs.

Introduction

Literary writers transmute the materials taken for artistic handling. Literary art presupposes conscious effort to transform the reality so that it will be aesthetically appealing to the readers and produce the desired effect on the minds of the connoisseurs. Far from making direct statements, artists prefer handling reality by means of indirection, suffusing it with emotion and imagination. For this purpose they use the emotive language rather than the referential one. Besides, through imagery – the various figures of speech – the use of appropriate diction, symbols, myths, proper manipulation of the syntactic structure, and various other literary and technical devices, the narrative, the dialogues, various points of view, insertion of poetic pieces, quotations, flash backs and epiphanies, the literary artist produces the transformed reality with an aura of novelty and charm, contributing to aesthetic pleasure which fascinates the readers when they subject them to a brown study. The use of a suitable style contributes much to this effect. If emotional handling renders deep feeling to the matter being handled, imaginative treatment recreates the whole with a different conception wherein the readers' flight on the wings of imagination and fancy enables them directly to reach at the underlying reality with enhanced effect despite the apparent differences or dissimilarities.

Thus, a deeper truth is excavated with the help of imagination and even a steady view of it as the sight of a distant light is possible for the artist who then makes prophetic statements. This prophetic vision is the product of such powerful imagination that apprises the readers of what is to happen or what might happen. In this attempt at a search for 'ideal probabilities' (as Aristotle said), the literary artist discovers truths which not even the scientists are capable of. Besides, a portrayal of human life either realistically or based on ideal probability, the literary artist is always intrigued by the mysterious working of the human psyche which is the focal area of literary artist's search to plumb its sombre depths of which other scholars have hardly any deep knowledge, barring probably the psychologists, philosophers, the religious thinkers, and to some extent a few social scientists. But even in this case, the unpredictable human nature has always been an enigma for the literary men as also for the others. Hence, it is a fertile field of constant inquiry and persistent search, a never-ending activity.

True artists endowed with an amazing degree of visionary, mystical powers share with readers the esoteric insights they get from their meditative acts, epiphany moments, deep psychological and spiritual insights. All these are very often need to be expressed in forms much unlike the direct statements. On the contrary, indirect utterances clad in a transformed language, and the background or setting specially prepared (wherein the spatio-temporal factors taking a changed appearance), are of prime significance for the literary artists, when they create a new imaginary world. This world has its own independent entity and should be viewed as such. Nevertheless, the art that has gone into the making of this verbal, textual world where the philosophy and social criticism are apparently hidden by the skill of the artist leaving the readers' reflective frame of mind to philosophize and infer from the incidents and happenings to arrive at the hidden springs of motives and thoughts which inform the undercurrent of the literary work, has to be critically examined to evaluate the merit of the artist's work. In other words, it is no less than a colossal task sifting the rational from the irrational elements to convert the 'aesthetic perception into intellectual terms', for transmutation is such that it gives the appearance of an altogether different reality with its own organic power. Much taste, sensibility, and logical insight should accompany this process of dismantling the artistic apparel which the process of artistic transmutation has clad the material and experience the artist had been trying to communicate to the readers. Much intricacy occurs when artistic transmutation is resorted to. This is an arduous task requiring tremendous effort as it implies an examination of the various technical devices used by the artist, as also other ways and means by which the artist has transmuted his subject matter including the philosophy of life and implied social criticism.

In the case of Francis Scott Fitzgerald who has not stated his philosophy of life directly in his writings at all, the task is further complicated. W.H. Hudson points to this difficulty, and the possibility of a philosophy of life in any novel, on closer examination, however transmuted it is: Like the drama, the novel is concerned with life – with men and women, and their relationships, with the thoughts and feelings, the passions and motives by which they are governed and impelled, with their joys and sorrows, their struggles, successes, failures. Since then, the novelist's theme is life, in one or several of its innumerable aspects, it is impossible for him not to give, express or by implication, some suggestion at least, if nothing more than a suggestion, of the impression which life makes upon him. Little as he may dream of using his narrative as the vehicle of any special theories or ideas, certain theories or ideas will nonetheless be found embodied in it, and even the slightest story will yield under analysis a more or less distinct underlying conception of the moral values of the characters and incidents of which it is composed. To this extent therefore, if no further, every novel, no matter how trivial, may be said to rest upon a certain view of the world, to incorporate or connote various general principles, and thus to present a rough general philosophy of life. (1996)

From the life portrayed differently in different works the reader has to infer and philosophize, and then look at it carefully so as to find out how he artistically transformed it concealing art itself. What is concealed has to be disclosed. How he concealed has to be analyzed and evaluated. Being a master artist, Fitzgerald seldom made any direct utterance of an abstract type to voice his philosophy and social criticism. Rather, he transmuted them into elegant artistic expressions especially in his novels which he considered a superior art form. Once Fitzgerald wrote: "...I had done very little thinking, save within the problem of my craft." (*Crack Up*, p. 49) Thus, Fitzgerald's thinking and social criticism is within the framework of his craft. In other words, they are all transmuted into his art. Very often he created situations that would speak for themselves. This too was a kind of transmutation. For this transmutation he made liberal use of indirection, and a metaphoric language vibrant with vividness and beauty.

He fashioned his ideas into artistically satisfying expressions with the aid of realistic imagination and emotion. His expressions throb with charm and gracefulness. There is intensity, power, and captivating force in the language he used. His phrases and words have a queer power of 'transport'. They carry the readers away to the world created by the writer. Many of his expressions are fresh and original and smack of his artistic talent and originality. His talent had a rare knack for recreation and transformation of the direct and less attractive observations into poetic truth – the imaginative and emotive rendering of the experience. This compels the readers' attention.

For instance, note the 'lingering' and 'transporting' effect of the passage at the end of *The Great Gatsby* where Nick, the narrator plunges into a meditative mood and muses:

Most of the big shore places were closed now and there were hardly any lights except the shadowy, moving glow of a ferryboat across the Sound. And as the moon rose higher the inessential houses began to melt away until gradually I became aware of the old island here that flowered once for the Dutch sailors' eyes-a fresh, green breast of the new world. Its vanished trees, the trees that had made way for Gatsby's house, had once pandered in whispers to the last and greatest of all human dreams; for a transitory enchanted moment man must have held his breath in the presence of this continent, compelled him into an aesthetic contemplation he neither understood nor desired, face to face for the last time in history with something commensurate to his capacity for wonder....Gatsby believed in the green light, the orgiastic future that year after year recedes before us...So we beat on, boats against the current, borne back ceaselessly into the past.(pp.144-145).

Here a historical fact, the interplay of the past and the present in terms of time, a geographic transformation (in terms of place) that has taken place alongside the past bewitching pastoral reality and the present not so beautiful condition of urbanized, treeless set-up replacing it, and all these dynamic changes which occurred over a period of time – all have been suggested, and the human endeavour to progress, but the mind's irresistible urge to recall the past with nostalgia and the resultant pull on the mind are all so artistically brought out that no better expression seems possible to bring about this emotional and imaginative experience and the similar level of effect. Such is the power of Fitzgerald's transmutation – whether philosophy or social criticism. In the above passage is implied a criticism of the present state of development at the cost of denudation of forests or tree-cover which brings about environmental problems. But man's greed for progress makes him ignore it. When the cities were built up, nature was ravished and her freshness was lost. Also are implied such philosophical questions as: Are we any better now than before? What was the cost we paid for our progress? Has our capacity for wonder ended with our quest for progress? Is the pastoral world we left behind a better option than the urban culture we have embraced? Maximum meaning has been achieved in minimum words. It is 'concentrated wisdom' as well. The use of the concrete, the imagery, is superb in communicating the abstract, and something almost incommunicable. The 'green light' symbol and the 'orgiastic future' along with 'green breast' symbol keep haunting us, and point to the human predicament – the illusion of the dream of a paradise on earth that is never attainable. 'So boats against the current we beat on', outstretching our hands towards the unattainable.

Much of what he wrote was transmuted autobiography. In many cases it was his own life with all its complexity that he tried to project into his writings. In Jerome Mandel's view: His method did not lend itself to the elegant transmutation of previous literary modes-the sort of thing one admires in Joyce, for instance. In his early works especially, Fitzgerald 'transmuted autobiography': that is, by combining 'his own emotions with the qualities of an actual figure'. (Bruccoli, *Grandeur*, p.125) or someone he had read about or even characters he had created earlier, he transmuted the events of his personal and his imaginative life into fiction. (1988)

Fitzgerald artistically transmuted his personal impressions and experiences. He desisted from mere copying of some models or even life. It was reported in the *Saturday Evening Post* that "Fitzgerald did not work directly from models; he did not attempt to copy life. 'Whether it's something that happened twenty years ago or only yesterday, I must start out with an emotion-one that's close to me and that I can understand.'"(March 4, 1933)

In his early novels- *This Side of Paradise* and *The Beautiful and Damned,* Fitzgerald's transmutation was not so objective and artistic as was his masterly transmutation in *The Great Gatsby.* In the former, he did not keep an aesthetic distance with the heroes; rather he merged himself into them. But in the latter, by using a First Person narrator (Nick Caraway), the author distanced himself from the hero to have a different look, making it attain more objectivity. In the words of William Troy:

Here is a remarkable instance of the manner in which adoption of a special form or technique can profoundly modify and define a writer's whole attitude toward his world. In the earlier books author and hero tended to melt into one because there was no internal principle of differentiation by which they might be separated; they respired in the same climate, emotional and moral; they were tarred with the same brush. But in *Gatsby* is achieved a dissociation, by which Fitzgerald was able to isolate one part of himself, the spectatorial or aesthetic, and also the more intelligent and responsible, in the person of the ordinary but quite sensible narrator, from another part of himself, the dream-ridden romantic adolescent from St. Paul and Princeton, in the person of the legendary Jay Gatsby. (1963)

Thus, the later novels can pride themselves of being more objective and artistic, and the climax of this achievement was *The Great Gatsby*. Though a greater level of artistic transmutation was achieved in *Tender Is the Night* compared with the earlier novels, yet it was not as perfect as *The Great Gatsby*. The last novel, *The Last Tycoon* is too incomplete to form a clear-cut opinion about it. Nonetheless, whatever of it is written is indeed written artistically and with a definite design behind it which is evident enough to infer that it also with its first person narrator, Cecilia Brady, is artistic and objective in its process of transmutation. Similarly, his short stories also contain his philosophy of life and social criticism artistically transmuted.

References

1. William Henry Hudson, *An Introduction to the Study of Literature*, 9th Indian Edition, reprinted, (1996), New Delhi: Kalyani publishers, p. 163.
2. Francis Scott Fitzgerald, *The Crack-Up*, with Other Pieces and Stories, New York: Penguin Books, (1965), p. 49
3. F. S. Fitzgerald, *The Great Gatsby*, (Indian Edition) New Delhi: Kalyani Publishers. (2000), pp.144-145.
4. Jerome Mandel, Article: *The Grotesque Rose: Medieval Romance and The Great Gatsby*, Modern Fiction Series, vol.34, Number 4, Winter, (1988), p.542.
5. *One Hundred False Starts*, 'The Saturday Evening post', March 4, (1933), pp.13, 65-66, New Essays, p. 8.

6 William Troy, Scott Fitzgerald – *The Authority of Failure*, Modern American Fiction, Essays in Criticism, (Ed) A Walton Litz, New York: Princeton University, OUP, (1963), p.133

7 N. P. Dawson, *The Beautiful and Damned*, New York: Globe and Commercial Adviser, March 4, (1922)

7. Mary Bell Swan, Article: *Author of This Side of Paradise Writes Satire on Modern Life*, Magazine: Buffalo Sunday Courier, April 30, (1922)

9 Ronald Berman, *The Great Gatsby and Modern Times*, Urbana and Chicago: University of Illinois Press, (1994)

10. Stephen Vincent Benet, quoted in American Novelists, 1910-1945, Part2: *F. Scott Fitzgerald* by O. E. Rölvaag, ed. James J. Martine, Detroit, Michigan; Gale Research Company, (1981)

6

Philosophic and Artistic Ambivalence of Fitzgerald's 'Double Vision'

Abstract

Francis Scott Fitzgerald's writings were much controverted on the ground that they did not proffer any clear-cut philosophic stance. Although it appears to be true, on closer examination it becomes evident that Fitzgerald had a philosophy of life just as any other literary men had, but the difference is that he did not cling to any one particular philosophy for long and that he had a shifting allegiance to different philosophical ideologies. What is remarkable about his philosophy throughout his career as a writer is that it had been conditioned by an ambivalence which had an artistic and philosophical aspect about it. His philosophy was a sort of "double vision". This paper tries to establish that Fitzgerald did have a philosophy of life, although he had frequently shifted his ideological allegiance from one to another. Further, the paper looks into the close connection between Fitzgerald's philosophy of life and his artistic and philosophical ambivalence which tempered his 'double vision'.

Key Words: Philosophy, art, ambivalence, double vision, existentialism, hedonism, cynicism, pessimism, transcendentalism.

Introduction

Some signal research has already been done on several aspects of F. Scott Fitzgerald's writings. Yet, there has hardly been any penetrating study made on Fitzgerald's philosophy of life and the ambivalence that marked his philosophy. There are even critics who felt Fitzgerald had no distinct philosophy of his own. But it is not reasonable to subscribe to such a view. Literary writers, no matter how insignificant they are, consciously or unconsciously incorporate in their writings their strongly-felt view of life or rather their 'philosophy of life'. Since the basic raw material of literature is 'life', writers can hardly refrain from revealing what they think of life. If literature is an 'imaginative recreation of life', then, literary men do strive to recreate life following their heart's dearly hugged wishes and inn conformity with their vision or philosophy of life. Generally artists are people discontented with the prevailing state of affairs. Their quest for perfection makes them raise their voice against the imperfections in life and the established system. Some might justify the prevailing system but many find fault with it and offer alternatives which their conviction holds to be better than the existing one. Writers are sensitive people endowed with the gift of deeper insights into reality. In their writings they encase these convictions and insights partly stemming from their sincerity to themselves and partly from their sense of social obligation to share the deeply-felt truths of life with their fellow beings in order to enrich their lives.

Philosophy of Life: An Integral Part of Literary Works

Artists normally find aesthetic relief only when they artistically express their philosophy, their view of life or interpretation of life. Direct statements of philosophy are repugnant to the spirit of art. Art implies indirection and conscious effort. It aims at producing a certain effect on the connoisseurs and does have a purpose, be it instruction or aesthetic delight or a combination of both. Since the expression given is artistic and indirect, the reader has to be highly discriminating when he/she peruses over a literary work so that the right messages and what the writer has intended will be properly grasped. But this process is difficult and demands from the discriminating reader artistic taste and metaphysical knowledge blended together in addition to some linguistic expertise. Both comprehension (intellectual understanding) and apprehension (intuitive understanding) are imperative to back up aesthetic sensibility. Intuitive understanding is a *sine qua non* in unlocking that mysterious world of transcendental reality whose vision the writers occasionally afford us through the epiphany moments they have experienced. Writers tend to believe that life is not something lived merely at the material, mundane, peripheral level, but something partaking of the higher metaphysical plane as well. They penetrate beyond the phenomenal world, and glimpse at the transcendental world whose magical vision they are very often unable to refrain from sharing with the readers. They feel impelled to unfold this world before the aspiring readers to enrich their perceptions of life. For writers both the 'nominal' and the 'phenomenal' worlds do count. Some writers give greater emphasis to the one or the other whereas some others display a balanced view. Yet some others vacillate and oscillate between the two. F. Scott Fitzgerald, it seems, belongs to this last group as a representative of the 'Lost Generation' with an ambivalent attitude.

Fitzgerald did not cling to any one particular philosophical ideology for long. His journey through life was marked by shifting thought-patterns toned by an ambivalence that made him move from one extreme position to another: from optimism to pessimism, from faith to cynicism, from materialism to idealism, from despair to hope, and from hedonism to stoicism. His different novels and stories mirror these shifts in philosophical stances in varying degrees. The basic cause of these shifts in stance can be attributed to his ambivalent attitude.

In different periods of his life Fitzgerald had been under the sway of different philosophical ideologies although he was not an enthusiast for philosophy as Coleridge or other Romantics were. He was a passionate artist for whom life was art and art was life. That is why his writings are highly autobiographical. As a literary artist he was a Romantic and later a matured one at that. He reached Keatsean level of objectivity and balance towards the end of his life. It started particularly with the publication of *The Great Gatsby* and reached the pinnacle in the novel, *The Last Tycoon* and the autobiographical piece, *The Crack-Up*. No doubt, Keats was his artistic model. But philosophically he shifted his allegiance to different schools of thought. Existentialism, Transcendentalism, Hedonism, Cynical materialism, Cynical Idealism, Pessimism, Optimism, Marxism, Socialism, Pragmatism and Individualism – all these had their impact on his mind at one time or other, directly or indirectly and his character s stand for these thought streams at one time or other.

Fitzgerald's Ambivalence and its Implications

Once Fitzgerald stated that "The test of a first-rate intelligence is the ability to hold two opposed ideas in the mind at the same time, and still retain the ability to function" (Fitzgerald, p.69). His philosophy of life is underscored by this ambivalent attitude. It is a kind of 'double-mindedness' – a dichotomous inner condition. It is productive of great irony because two mutually contradictory things or states are counterbalanced without any tilting for one or the other. He had the rare gift to hold two opposed views in perfect balance. He never uttered his view of life with perfect certainty because he was not sure which one was the truth. This uncertainty was the outcome of both internal and external problems, and factors internal and external.

His peculiar psyche, his complex personality had a split nature, a schizophrenic tendency, an inherited factor from his mother. Moreover, his childhood experiences and the way his mother had brought him up in an overprotective manner, his own father's cool nature, his education at St. Paul Academy (1908-10), at Newman School (1911-13), and later at Princeton – all these had their due impact on his mind in forming the type of attitude he developed in his life. This attitude marked by ambivalence, a kind of dualism, conditioned his philosophy, art and approach to everything in life – temporal, spatial, and ideological.

In *The Ice Palace* Fitzgerald shows marked ambivalence towards the South, whereas in *May Day* he reveals his pronounced ambivalence towards Marxism. 'South' is spatial and 'Marxism' ideological. His treatment of the industrial versus agrarian eras and their comparative studies reveal his temporal ambivalence. This ambivalence explains for the 'double vision' that Fitzgerald projects in his writings. This makes him free from fanatic and pedantic insistence on any particular view or idea. He was happy to present the pleasures and delights of being rich but at the same time he did not shy away from pointing out its hollowness and hidden dangers. His ambivalent attitude had its own reasons: "Fitzgerald was the only son of an unsuccessful, aristocratic father and an energetic, provincial mother. Half the time he thought of himself as the heir of his father's tradition, which included the author of 'The Star-spangled Banner', Francis Scott Key, after whom he was named, and half the time as 'straight 1850 potato-famine Irish'. As a result he had typically ambivalent American feelings about American life, which seemed to him at once vulgar and dazzlingly promising". (The *New Encyclopaedia Britannica,* p.805). But external problems and factors had also contributed to strengthen that tendency to view everything with uncertainty, suspicion, and lack of conviction. The jazz Age, the post war period, had naturally developed a tendency to doubt the precepts and practices of the older generation, because it plunged the world into an unnecessary and devastating war in which many youth lost their lives. Thus, from a complex set of factors Fitzgerald had developed this habit of 'ambivalence' which fond its expression mainly in art and philosophy.

In 'art', his ambivalent attitude has displayed the power to hold two opposed view points and develop them with equal ease without jumping into value judgments and siding with one or the other in a pronounced manner. He held it to be the evidence of a 'first rate intelligence'. In 'philosophy', he would deal with diverse views but always resorted to 'suspended' judgments. He desisted from sweeping value judgments. This is the sign of a philosophic mind. The philosophic attitude is one of 'suspended' judgment. He had this rare quality of refraining from hurried and rash judgments based on superficial evidences. He was not dead cert where truth resided. So he had a skeptical frame of mind. He seemed to be an admirer of both the material and the transcendental world. Yet he seemed to doubt both and lacked conviction as to which one is the real. He took antithetical stances by examining contradictory ideologies like socialism and capitalism, idealism and materialism, transcendentalism and pragmatism, Marxism and individualism, theism and atheism, romanticism and realism, spiritualism and Hedonism, etc, in the same works and any one of these ideologies dominating a given work.

Andrew Hook's observation in this regard is pertinent: "In fact, one of the most appealing aspects of Fitzgerald's early novels is precisely a question of his uncertainty, or lack of conviction, about what is right and what is wrong. The texts refuse judgment because the author is concerned to delineate experience without any absolute confidence about which aspects matter more than others. Hence the moral absences those traditional critics have seen as damaging flaws. The position is complicated by the obvious contradictions within Fitzgerald himself. Clearly his temperament included quite a powerful impulse towards judgment... as an artist Fitzgerald allowed other dimensions of his own responsive openness to life and experience to emerge in what he wrote" (Hook, pp.24-25).

He also reminds one of S. Radhakrishnan's words, "Modern man is vacillating between vague apocalyptic fears and deep mystical yearnings." But this vacillation is typical of the modern generation of which Fitzgerald was a member. The changed circumstances of the period had sufficient justification as to why things should be so. Therefore, we cannot blame the writer or his contemporaries for being one or the other. "Several peers emphasized this dualism in his works after Fitzgerald died: for John Passos, it was 'a combination of intimacy and detachment'; for Malcolm Cowley, it was 'double vision'. They believed that Fitzgerald's simultaneous involvement in and observation of fictional situations, his participating self and scribal self, helped to explain his most impressive work."(Kuehl, p. 45)

Although Fitzgerald's philosophy was marked by ambivalence, he was deeply solicitous about the degeneration in society also. This social concern was the dynamic side of his philosophy despite his periodic, ideological vacillations. In addition to philosophic ambivalence, as pointed out earlier, Fitzgerald displayed moral and artistic ambivalence, too. Although he has been criticized on this point, it is generally accepted as the mark of a true artistic genius blessed with a 'negative capability' and Fitzgerald is rightly one. His writings attest to the veracity of this critical consensus.

Conclusion

To sum up, Fitzgerald's philosophy of life was marked by shifting ideological allegiances as an inevitable offshoot of the turbulent age of confusion in which he lived and also as outcome of his childhood experiences he had in his family. Further, the ambivalence he displayed in his philosophy was also complex with its artistic, moral, temporal, spatial, and philosophical implications. A study of these aspects points to the inextricable connections between his philosophy of life and ambivalence and contributes to a better understanding of the multifaceted artistic genius of Fitzgerald with a 'double vision'.

References

1. Fitzgerald, F. Scott, "The Crack-Up", in *The Crack-Up,* (ed.) Edmund Wilson, 1945, (reprint, New York: New Directions, 1956).
2. *Fitzgerald F(rancis) Scott (Key),* The New Encyclopedia Britannica, vol.4, Micropaedia, (Chicago: Encyclopedia Britannica, Inc., 1997).
3. Hook, Andrew, Cases for Reconsideration: Fitzgerald's 'This Side of Paradise' and 'The Beautiful and the Damned', *'Scott Fitzgerald: The Promises of Life'* (ed.) A Robert Lee, (London: Vision Press, 1989).
4. Kuehl, John Richard, *F. Scott Fitzgerald- A Study of the Short Fiction,* (Boston: Twayne Publishers, 1991)

SECTION-C

FACETS OF ENGLISH LANGUAGE TEACHING/ LEARNING

1

.. How I Made My Students Speak English Better

My teaching experience which by now spans a period of over two decade has given me some valuable insight into effective teaching techniques. I realized that despite the richness of the current teaching methodology, the actual experience of teaching-learning is, generally bereft of the anticipated outcome. This observation urged me to device an entirely personal technique of teaching in which my own inner resources would make my teaching attractive, impressive and effective. In my method I drew upon the existing techniques and methods, but substantially adapted them to make my teaching interesting.

I am fully convinced that language learning involves habit formation as well as mental activity. In the learning process mental activity takes precedence over mere habit formation. Yet both contribute to each other. In any active learning process all the psychic potentialities of the learner are to be brought into play. The greater the teacher's ability to get the learner absorbed in the learning activity, the better will be the effect. For this every class should be thought-provoking as well as fascinating. The teacher through his psychological insight should make sure that the learner focuses all his inner power on the learning activity which calls for concentration of thought, attention, memory, perception, imagination, intellect and intelligence. The teaching must arouse the curiosity of the learner and grip his attention. This depends more on the individual powers of the teacher than on the adoption of mere methods. The teacher himself must be adequately braced up with knowledge which should excite wonder in the learner's mind. Besides, the teacher's moral qualities and psychological insight along with a powerful core will serve as a formative and positive influence on the students.

I realized in course of my teaching that language learning process involves both written and spoken activities simultaneously. The learner who aspires to have mastery of written English stands to gain more skill if only be practices some spoken English, too. In the same way, one who wishes to learn Spoken English could do better if one resorts to some writing as well. It implies that both written and oral practice should go hand in hand in proper mastery of the English language. It points to the necessity of learning a finite set of grammar rules through proper written and oral practice so as to be capable of generating an infinite number of sentences which make communication easy.

Since linguistic communication is basically done through oral and written sentences learners should be made to be adept at making sentences. No doubt, sentences are made of words and strengthening vocabulary is essential for sentences making. But this can be done white the process of sentence construction is underway. Therefore, the focus should be on sentence construction, and in the Indian context the learners have to be made aware of the difference between the sentences patterns of Indian languages and that of the English language. The Indian languages follow "SVO" (Subject-Verb-Object) pattern whereas English follows "SVO" (Subject-Verb-Object) pattern. Thinking and ordering words in the pattern followed by English pause initial problems for Indian students and that has to be solved through plenty of drilling (both oral and written) and this makes English learning easy.

I made the students arrange words in the English word order and taught them the common English sentence patterns such as SV, SVO, SVC, SVOC, SVOA, ASVO, SVOO, etc. Terms like the Subject, Verb, Object, Complement, Adjunct,

Direct and Indirect Objects were explained and the words which perform these functions were identified. Plenty of drilling was given in each case so that there would be no doubt left regarding any particular slot in a sentence. More drilling increased their speed of speaking as well as writing. I started from the simple level of 'SV' and made them forge ahead. For eg: I took two small words like 'Suma' and 'sleeps'. The students were helped to arrange these words like the English patters of SV and the result was 'Suma sleeps' (SV). A large number of such sentences were made, such as: He sits: She dreams. It barks: They swim: He laughs: Tom laughs: Birds fly: etc...No doubt, a little explanation had to be given as to what 'subject', 'object', 'verb', 'complement' or 'adjunct' mean. The learners were told that these are a few slots in the sentence. Further, I pointed out to them that a 'noun', 'pronoun' or a 'noun phrase' could perform the function of the subject of object. Through several examples such as the following, the point was established:

S (N)	(V)		
Ramu	laughs.		[pattern: S V]
S-(Pronoun)	(V)		
He	runs.		[pattern: SV]
S-(n-phrase)	(V)		
A fat man	sleeps.		[pattern: SV]
S [n]	(V)	O [n]	
Tom	plays	football.	[pattern: SVO]
S [n]	(V)	O [n-phrase]	
Sheela	helps	her mother.	[pattern: SVO]
S [pron.]	(V)	(O) [n}	
She	drinks	milk.	[pattern: SVO]
S [pron.]	(V)	O [pronoun]	
We	saw	him.	[pattern: SVO]

This identification enabled the students to use noun or noun phrase or pronoun as subject and object. Once the learners are given sufficient practice (oral & written) so that it enables them to understand the subject and object areas, and the words or phrases which occur there, and a little explanation of what a 'noun', 'pronoun' or a 'noun phrase' means, one can focus one's attention on the various aspects of the next and the most important slot in the syntactic structure, namely, the 'verb'.

After defining the 'verb' by drawing attention to the 'static' and 'dynamic' types, I found that teaching of the five elementary forms of the verb, namely, the 'base form', the '-s/-es form', the '-ing form' (present participle), the 'past form', and the 'past participle' would be highly useful, since these forms are are crucial to making tenses and many grammatical constructions. Plenty of examples were given to learners to convince them of the contexts of occurrence of these forms as well as their uses. For example:

(base form)
They play cricket. (Tense: Simple Present)
(-s form)
She sings a song. (Tense: Simple Present)
(-ing form)
They are playing cricket (Tense: Present Progressive)
(past participle)
They have written the examination. (Tense: Present Perfect)

In this way, the children were made to understand how each tense was form. They were told that many sentences could be made using these forms in different positions as the underlined ones in the following examples:

Sit here. (Base form)

Wear it, please. (Base form)

Smoking is injurious to health. (-ing form as 'verbal noun')

Reading a book, he fell asleep. (-ing form as 'present participle')

Helped by a friend, he completed his studies. ('Past participle')

I saw him swimming in the lake. (-ing form as 'present participle')

He is a noted writer. (Past participle as 'adjective')

That is a waiting shelter. (-ing form as 'adjective')

Giving numerous examples of each type simply strengthened the students' power of sentence construction. Oral and written practice helped them fix these types in their minds for handy expressions. After they were taught the 'elementary forms' of the verbs, they were asked to learn 'Regular Verbs' and 'Irregular Verbs'. A list of irregular verbs was given to each learner and they were asked to memorize the Principal forms of the verbs, namely, the present (base form), the past form, and the past participle, since lack of knowledge of these forms is a barrier to easy speech when ideas are expressed in the past or using perfect tenses or present or future simple tenses.

A very significant step in helping learners to forge ahead in Spoken English is by way of introducing the Auxiliary Verbs/Anomalous Finites. Mastery of the Auxiliaries holds the key to easy Spoken English. The reasons are many.

Firstly, Auxiliaries are needed to frame any type of questions (and asking questions is a very important thing in Spoken English). For example, all the underlined words in the following:

Are you happy?

Is it your house?

Am I troubling you?

Do you visit that place?

How do you go there?

Where will you sit?

What should I do for you?

Secondly, Auxiliaries (as the underlined ones below) are needed to make affirmative sentences negative. For example:

I go there. (Affirmative)

I do not go there. (Negative)

She speaks English. (Affirmative)

She does not speak English. (Negative)

They finished their work. (Affirmative)

They did not finish their work. (Negative)

Thirdly, Auxiliaries are needed to frame 'Tag Questions'. For example:

You know English, don't you?

She behaves herself well, doesn't she?

They will come here later, won't they?

Fourthly, Auxiliaries are indispensable in Passive voice. A suitable form of 'be' and the past participle of the main verb are obligatory elements in passive constructions. For example:

Suma organizes a meeting. (Active)

A meeting is organized by Suma. (Passive)

Fifthly, 'Short Replies' which are commonly found in Spoken English usually end with the auxiliaries as the underlined ones in the following examples:

Do you enjoy poetry?

Yes, I do? (Short Reply)

Will you help me?

Yes, I will. (Short Reply)

(*Note:* - In negative replies, the auxiliaries combine with the abbreviated form of 'not', namely, n't)

Eg: Can you meet him?

No, I can't. (Negative Reply)

In short, a careful and elaborate study of the auxiliaries will help the students speak English faster and easier. Hence I always insisted the learners on their mastering the auxiliaries properly. Auxiliaries will help the learners in performing many language functions such as *offering help, seeking advice, offering advice, seeking permission, making polite requests, inviting someone,* etc. The learners were later given more classes on these language functions which augmented the *appropriateness* and *acceptability* of their Spoken English expressions. Since mastery of the auxiliaries helped the students ask all sorts of questions - *Wh-questions, Yes/No questions, Tag Questions*, and *embedded questions*, they would carry on carry on a conversation smoothly. Asking questions and answering them are the most important areas of any conversation. Grammatical knowledge and repeated practice enabled them to answer without errors, and oral and written drills increased their speed.

In addition to the noun, the pronoun, the verb, and the adverb, other word classes of the parts of speech such as the adjective, the preposition, the conjunction, and the interjection were also taught by placing them in the lexical and the syntactic contexts. This strengthened not only their morphological and syntactic knowledge, but their vocabulary and grammar should go hand in hand for speedier and correct expression. The word in the right context increases the learner's facility and felicity of expression.

As the secondary measure to enhance the beauty of the spoken word, pronunciation was stressed. In all my Spoken English classes I introduced phonetics and phonology as an integral part of the course. Theoretical knowledge of the organs of speech, classification and description of vowels and consonants, stress, rhythm, and intonation was followed by practical classes for better articulation, accentuation, rhythm, and intonation. In this regard, J. D. O'Connor's book, '*Better English Pronunciation*', and '*Spoken English*' (three books) by CIEFL, dealing with Consonants, Vowels, and Stress, Rhythm and Intonation proved to be highly useful. B. B. C. Spoken English Text with CDs, a few Indian CDs, a few phonetic charts were used as teaching aids in addition chalk and talk. A few classes of discussion, speech practice, interview training, and conversation practice based on imaginary situations etc., strengthened the creativity of students and communication skill. In this way, I made my students speak English better.

References

1. Chomsky, Noam. (1957), *Syntactic Structures,* Mouton: The Hague.
2. Chomsky, Noam. (1972), *Language and Mind,* New York: Harcourt Brace Jovanovich.
3. O'Connor, J. D. (1973), *Phonetics,* Harmondsworth: Penguin Books.
4. O'Connor, J. D (1980), *Better English Pronunciation,* Cambridge: Cambridge University Press.
5. Thomson, A. J & A. V. Martinet (1986), *A Practical English Grammar,* New Delhi: Oxford University Press.
6. Stannard, Allen, W. (2009), *Living English Structure, New Delhi: Dorling Kindersley (India) Pvt. Ltd.*
7. CIEFL, Spoken English (Vowels) (Practice Series). Hyderabad.
8. CIEFL, Spoken English (Consonants) (Practice Series). Hyderabad.
9. CIEFL, Spoken English (Stress, Rhythm & Intonation) (Practice Series). Hyderabad.

2

'Communicative Approach' as the Most Effective Modern Approach to the Teaching and Learning of English

Introduction

Easy and effective language mastery has been a long-sought-out proposition which remains till date a hard nut to crack. Numerous methods, approaches and techniques had had their day and like any craze or fashion, after the initial appeal, they disillusioned the adherents, and language asserted as ever its tough nature, if not invincibility, like an untamed pachyderm. Of the various approaches that have tried to make the English language learning a fruitful effort in recent times, it is the Communicative Language Teaching that has proved to be the most effective and highly productive approach. Not that it is free from flaws, but that it has an edge over all other well-intentioned approaches and seems to be an improvement over the earlier approaches in that it tries to fill the lacunae of such approaches and methods in faster language learning. It is not a method, nor is it a technique, but an approach, rather a set of approaches. As the title CLT suggests 'communication' is at the core of this approach; language learning is learning to 'communicate'. Its desired goal is 'communicative competence'. CLT is insistent on learners' language experience rather than learning about language which was traditionally done to a great extent under methods like Grammar-Translation Method, the Oral Method, Situational Approach, The Audio Lingual Method, etc. Unlike many other methods it is highly learner-centred and so marks the beginning of a paradigm shift. This approach has now gained considerable global currency and great popularity because of its learner-friendly nature. The following are the more notable of the various Communicative Approaches being practised:

(1) Communicative Language Teaching (CLT)

This approach emphasizes the functional and communicative aspects of language. It stresses meanings behind the structures of language. So it is notional too. Both the American and British proponents now see it as an approach (and not a method) that aims to (a) make communicative competence the goal of language teaching and (b) develop procedures for the teaching of the four language skills that acknowledge the inter dependence of language and communication. There is no single text of authority on it, nor any single model that is universally accepted as authoritative. Many view it as an integration of grammatical and functional teaching. Littlewood (1981:1) states, "One of the most characteristic features of communicative language teaching is that it pays systematic attention to functional as well as structural aspects of language". For some people CLT means using procedures where learners work in pairs or groups employing available language resources in problem solving tasks. In such cases, what is important is transaction or interaction of some kind with an intention and responses to it. CLT stresses contextualization of the language items. Much more than language mastery, effective communication is emphasized. CLT aims at a comprehensible pronunciation rather than native-speaker like pronunciation. Rather than accuracy in formal correctness, the primary goal of CLT is fluency and acceptable language. Thus, in all these, it stands in striking contrast to the much-vaunted Audio-lingual Method popularly used in the U.S.A. Hence, it was developed to make up for the weaknesses of the Audio-lingual Method. CLT is learner-centred and it takes an experience-based view of second language teaching. Its chief goal is "communicative competence". The learner's role is that of a negotiator, and he learns in an inter-dependent way. The teacher has to play twin roles of that of a facilitator and an independent participant within the learning–teaching group. In addition, he is also a 'needs analyst, counselor, and group process manager'. There are three kinds of materials used in CLT. They are labeled as "text- based, task-based and realia" materials.

(2) The Natural Approach

This approach was developed by Tracy Terrel and Stephen Krashen. "In the Natural Approach there is an emphasis on exposure, or *input*, rather than practice; optimizing emotional preparedness for learning; a prolonged period of attention to what the language learners hear before they try to produce language; and a willingness to use written and other materials as a source of comprehensible input. The emphasis on the central role of comprehension in the Natural Approach links it to other comprehension-based approaches in language teaching." (Jack C. Richards and Theodore S. Rodgers, 2007, p.179) This approach tries to teach communicative competencies. The emphasis given to lexicon outweighs the importance attached to grammar. Primacy of meaning is justified on the ground that lexicon carries the largest volume of information compared to any other part of the language. Learners are supposed to actively take pat in communicative activities. This gradually reduces their emotional problems and strengthens their inner freedom and builds up the confidence level. The teacher is expected to provide comprehensible input, play a friendly, interesting role in the classroom and choose or devise a rich mix of classroom activities for the success of this approach.

(2) Co-Operative Language Learning (CLL)

It is also known as Collaborative Learning (CLL). This instructional approach makes maximum use of co-operative activities involving pairs and small groups of learners in the classroom. It aims at raising the achievement of all students both bright and weak ones alike. Such learning helps the teacher develop positive relationships among students. From such relationships arise healthy social, psychological and cognitive development. Competition is soon replaced by co-operation which results in general high performance. The interactive pair and group activities provide opportunities for naturalistic second language acquisition. CLL also aims at enabling students' focused attention to particular lexical items, language structures and communicative functions through the use of interactive tasks. Learner stress is the minimum in CLL and motivation fairly high. It is conducive to develop critical thinking skills and communicative competence besides social skills. In this teacher's role is that of a facilitator unlike the traditional authoritarian role.

(3) Content Based Instructions (CBI)

In this approach teaching is organized around the content or information that students will acquire, rather than around linguistics of other type of syllabus. The language that is being taught could be used to present subject matter, and the students would learn the language as a by-product of learning about real- world content. An integrated skills approach is an important part of CBI. Language is both text and discourse based. It is purposeful as well. According to CBI people learn a second language most successfully when the information they are acquiring is perceived as interesting, useful, and leading to a desired goal. Learner autonomy is emphasized by CBI. Also "learning by doing" is stressed. Teachers are expected to be knowledgeable in the subject matter. They have to create a truly learner-centred classroom. They have to contextualize the lessons. They must make use of group-work and team building techniques. The materials used for teaching should be remarkably varied, highly comprehensible, and authentic. CBI is highly communicative.

(4) Task-Based Language Teaching (TBLT)

This approach makes use of tasks as the core unit of planning and instruction in language teaching. The activities used should be those that promote real communication. Much linguistic communication is to be done during activities and only those activities with much real communication are to be chosen. Such communication can promote learning. Any meaningful language utterance supports learning process. It is generally held by the advocates of this approach and several educationists that engaging learners in tasks provides a better context for the activation of learning processes than form-focused activities. Therefore, this finally provides better opportunities for language learning to take place. A task is, after all, an activity or goal that is carried out using language, such as finding a solution to a puzzle, reading a map and giving directions, making a telephone call, writing a letter, or reading a set of instructions and assembling a toy: "Tasks...are activities which have meaning as their primary focus: success in tasks is evaluated in terms of achievement of an outcome, and tasks generally bear some resemblance to real life language use. So, task-based instruction takes a fairly strong view of communicative language teaching". (Skehan 1996 p. 20) TBLT is motivated primarily by a theory of learning rather than a theory of language. The unique principles of their theory of learning are: a) Tasks provide both the input and output processing necessary for language acquisition b) Task activity and achievement are motivational c) Learning difficulty can be negotiated and fine-tuned for particular pedagogical purposes.

To conclude, all these communicative approaches minimize the teacher roles and try to effect maximum learning outcomes ensuring active learner participation and real language experience.

References

1. Jack C. Richards and Theodore S. Rodgers (2007) *Approaches and Methods in Language Teaching* (Second Ed.) Cambridge University Press.
2. .Jo McDonough and Christopher Shaw (2003), *Materials and Methods in ELT (Second Ed.): A Teachers Guide,* Blackwell Publishing, Malden, U.S.A.
3. Nancy Frankfort, Joan Dye, (1994): *A Communicative Course in English* (Teacher's Ed.) Prentice Hall Regents (U.S.A.)
4. Bhatnagar and Bell, (2004), *Communication in English,* Orient Longman Private Limited, New Delhi.
5. Susan M. Gass, Jacquelyn Schachter, *Linguistic Perspectives on Second Language Acquisition* (1989), (Editors), Cambridge University Press, Cambridge U.K.
6. R.K. Singh (2005), *Teaching English for Specific Purposes – An Evolving Experience,* Book Enclave, Jaipur.
7. A.K. Banerjee (2002) *New Directions in Grammar and English Language Teaching,* Aavishkar Publisher, Jaipur.
8. Patricia K. Werner, Mary Mitchell Church & Lida R. Baker (1996), *A Communicative Grammar,* McGraw-Hill, Boston.
9. Diane Larsen-Freman (2004), *Techniques and Principles in Language Teaching,* (Second Ed.), OUP
10. S.C. Chaudhary (2002), *Teaching English in Non-native Contexts,* Orient Longman, Chennai.

3

Exploring Learner-Centred Approaches to English Language Teaching

Abstract

The teaching of English language in non-native contexts is hemmed in by a confused array of problems. No single method used so far can plume itself on any magical learning outcome as it has laid claim to. The traditional lecture method being overused and dubbed faulty on account of its teacher-centric nature is slowly giving way to learner-centred pedagogy. In a teacher-centred approach, the teacher grabs the central attention and the students are pushed to the periphery. They are forced to remain glued to their seats within the four walls of the classroom like dumb prisoners. Hardly is there a chance available for the students to express themselves well and articulate their responses. Their critical faculties are often silenced by the imperious approach of the teacher. Under the use of this dictatorial method the students enjoy no democratic environment to experience learning. They are "cabined, cribbed, and confined". On the contrary, several modern learner-centred approaches have ushered in a new dawn of freedom for the students ensuring the joy of learning unfettered by any restrictions, and affording the delight of active involvement. Of late, the teacher has to assume the role of a facilitator, a guide, and counselor.

This paradigm shift from the teacher to the learner has been brought about by the following approaches: 1) Communicative Language Learning 2) Co-operative Language Learning 3) Task-Based Language Learning/Teaching 4) Content-Based Instruction 5) Syncopated Approach 6) Computer Assisted Language Learning (CALL) 7) E-Learning 8) Interactive Teaching Learning Methods 9) Multi-media-Guided Language Learning 10) The Use of Modern Educational Resources 11) Technology Assisted Language Learning, etc. Other alternative approaches that help the learner–

centred language teaching are: 1) Total Physical Response 2) The Silent way 3) Community Language Learning 4) Suggestopedia 5) Whole Language Approach 6) Multiple Intelligences Approach 7) Neurolinguistic Programming 8) The Lexical Approach 9) Competency-Based Language Teaching, etc. All the above-mentioned approaches and methods shift the focus from the teacher to the learner. Teaching and Learning are two complex processes, the two sides of the same coin, posing great difficulties which have vexed our education system for long. Effective teaching-learning calls for an eclectic approach wherein a fine blend of methods, genuine effort from learners and teachers, innovative methods by both, life-long learning by teachers and learners, etc are all judiciously used.

This paper attempts to explore the above mentioned learner-centred approaches which currently dominate the English language teaching arena, and promise more fruitful language experience as well as better language production.

Introduction

The teaching of English language in non-native contexts is hemmed in by a confused array of problems. No single method used so far can plume itself on any magical learning outcome it lays claim to. The traditional lecture method being overused and dubbed faulty because of its teacher-centric nature is slowly giving way to learner-centred pedagogy. In a teacher-centred approach, the teacher grabs the focal attention and the students are pushed to the periphery. They are forced to remain glued to their seats within the four walls of the classroom like dumb prisoners. Hardly is there a chance available for the students to express themselves well and articulate their responses. Their critical faculties are often silenced by the imperious approach of the teacher. Under this dictatorial method the students enjoy no democratic environment to experience learning. They are "cabined, cribbed, and confined". On the contrary, several modern learner-centred approaches have ushered in a new dawn of freedom for the students ensuring the joy of learning unfettered by any restrictions, and afford the delight of active involvement. Of late, the teacher has to assume the role of a facilitator, a guide, and counselor. This paradigm shift from the teacher to the learner has been brought about by the following approaches: 1) Communicative Language Learning 2) Co-operative Language Learning 3) Task-Based Language Learning/ Teaching 4) Content-Based Instruction 4) Community Language Teaching 5) Technology Assisted Language Learning, etc. Other alternative approaches that help the learner–centred language teaching are: 1) Total Physical Response 2) The Silent way 3) Community Language Learning 4) Suggestopedia 5) Whole Language Approach 6) Multiple Intelligences Approach 7) Neurolinguistic Programming 8) The Lexical Approach 9) Competency-Based Language Teaching, etc.

Here I would like to explore the various learner-centred approaches within the constraints of this paper.

(1) Communicative Language Teaching. (CLT)

This approach emphasizes the functional and communicative aspects of language. It stresses meanings behind the structures of language. So it is notional too. Both the American and British proponents now see it as an approach (and not a method) that aims to (a) make communicative competence the goal of language teaching and (b) develop procedures for the teaching of the four language skills that acknowledge the inter dependence of language and communication. There is no single text of authority on it, nor any single model that is universally accepted as authoritative. Many view it as an integration of grammatical and functional teaching. Littlewood (1981:1) states, "One of the most characteristic features of communicative language teaching is that it pays systematic attention to functional as well as structural aspects of language". For some people CLT means using procedures where learners work in pairs or groups employing available language resources in problem solving tasks. In such cases, what is important is transaction or interaction of some kind with an intention and responses to it. CLT stresses contextualization of the language items. Much more than language mastery, effective communication is emphasized. CLT aims at a comprehensible pronunciation rather than native-speaker like pronunciation. Rather than accuracy in formal correctness, the primary goal of CLT is fluency and acceptable language. Thus, in all these, it stands in striking contrast to the much-vaunted Audio-lingual Method popularly used in the U.S.A. Hence, it was developed to make up for the weaknesses of the Audio-lingual Method. CLT is learner-centred and it takes an experience-based view of second language teaching. Its chief goal is "communicative competence". The learner's role is that of a negotiator and learn in an inter-dependent way. The teacher has to play twin roles of that of a facilitator and an independent participant within the learning–teaching group. In addition, he is also a 'needs analyst, counselor, and group process manager'. There are three kinds of materials used in CLT. They are labeled as "text- based, task-based and realia" materials.

(2) Community Language Learning (CLL)

Developed by Charles A. Curran and his associates from Chicago, the CLL relies on counseling techniques. The role of the teacher is redefined as 'counselor' and that of the learner 'client'. CLL is closely associated with what is called 'humanistic techniques' (Moskowitz 1978). CLL views language as social process. It is much more than mere communication. "Language is people; language is persons in contact; Language is persons in response" (La Forge, 1983: 9). CLL views human learning as both cognitive and affective. The learners are required to make personal commitments so as to facilitate the language acquisition process. CLL does not use conventional language syllabus. Rather, the learners suggest the things they wish to talk about. The teacher just facilitates the conveyance of their meanings depending on the standard of the learners. The progression is based on the topic. The teacher's reformulations in the target language helps the learners express in more refined manner later. Grammar and lexis are occasionally taken up for clarification.

CLL combines innovative learning tasks and activities with conventional ones. The combination is something like: "Translation, Group work, Recording Transcription, Analysis, Reflection and Observation, Listening, and Free conversation". Learners are like members of a community and learn through interaction. Learning is thus a group achievement rather than merely personal. CLL makes high demands on language teachers. If they are proficient and sensitive, learners stand to gain, otherwise, not.

(3) Co-Operative Language Learning (CLL)

It is also known as Collaborative Learning (CLL). This instructional approach makes maximum use of co-operative activities involving pairs and small groups of learners in the classroom. It aims at raising the achievement of all students both bright and weak ones alike. Such learning helps the teacher develop positive relationships among students. From such relationships arise healthy social, psychological and cognitive development. Competition is soon replaced by co-operation which results in general high performance. The interactive pair and group activities provide opportunities for naturalistic second language acquisition. CLL also aims at enabling students' focused attention to particular lexical items, language structures and communicative functions through the use of interactive tasks. Learner stress is the minimum in CLL and motivation fairly high. It is conducive to develop critical thinking skills and communicative competence besides social skills. In this teacher's role is that of a facilitator unlike the traditional authoritarian role.

(4) Content Based Instructions (CBI)

In this approach teaching is organized around the content or information that students will acquire, rather than around linguistics of other type of syllabus. The language that is being taught could be used to present subject matter, and the students would learn the language as a by-product of learning about real- world content. An integrated skills approach is an important part of CBI. Language is both text and discourse based. It is purposeful as well. According to CBI people learn a second language most successfully when the information they are acquiring is perceived as interesting, useful, and leading to a desired goal. Learner autonomy is emphasized by CBI. Also "learning by doing" is stressed. Teachers are expected to be knowledgeable in the subject matter. They have to create a truly learner-centred classroom. They have to contextualize the lessons. They must make use of group-work and team building techniques. The materials used for teaching should be remarkably varied, highly comprehensible, and authentic. CBI is highly communicative.

(5) Task- Based Language Teaching (TBLT)

This approach makes use of tasks as the core unit of planning and instruction in language teaching. The activities used should be those that promote real communication. Much linguistic communication is to be done during activities and only those activities with much real communication are to be chosen. Such communication can promote learning. Any meaningful language utterance supports learning process. It is generally held by the advocates of this approach and several educationists that engaging learners in tasks provides a better context for the activation of learning processes than form-focused activities. Therefore, this finally provides better opportunities for language learning to take place. A task is, after all, an activity or goal that is carried out using language, such as finding a solution to a puzzle, reading a map and giving directions, making a telephone call, writing a letter, or reading a set of instructions and assembling a toy: "Tasks...are activities which have meaning as their primary focus: success in tasks is evaluated in terms of achievement of an outcome, and tasks generally bear some resemblance to real life language use. So, task-based instruction takes a fairly strong view of communicative language teaching" (Skehan 1996 p: 20) TBLT is motivated primarily by a theory of learning rather than a theory of language. The unique principles of their theory of learning are: a) Tasks provide both the input and output processing necessary for language acquisition b) Task activity and achievement are motivational c)Learning difficulty can be negotiated and fine-tuned for particular pedagogical purposes.

Alternative Approaches

There are also many alternative approaches and methods to language learning which are also learner-centered. These approaches which developed from 1970 to 1990 are the outcome of a quest for alternatives to grammar-based approaches and methods. Hence alternative approaches are basically communicative in nature. They are briefly explored here:

(1) Total Physical Response

This language teaching method is built around the co-ordination of speech and action. It attempts to teach language through physical (motor) activity. This theory was developed by James Asher, a professor of psychology. He observed that like children who respond to commands physically without producing verbal responses, adults also can learn a second language by following a string of imperative sentences. Asher recognized the important role of the affective realm in language learning. Hence he encouraged game-like movements that reduce learners' stress and create a positive mood in the learner which solicit learning. Listening should be accompanied by physical movement. Speech and other productive skills should some later. Asher believes in the existence in the human brain of a bio-program for language which defines an optimal order for first and second language learning. Asher sees his TPR as directed to right-brain learning (brain lateralization) whereas most second language teaching methods are directed to left-brain learning. TPR helps through motor movement the right hemisphere activity before left hemisphere can process language for production. Reduction of stress is also a great advantage of this learning process.

(2) The Silent Way

Developed by Caleb Gattegno, the Silent Way holds that the teacher should be silent as much as possible in the classroom and the learner should be encouraged to produce as much language as possible. The learner has to discover or create rather than remembering and repeating what is to be learned. Accompanying physical objects can help learning. Problem solving, involving the material to be learned, also facilitates learning, according to the advocates of this theory. The silent way encourages oral responses of students. It also promotes learner autonomy and co-operative learning.

(3) Suggestopaedia /Desuggestopaedia

The Bulgarian psychiatrist-educator Georgi Lozanov developed this method. He defines it as a "science....concerned with the systematic study of the non-rational and / or non-conscious influences that human beings are constantly responding to (Stevick 1976:42). Suggestopaedia tries to harness these influences and redirect them so as to optimize learning. The distinctive feature of suggestopaedia is the profuse use of decoration, furniture, arrangement of the classroom, the use of music, and the authoritative behaviour of the teacher. "Memorization in learning by the suggestopaedic method seems to be accelerated 25 times over that in learning by conventional methods" (Lozanov 1978: 27) Music and musical rhythm are central to suggestopaedia. This relaxes learners. Suggestopaedia puts to good use a modified version of hypnotic suggestion. Suggestion, in hypnotic theory means that "an idea realizes in itself". There are six principle theoretical components through which desuggestion and suggestion operate and that set up access to reserves. They are: 1) authority 2) infantilization, 3) double-planedness 4) Intonation 5) rhythm 6) concert pseudo-passiveness.

(4) Whole Language

The whole Language movement holds that language should be taught as a "whole". This theory emphasizes learning to read and write naturally with a focus on real communication, and reading and writing for pleasure. It shares the view of Communicative Language Teaching that meaning is central to language. This approach insists that all the four language skills be integrated in teaching-learning. Their view of language is interactional in perspective. Thus, language is a vehicle for human communication. They also view language psycho-linguistically as a vehicle for internal "interaction" and it emphasizes the use of authentic literature and real events. Reading for comprehension, integration of skills, use of student produced text, student–centred learning, collaborative learning etc are its main characteristics. The use of student produced text is criticized by many on the ground of possibility of inaccuracy.

(5) Multiple Intelligences

It is based on a learner-centred philosophy that human intelligence has multiple dimensions that must be acknowledged and developed in education, The traditional I.Q tests are based on the view that intelligence is a single, unchanged, inborn capacity. But, it only measures logic and language whereas M.I views that the brain has other equally vital types of intelligence. All these can be developed through training and practice. M.I considers learner differences, different learning styles, varied preferences and diverse intelligences. Teaching should recognize these learner variations. Gardner (1993) proposed a "Multiple Intelligences Model". He posits eight native intelligences. They are: 1) Linguistic 2) Logical/Mathematical 3) Spatial 4) Musical 5) Interpersonal 6) Bodily Kinesthetic 7) Intrapersonal and 8) Naturalist intelligences. Some other intelligences are also noted. They are: Emotional Intelligence, Mechanical Intelligence and Practical Intelligence. Teaching should be in such a way that all these are proportionately developed.

(6) Neuro-linguistic Programming:

It was developed by John Grindler and Richard Bandler in the mid 1970's, as a system of techniques that therapists use in building rapport with clients gathering information about their internal and external views of the world and helping them achieve goals and bring about personal change. They sought to fill what they perceived to be a gap in psychological thinking and practice of the early 1970's by developing of step by step procedures that would enable people to improve themselves. "NPL.... is a collection of techniques, patterns, and strategies for assisting effective communication, personal growth and change, and learning. it is based on a series of underlying assumptions about how the mind works and how people act and interact."(Revell and Norman, 1997:14) Despite its therapeutic origin it had some appeal within language teaching to those interested in what is called humanistic approaches—that is, approaches that focus on developing one's sense of self-actualization and self-awareness, as well as to those drawn to what has been referred to as New Humanism.

(7) Technology Enabled Language Learning:

The learners of today are turning more and more to educational technology available through the ICT especially the internet, the computers, the e-learning facilities like the mobile phones, the cable T.V, the radios etc. All the teaching aids and the CD-ROMs, multi-media packages, cassettes, etc., enable language learners to have better learning experience. Not only are the learners in position to have better information but are less teacher-dependent as well. The reason is that these are learner-friendly and in keeping with fashion of the day. The teacher is metamorphosed into a facilitator now. Nevertheless, his role can in no way underestimated.

Conclusion

In conclusion, all the above-mentioned approaches and many more minimize the role of the teacher and put the learner in the limelight ensuring him/her a lot more freedom than of yore. These approaches are likely to better the learning experience. Teacher's bracing himself up with the changed circumstances will not only benefit the students more but open more avenues for him/her to improve the career prospects and win the encomium of the learning community!

References

1. Patricia K. Werner, Mary Mitchell Church & Lida R. Baker (1996) A Communicative Grammar, McGraw-Hill, Boston
2. Jo McDonough and Christopher Shaw (2003), Materials and Methods in ELT (Second ed.): A Teachers Guide, Blackwell Publishing, Malden, U.S.A.
3. Nancy Frankfort, Joan Dye, (1994): A Communicative Course in English (Teacher's Ed.) Prentice Hall Regents (U.S.A)
4. Bhatnagar and Bell (2004), Communication in English, Orient Longman Private Limited, New Delhi
5. Susan M. Gass, Jacquelyn Schachter, Linguistic Perspectives on Second Language Acquisition (1989) (Editors), Cambridge University Press, Cambridge U.K
6. R.K. Singh (2005), Teaching English for Specific Purposes - An Evolving Experience, Book Enclave, Jaipur
7. A. K. Banerjee (2002) New Directions in Grammar and English Language Teaching, Aavishkar Publisher, Jaipur
8. Jack C. Richards and Theodore S. Rodgers (2007) Approaches and Methods in Language Teaching (Second Ed.), Cambridge University Press.
9. Diane Larsen-Freeman (2004), Techniques and Principles in Language Teaching (Second Ed.), OUP
10. S. C. Chaudhary (2002), Teaching English in Non-native Contexts, Orient Longman, Chennai

4

Linguistic Variables that Impede the English Language Learning Process of Tribal Students: A Case Study

Abstract

English language learning is hampered by several factors - linguistic, psychological, sociological, historical, etc. In this paper some of the important linguistic variables are closely examined. These factors are related to Phonetics, Phonology, Morphology, Syntax, Graphology, Lexicology, etc. Expertise in these branches contributes to linguistic mastery, and lack of knowledge in these areas hampers language learning. Most tribal students have problems related to these areas. A study conducted in Gadchiroli district in Maharashtra has attested to the veracity of the hypothesis that several linguistic factors impede the language learning process of students especially that of the tribal students.

Introduction

Knowledge of and competence in linguistic variables like Phonetics, Phonology, Morphology, Syntax, Semantics, Graphology, Lexicology, etc. is very important in mastering a language like English. But students in tribal areas have neither adequate knowledge nor competence in these areas. In fact, their linguistic knowledge is abysmally poor. Therefore, these linguistic barriers baulk their English learning process. The most important area of linguistics is that of grammar in which Morphology and Syntax come together and other branches overlap with grammar to some extent. Knowledge of the grammar of words (Morphology) and that of sentences (Syntax) is central to language mastery in both written and spoken forms, though recently many have tried to underestimate grammar focusing on communication and functional aspects. As Sperber and Wilson put it:

> [A] language ... is a grammar-governed representational system... [T]he property of being a grammar-governed representational system and the property of being used for communication are not systematically linked. They are found together in the odd case of human natural languages, just as the property of being an olfactory organ and the property of being a prehensile organ, though not systematically linked in nature, happen to be found together in the odd case of the elephant's trunk... [I]t is as strange for humans to conclude that the essential purpose of language is for communication as it would be for elephants to conclude that the essential purpose of noses is for picking things up. (1986, pp. 173-74)

Gregg warns the academicians, sensing the latest tendency to reduce the importance of grammar in language learning, and in the written form making use of the graphic substance: "We cannot escape from grammar; no matter how hard we try to subsume it under some other category like 'communication' or 'discourse function,' it just won't go away." (1989, p.27)

Similarly, pronunciation is equally important in oral expression of the language that makes use of the *phonic* substance. If spoken English is to be clearly understood, the oral rendering should be in the generally accepted mode of pronunciation that leads to intelligibility. But EFL/ESL learners have several problems in this area. O' Connor aptly observes:

> "It is well-known that a child of ten years old or less can learn *any* language perfectly, if it is brought up surrounded by that language, no matter where it was born or who its parents were. But after this age the ability to imitate perfectly becomes less, and we all know only too well that adults have great difficulty in mastering

the pronunciation (as well as other parts) of foreign languages. Some people are more talented than others; they find pronouncing other languages less difficult, but they never find them easy. Why is this? Why should this gift that we all have as children disappear in later life? Why can't grown-up people pick up the characteristic sound of a foreign language as a child can?

The answer to this is that our native language won't let us. By the time we are grown-ups the habits of our own language are so strong that they are difficult to break. In our own language we have only a fairly small number of sound-units which we put together in many different combinations to form the words and sentences we use every day. And as we get older we are dominated by this small number of units." (2008, pp.1-2)

The students of the tribal Gadchiroli district had many linguistic/grammatical impediments thwarting their development in English language. A series of questions were asked to the Final Year B. A students of the selected colleges (some 12 Arts Colleges) to elicit their responses to assess the role of the major linguistic factors in hindering the language learning process of the tribal students of Gadchiroli district. The Questionnaire was intended to isolate the *Linguistic Variables* that are supposed to thwart the language learning process of the tribal students of Gadchiroli district.

The questions asked were so framed as to elicit information covering most areas of Linguistics: The study yielded amazing results in relation to the following linguistic aspects. The study supports the hypothesis that students generally have numerous and serious linguistic problems especially in the three knowledge areas and in the four skill areas. The hypothesis is greatly validated in nearly all cases.

A Few Linguistic Problems in Relation to Phonetics/ Phonology

Most students are unable to pronounce English well. Their pronunciation is marred by Mother Tongue

Interference (M. T. I). They tend to substitute the sounds of their mother tongue Marathi (or Telugu in the case of many students in Sironcha, bordering Andhra Pradesh) for many English sounds which do not have equivalents in their mother tongue, thus causing problems of intelligibility to non-Marathi speakers of English. Some of their problems have been identified. The following five questions were asked to find out the level of phonetic/phonological knowledge they have presently and a few problems these students in the tribal regions of Gadchiroli district face.

The study reveals that **82.80%**students who participated in the survey expressed the view that they find pronunciation mastery very difficult. Only **17.20%,** a negligible number of students opined that it was not difficult. Thus, the study clearly proves the hypothesis that several linguistic factors impede the English language learning process in the tribal areas.

Q1. Do you find it difficult to master the pronunciation of English words?

Sample	X	Y
No of items	12	12
Sum	231.0	48.0
Mean	19.25	4.0
Median	20.0	2.5
Variance	97.66	13.64
Standard Deviation	9.88	3.69

Graphic Representation:

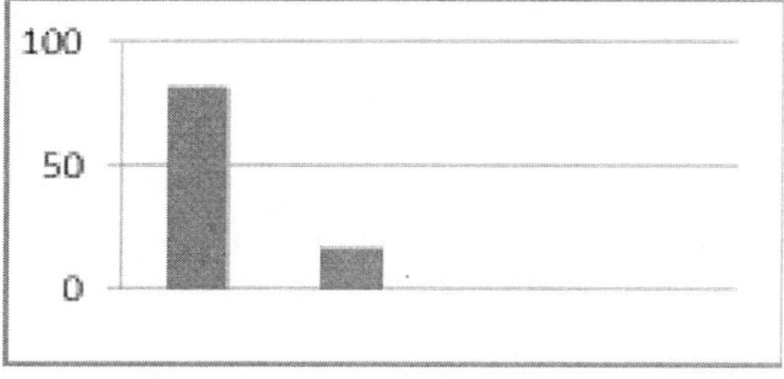

YES= 82.80% NO= 17.20%

Q2. Do you know that there are 44 sounds in English although there are only 26 letters?

As the responses to the second question reveal, majority of the students **(68.10%)** did not know the difference between letters and sounds, and only a few **(31.0-%)** knew that English RP has 44 sounds despite the fact that there are only 26 letters. The hypothesis in this case is adequately validated.

Sample	X	Y
No of items	12	12
Sum	89.0	19.0
Mean	7.42	15.83
Median	4.0	13.0
Variance	74.81	96.51
Standard Deviation	8.65	9.82

Graphic Representation:

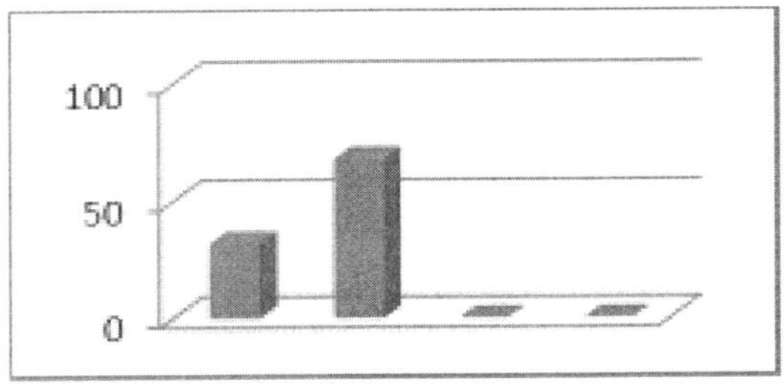

YES= 31.90% **NO= 68.10%**

Q. 3. Has any teacher told you so far that there are 20 vowel sounds and 24 consonant sounds in the sound system of English?

A notable majority of students (some **75.99%**) did not know that there are 20 vowel sounds and 24 consonant sounds in English RP. Only **24.01 %** knew about it. This throws light on the fact that the teachers themselves either did not care to teach them these details or probably, they themselves did know about it. The hypothesis is highly validated.

Sample	X	Y
No of items	12	12
Sum	67.0	212.0
Mean	5.59	17.67
Median	3.0	17.5
Variance	64.08	93.52
Standard Deviation	8.0	9.67

Graphic Representation

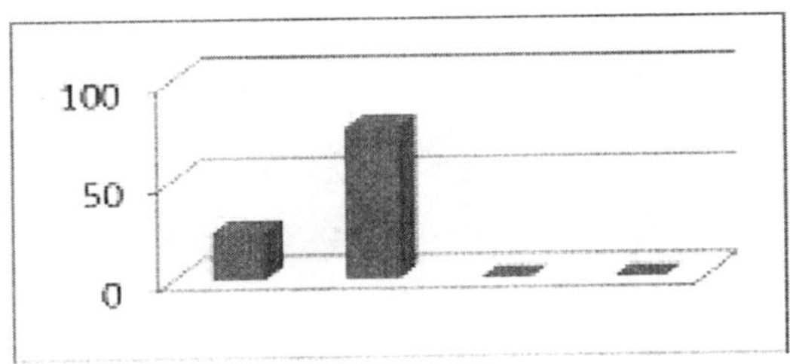

YES= 24.01% **NO= 75.99%**

Q4. Have you ever been taught how to articulate or produce the English sounds correctly?

No less than **85.67%** students revealed that they were not taught how to articulate the sounds in English. Only **14.33%** claimed they were taught how to articulate the English sounds correctly. Hence the students always substituted the sounds of their own Mother Tongue for actual sounds of English. This datum again shows that students are deeply ignorant of matters related to pronunciation partly whose blame goes to the teachers who did not teach them, may be because they themselves did not get training in Phonetics, or probably they did not pay any attention to this aspect. The hypothesis is, again, highly validated her

Sample	X	Y
No of items	12	12
Sum	40.0	239.0
Mean	3.33	19.92
Median	1.5	19.5
Variance	29.15	58.45
Standard Deviation	5.39	7.64

Graphic Representation:

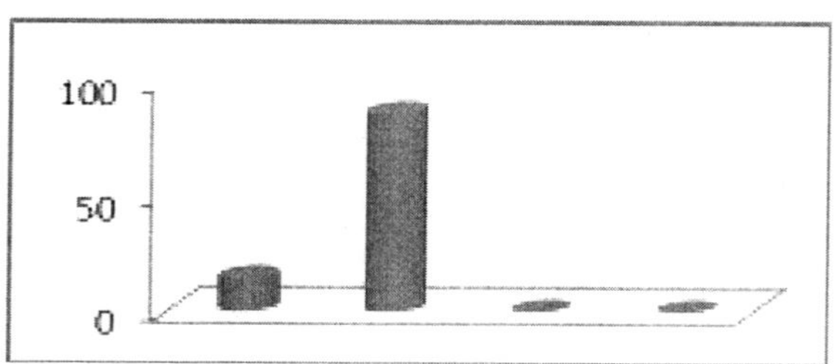

Yes= 14.33 % **No= 85.67%**

Q5. How do you pronounce the word *'zoo'*? :

***'soo' 'zoo' 'joo'*? (Tick your choice).**

Nearly fifty percent **(49.82%)** students could not pronounce the /z/ in *'zoo'* correctly. But an equal percent **(49.82%)** claimed they were able to pronounce it correctly. Only one student answered *'soo'* forming **0.35%.** Had the students been trained well, they would have been able to get rid of the mother tongue influence under which they substituted a wrong sound /d3/ for /z/ in "zoo'. That nearly 50% students mispronounce is evident here and proves the validity of the hypothesis to a good extent.

Sample	X	Y	Z
No of items	12	12	12
Sum	1.0	139.0	139.0
Mean	0.083	11.58	11.58
Median	0.6	10.5	10.5
Variance	0.083	83.90	41.71
Standard Deviation	0.028	9.16	6.46

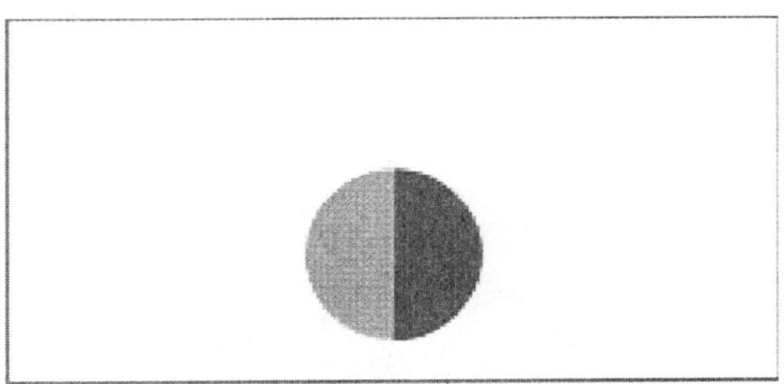

Graphic Representation

***Soo*= 0.35%** ***zoo*= 49.82%** ***joo*= 49.82%**

A Few Linguistic Problems Related to Morphology:

Students of the tribal areas have very poor knowledge of the structure of words in terms of morphemes. Not only do they lack knowledge of the parts of speech, but they abysmally lack knowledge of derivations using suffixes and prefixes. The following three questions were asked find out the morphological problems of these students.

As for Prefixes and Suffixes, as the study reveals, **83.51%** did not know what prefixes and suffixes are. Only a small percentage of just **16.49%** said they knew what these were. The validity of the hypothesis proved beyond doubt in this case.

Q6. Do you know what *prefixes* and *suffixes* are?

Sample	X	Y
No of items	12	12
Sum	46.0	233.0
Mean	3.83	19.42
Median	1.0	21.0
Variance	54.69	70.45
Standard Deviation	7.39	8.39

Graphic Representation

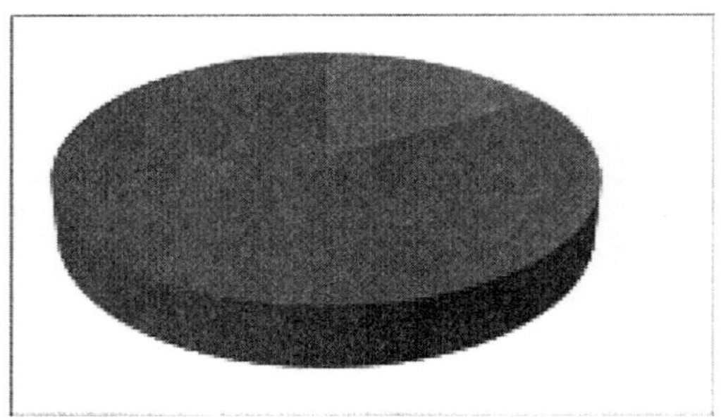

Yes= 16.49% **No= 83.51%**

Q7. Do you know that words also have a structure like that of sentences?

The above question was intended to test if they had some knowledge about Morphology. It was assumed that they lacked it. And attesting to the truth of the assumption, a shocking **88.53%** of the participating students answered the question in the negative. Only a negligible percentage of just **11.46%** knew that words also have a structure. The hypothesis is highly validated here.

Sample	X	Y
No of items	12	12
Sum	32.0	247.0
Mean	2.67	20.58
Median	2.0	22.0
Variance	8.06	78.99
Standard Deviation	2.83	8.89

Graphic Representation:

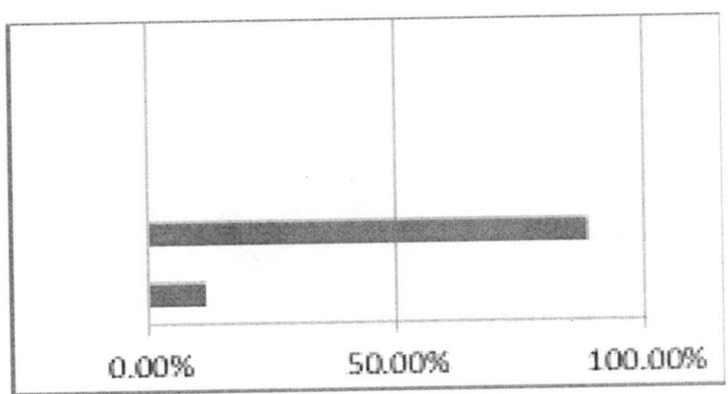

Yes = 11.46% **No= 88.53%**

Q8. Do you know the parts of speech/word classes in English?

It was really intriguing to find that majority of the students **(68.11)** were ignorant of one of the basic grammar topics in English -*Parts of Speech*- underlining their linguistic (here morphological) impediment in mastering English. Even towards the close of the UG programme, only **31. 89%** had knowledge about parts of speech/word classes in English. The hypothesis is highly validated in this case.

Sample	X	Y
No of items	12	12
Sum	89.0	190.0
Mean	7.42	15.83
Median	7.5	18.0
Variance	30.63	53.61
Standard Deviation	5.53	7.32

Graphic Representation:

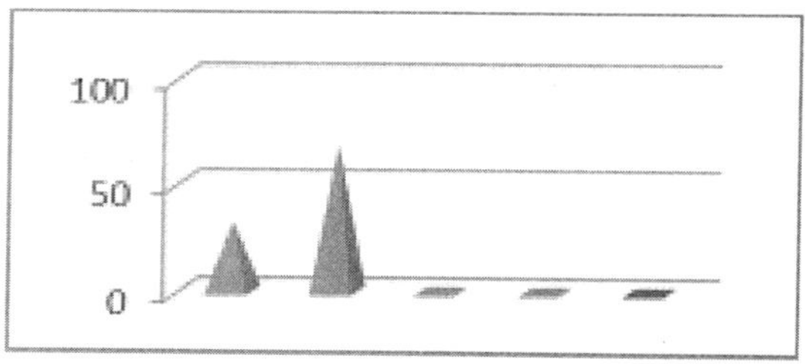

Yes= 31.89% **No= 68.11%**

A Few Linguistic Problems Related to Syntax:

Syntax, being the most important branch of Grammar, is to be mastered for good knowledge of the English language. The following two questions were asked to check their syntactic knowledge.

In order to test their basic syntactic knowledge the following simple question was asked. Surprisingly most of them **(75.26%)** identified the commonest English sentence pattern to be the **SVO** pattern. This reveals that they had at least known the English order of sentences/ word order. Only **24.74%** (i.e.13.97+10.75) were not sure which the commonest English pattern is. The hypothesis is barely validated in this case. The following table and diagram illustrates the study:

Q9.Which is the commonest sentence pattern in English?—(i) SV (ii) SVO (iii) ASVO

(*Tick your choice).*

Sample	X	Y	Z
No of items	12	12	12
Sum	39.0	210.0	30.0
Mean	3.25	17.5	2.5
Median	2.5	18.5	2.0
Variance	10.75	53.73	3.54
Standard Deviation	3.28	7.33	1.88

Graphic Representation:

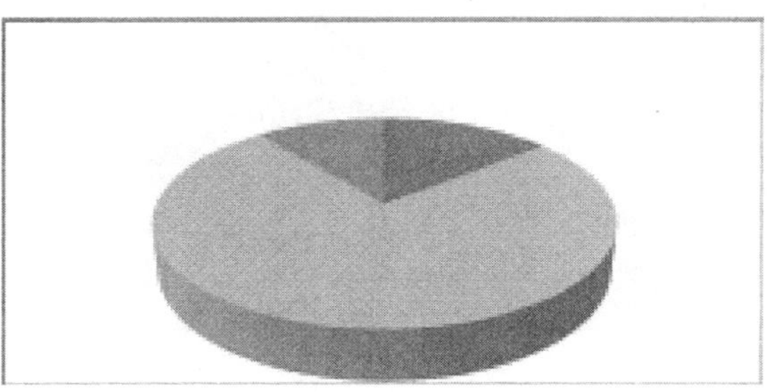

SV= 13.97%, SVO= 75.26%, ASVO= 10.75%.

Q10. Which do you think can function as the 'subject' and 'object' in a sentence?—(a) Noun (b) Verb (c) Preposition (*Tick your choice*).

The second question was intended to test the syntactic knowledge of the students. It revealed that a greater number of students **(56.63%, i.e. 50.54+6.09)** did not know that it is a *noun* that can function as the subject and object in a sentence. This shows that their knowledge of syntax is also not up to the mark. Only **43.37%** gave the right answer to the question. Here too the hypothesis is validated. The following table and diagram illustrate the point:

Sample	X	Y	Z
No of items	12	12	12
Sum	121.0	141.0	17.0
Mean	10.08	11.75	1.41
Median	8.0	12.0	1.0
Variance	60.99	57.84	2.26
Standard Deviation	7.81	7.60	1.50

Graphic Representation:

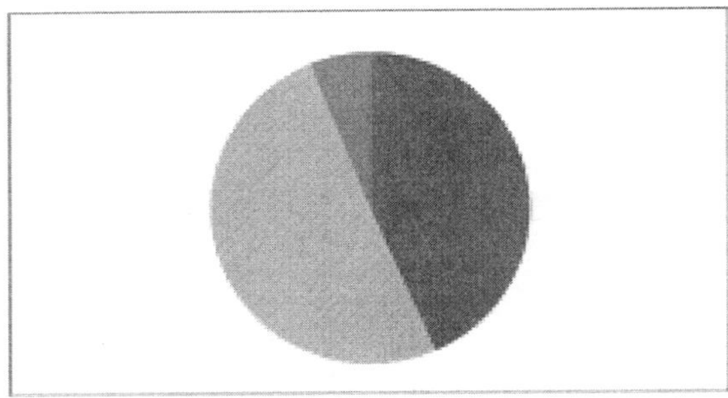

Noun= 43.37%, Preposition= 06.09%, Verb= 50.54%

The Main Graphological Issue:

Another linguistic area where the tribal students had difficulty was related to Graphology. Most students proved to have serious spelling problems. The fact that **70.61%** did not know the spellings of commonly used words reveals this great difficulty. Only some **29.39%**students knew the spellings of ordinary/commonly used words in English. This finding too highly validates the hypothesis.

Q11. Do you know the spellings of most of the commonly used words in English?

Sample	X	Y
No of items	12	12
Sum	82.0	197.0
Mean	6.83	16.41
Median	5.5	17.5
Variance	35.42	82.81
Standard Deviation	5.95	9.10

Graphic Representation:

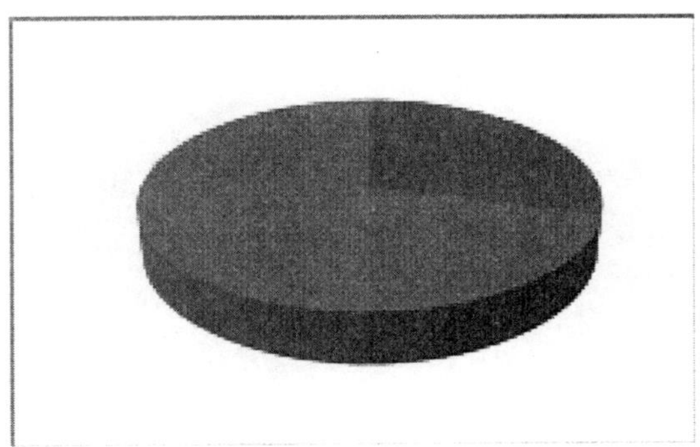

Yes= 29.39% **No= 70.61%.**

The Main Linguistic Problem Related to Semantics:

The tribal students generally had a poor vocabulary because they did not know the meanings of most ordinary words. The following question was asked to check whether they knew the synonyms of some commonly used words. Their responses revealed that a shocking **87.82%** of the participants admitting that they did know at all. This attests to the veracity of the hypothesis. Only **12.18%** said they knew it. This is illustrated by the following table as well as the diagram:

Q12. Do you know the synonyms of commonly used words like 'wonderful', 'attractive'?

Sample	X	Y
No of items	12	12
Sum	34.0	245.0
Mean	2.83	20.41
Median	2.0	21.0
Variance	6.88	81.90
Standard Deviation	2.62	9.04

Graphic Representation:

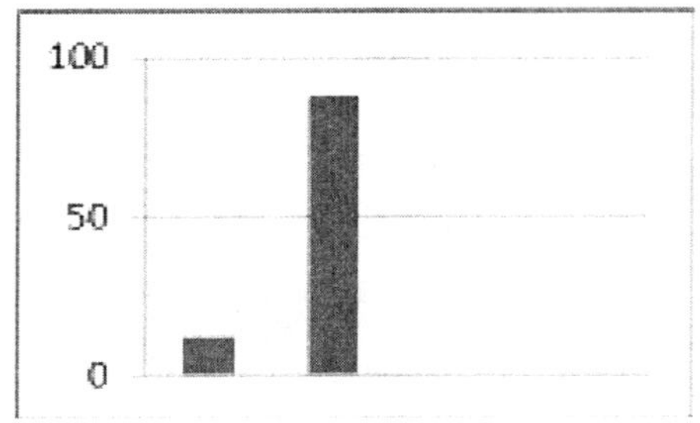

Yes=12.18% **No= 87.82%**

Main Linguistic Issues Related to Lexicology:

One reason why students of tribal areas is poor at English is that they do not have the habit of looking up a dictionary to find the meanings of words or phrases and search for more details about the words they encounter. This habit has to be broken. Two questions were asked to identify the lexicological issues of these students.

The study revealed that a vast majority of them do not know how to refer to a dictionary to glean information about the words such as meanings, opposites, grammatical aspects, pronunciation etc. Those who responded in the 'negative' formed an appalling **89. 24%.** This is a lexicological vacuum to be filled at any cost. Only a small percentage of **10.76%** knew how to refer to a dictionary speedily! What is more? **55.20%** of the students did not have a personal dictionary. Both the findings validate the hypothesis. The following tables and diagrams represent the findings:

Q13. Do you know how to refer to a dictionary properly and find out the meanings or opposites or such other information quite speedily?

Sample	X	Y
No of items	12	12
Sum	30.0	249.0
Mean	2.5	20.75
Median	2.5	21.0
Variance	3.91	81.66
Standard Deviation	1.98	9.03

Graphic Representation:

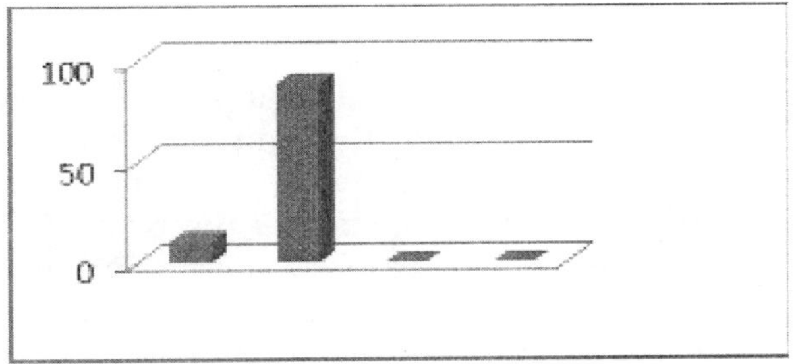

Yes= 10.76% **No= 89.24%**

Q14. Do you have a personal dictionary?

Sample	X	Y
No of items	12	12
Sum	125.0	154.0
Mean	10.4	12.83
Median	9.5	15.0
Variance	25.54	66.33
Standard Deviation	5.05	8.14

Graphic Representation:

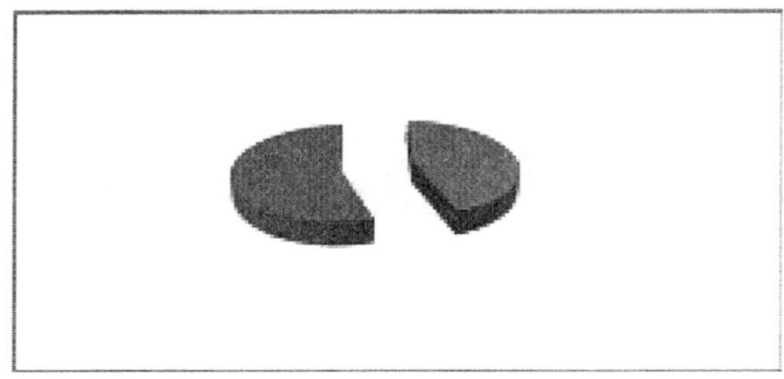

No= 55.20% **Yes= 44.80**

The Main Issue Related to Reading Skill:

Reading is one of the most important channels through which knowledge flows into the human mind. But mere reading will not do the magic. Reading should be perceptive and for that it should be done with rapt attention and full concentration. Further knowledge of the medium through which knowledge is transferred is of paramount significance. Mastery of the medium leads to proper understanding. Its absence leads to incomprehension and perceptional problems. Mastery of the medium implies mastery of vocabulary and grammar - Morphology, Semantics and

Syntax. Thus reading skill for comprehension is closely related to linguistic mastery. Since English is the most important medium of global knowledge, its mastery leads to better comprehension and absorption of knowledge. Poor knowledge of English leads to terrible loss by way of non-understanding of the texts read.

The study reveals that **87.82%** students do not understand what they generally read in English. Only a negligible **12.18%** understood what they read. This greatly supports the Hypothesis that tribal students have linguistic problems which impede their English language learning process. This once again proves that the students have very poor mastery of English.

Q15. Do you understand what you generally read in English?

Sample	X	Y
No of items	12	12
Sum	34.0	245.0
Mean	2.83	20.42
Median	2.0	22.0
Variance	6.88	70.99
Standard Deviation	2.62	8.42

Graphic Representation:

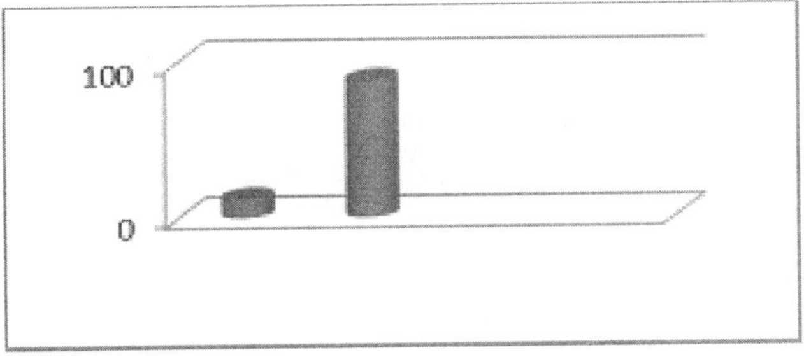

Yes= 12.18 **No= 87.82**

Conclusion

It is clear from the above study that the tribal students confront numerous linguistic problems while learning the English language. Only a few of the important problems are subjected to a close study here; there are many more to be studied. However, the study proves beyond doubt that the tribal students face several linguistic problems while learning English. These impede their speedy mastery of the language. Unless effective steps are taken both by the teachers and the government, these students will find learning English a wild goose chase!

References

1. Sperber, D, and D. Wilson (1986), *Relevance: Communication and Cognition*, London: Blackwell.
2. Gregg, K.R. (1989) Second Language Acquisition Theory: the Case for a Generative Perspective. In *Linguistic Perspectives on Second language Acquisition*, Susan M. Gass & Jacquelin Schachter (eds.), Cambridge, UK: Cambridge University Press.
3. O' Connor, J. D (1980) *Better English Pronunciation* (Second Edition) London: Cambridge University Press, Reprint, 2008.
4. Lyons, John (2007) *Language and Linguistics: An introduction*, United Kingdom: Cambridge University Press.

5

Psychological Factors that Hinder the English Language Learning Process of Students: A Case Study

Abstract

It has been observed that the pace at which the tribal students learn English is abysmally slow in comparison with that of other students. Hence a study was conducted among the tribal students of Gadchiroli district to verify the observation and to isolate the impeding factors that baulk their English language process. The study revealed some interesting facts. They are discussed in this paper. If the ESL students have several difficulties in learning the English language, the situation of the rural and tribal students is much more so. These difficulties stem from both heredity and the environment which they are heir to or exposed to. Being the children of the first generation parents and born in straitened and hostile circumstances, these rural and tribal students have inexplicable difficulties when learning the English language. Centuries of intellectual deprivation of their forefathers and the tremendous exploitation of their frailties have deadened their sensibilities and drained their psychic potentialities. Cultural, economic, social and historical factors have conditioned their minds. Of the numerous problems they face the psychological and linguistic factors are of paramount significance. In this paper the psychological issues are discussed. The study revealed that psychological factors such as i) Prejudice ii) Hatred/dislike iii) Negative attitude iv) Fear v) Uncertainty vi) Confusion, vii) Anxiety viii) Inferiority Complex ix) Indolence x) Lack of interest xi) Shyness and hesitation and xii) Lack of motivation adversely affect the English language learning process of students, especially the tribal students.

Introduction:

Learning is very much conditional upon healthy emotional factors and proper thinking habits. There are many psychological variables which make or mar the language learning process of learners. Good motivation and positive emotions go a long way in mastering the English language or any other language. Speaking of 'approach and avoidance motivation', a group of psychologists state that "Motivation impels us towards some things and away from others. We seek to maximize pleasures and minimize pain, gravitate towards rewards and avoid punishment and deprivation. These seemingly universal tendencies reflect the activity of two distinct neural systems in brain." (Michael *et al*, 2009, p.476). When the psychological factors are favourable for the learners, actual learning takes place. True learning is sure to leave an indelible mark on the future course of actions of the learner. "All knowledge, however acquired, all skill resulting from motor activity, all habits, all acquaintances with people and things, all attitudes built up in dealing with people and things, have been learned in the broad sense of the term...Learning , then is an activity that produces a relatively permanent effect on later activity" (Woodworth, 2001, p. 288).

A learner should have good and positive attitudes towards his/her subjects under study as also towards the teachers and the peers. Further, motivation plays a crucial role in forging ahead in one's studies. Without the necessary extrinsic and/or intrinsic motivation students will not be interested in their studies. Clear thinking is yet another factor in good learning. Clear thinking requires that the mind be quite clear. The mind that is clouded by emotions of any sort cannot think clearly. Emotions especially negative ones blur clear thinking. Only clear thinking leads to real learning process just as clear thinking helps logical processes of discovering truth. Clear thinking is a precondition for clear perception which in turn is a prerequisite for acquiring a language too.

Mind needs freedom, freedom from the shackles of negative emotions such as fear, hatred, doubts, uncertainty, hesitation, anxiety, helplessness, inferiority complex, and the like. Positive emotions can aid clear thinking. If principles of language are to be internalized they have to be perceived well. Only a tranquil mind can easily grasp the complexities of a language. Fortunately, human beings are endowed with a capacity for learning languages. In learning a language internalization of grammar is essential. This enables the learners to use the language effectively. Grammatically enabled learners are the outcome of learning grammar. Nevertheless, language is a mental phenomenon as Chomsky asserts. In his attempt to differentiate between 'ideation and ideology', following a 'formal linguistics' view as against Halliday's 'functional linguistics', Prabhu comments: "The distinction is relatable here to linguistic competence as a mental phenomenon and language as a social phenomenon. It is thought that human beings are endowed with a specific capacity for language, that is to say, a specific set of expectations, options, constraints, etc, on the strength of which each child is able to construct in its own mind the complex grammar of the language it is exposed to. Grammar is a system of rules or relations that operates in each individual's mind and enables that individual to use the language grammatically and tell grammatical from ungrammatical sentences". (Prabhu, 2002, pp.14-15)

Very often the second language learners do not have unburdened, unruffled, and clear minds. Their minds are rather weighed down by numerous problems, mostly psychological. Most problems originate from the families from where they come. Some problems are the products of their own environment and/or heredity. The hypothesis was that these psychological factors enfeeble their mental faculties and hinder them from acquiring the second language easily. Hence it is reasonable to have a closer look at some of these important problematic variables. The major psychological problems identified are: i) Prejudice ii) Hatred/ dislike iii) Negative attitude iv) Fear v) Uncertainty vi)

Confusion, vii) Anxiety viii) Inferiority Complex ix) Indolence x) Lack of interest xi) Shyness and hesitation and xii) Lack of motivation. These should be examined closely:

Some **12** colleges of the tribal district of Gadchiroli (Maharashtra) were selected for study. The students (the sample population - some **279** - in number) were from the Final Year BA classes of these colleges. The participants were the students available in the class at the time of the survey conducted in the colleges using questionnaires. In some cases the number of participants was quite small. The reason was that the researcher could not reach the institution when all students were available (because of the long distance he had to travel between colleges).

The Major Impeding Psychological Variables

The following psychological variables have been identified (through the questionnaire) as the major impeding factors in English language learning process:

1. Prejudice

Prejudice is a major obstacle in learning process and especially in language learning process. Many students come to educational institutions with highly prejudiced minds. When people are prejudiced they will not be able to cope with the reality which they encounter later, because prejudice is a judgment formed in advance without having sufficient experience, or rather it is a preconceived notion. This judgment or preconceived idea is very often at variance with reality. When they come to grip with the reality later, they will find it very difficult to accept the situation or reality. Often such prejudices mar learning activity and lead to disillusionment. Hence students should approach educational institutions without prejudices and with an open mind for studies and accepting the prevailing realities as they are. Or they should be ready to cast off their prejudices as soon as they come to know about the realities. A fair mind, to accept reality as it is, is a sine qua non to fare well in learning process. Teachers should interact with the students to find out their prejudices and correct them at the earliest. But there are also exceptionally good and ideal students who come unprejudiced and are on the search for acquiring knowledge and modifying their very lives. They know that the path to acquiring knowledge is not easy and smooth. They are by nature ready to take up the arduous task as it is. They do not get discouraged by the challenges posed by studies. Like adventure-seeking mountaineers, they aim to reach great heights and forge ahead taking the best route possible to attain to their goal and enjoy the very process. But such students do not form a majority, especially in the rural tribal background. The language learning process of most students is impeded by all or some of the following psychological variables, as the study will prove later

Many students in the tribal area of Gadchiroli had the prejudice that English is a difficult language. The study conducted through the questionnaire confirmed it. The data was collected from the Final B.A *(Compulsory English*) students. They were asked the question: *Do you think English is a very difficult language?* The vast majority of the students (i.e., 214), which is 77% of the participants, replied that they thought English is a very difficult language clearly proving the hypothesis that most students are prejudiced against English and that this prejudice is a hindrance to their English language learning process. Probably, they repeatedly hear others or even teachers affirm that English is a difficult language. This might have made them prejudiced. (Some 214 students said '*Yes*' in answer to the question and only 65 said: '*No*'.) The finding can be analyzed as follows using the statistical method and be represented by the Pie Diagram:

Question-1: ***Do you think English is a very difficult language?***

Sample	X	Y
No. of items	12	12
Sum	214	65
Mean	17.83	5.42
Median	18.5	5.0
Variance	53.06	19.90
Standard Deviation	7.28	4.45

Diagrammatic Representation:

YES=77% (the blue segment), NO=23% (the orange segment)

2. Hatred/Dislike

One of the major stumbling blocks in English language learning process is hatred or dislike. There are a few objects the students may hate or dislike. They may hate the very institution for one reason or another. It may be caused by some bitter experience in the institution or it may be because of the negative opinions about the institution heard from others. Whatever be the reason, if they do so, their interest in studies may diminish and learning English language is part of their studies which is also likely to be affected considerably. Their hatred may also be that of the teacher due to some reasons. In that case also students may not learn the language well. Another possibility is that of hating or disliking the English language itself for one reason or another. In this case also learning English becomes very difficult. We never pay due attention to the thing or person we hate or dislike. Hence the first thing to overcome this block is to start loving or liking the English language itself.

The study proves that the majority of students, 180 (64.51%), dislikes English. But only 99 students (just 35.49%) said they do not hate English. Thus, the study proves the hypothesis that hatred/dislike of the language as a psychological factor is a hindrance to language learning. The following analysis of the data and the Pie Diagram bring out the details of this enquiry.

Question: 2: ***Do you dislike/ hate English for one reason or another?***

Sample	X	Y
No of items	12	12
Sum	180	99
Mean	15	8.25
Median	12	5.0
Variance	56.72	74.57
Standard Deviation	7.53	8.64

Diagrammatic Representation:

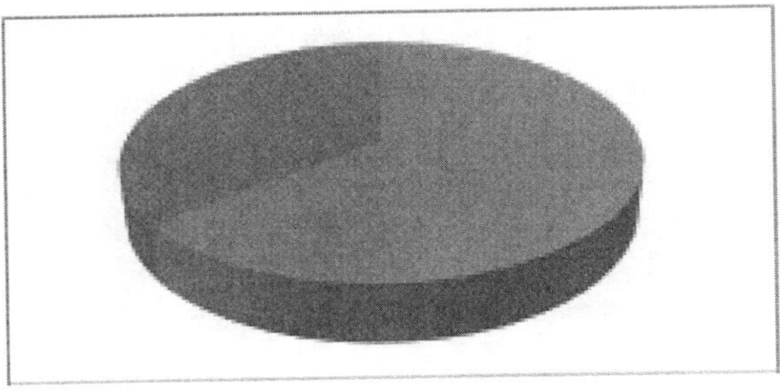

YES=64.51% NO= 35.49%

3. Negative Attitude

If students have a negative attitude towards English language, they will not put in the required effort in learning the language. The attitudes of many students are negative when it comes to learning English. They are cynical about it, attributing to its propagation some hostile motives like the hidden British agenda of English language as a vehicle to transmit culture, etc, about which the public speakers or the media must have apprised them, like Macaulay's *Minutes*. In such cases, the students develop negative attitudes which prevent them from approaching the language with a thirst for mastering it.

The study revealed that 38% students were told by teachers or others that English is a colonial language, thus, creating in them a negative attitude towards English. Fortunately, 62% are free from such negative attitudes. The hypothesis was fairly validated, (if not to a great extent), since it is applicable to a reasonable number of students, namely, 38%.The following analysis and the diagram clearly bring out the details of the study in relation to the question given below:

Question: 3. ***Have you ever been told (by teachers or others) that English is a colonial language?***

Sample	X	Y
No of items	12	12
Sum	105.0	174.0
Mean	8.75	14.5
Median	4.5	12.0
Variance	83.30	95.18
Standard Deviation	9.13	9.76

Diagrammatic Representation:

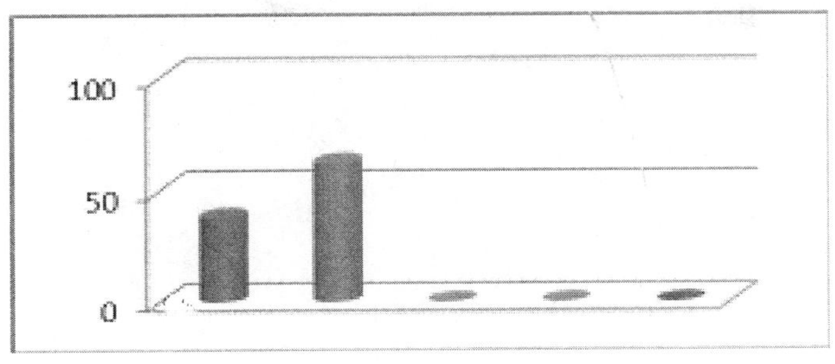

YES= 38% NO= 62%

4. Fear

Many students have vague and irrational fears towards English. They fear that it is a language that is likely to bring about their possible failure in the examinations and obstruct their progress in life. Some fear that it is so tough a language that they cannot master it in their life time. Others fear that learning English is likely to retard their knowledge of or interest in their own Mother Tongue. They fear English may snatch them away from their interest in the local language. This fear may be injected into them by the elders or teachers or those zealots of patriotism. Once the mind fears something it tends to avoid contact with it. Further, fear makes clear thinking impossible. Thus, English learning is adversely affected.

The study revealed that majority of students (57%) have a fearful attitude towards English and only 43% said they did not have such a fear. Thus, the hypothesis stands highly validated. The following analysis and the subsequent diagram clearly bring out the results of the inquiry

Question 4: ***Is your attitude towards English one of fear?***

Sample	X	Y
No of items	12	12
Sum	159.0	120.0
Mean	13.25	10.0
Median	8.0	8.5
Variance	94.93	45.82
Standard Deviation	9.74	6.77

Diagrammatic Representation:

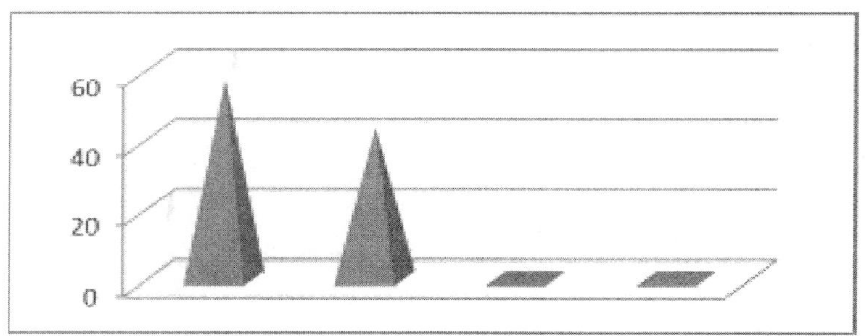

YES= 57%   NO=43%

5. Uncertainty and Confusion

Several students know English well but are not sure if what they speak or write is correct. Their knowledge is not strengthened by the required level of practice. Lack of written and spoken practice and lack of language exposure makes them doubt whether they are using the right expressions or correct usage. So they are hesitant to speak or write confidently and courageously. This uncertainty is all the more manifest in their speaking when they have to enter into a face-to-face conversation with someone or a group. When facing people the question of self-esteem and ego finds its place in the mind and thereby aggravating the uncertainty factor and causing greater doubt about one's knowledge.

In the absence of proper practice and constant usage the numerous and diverse vocabulary items cannot be properly digested by the students. Equally true is the case of grammar items and other linguistic elements. This vague perception of things in the absence of the much needed speaking and writing practice makes the students feel highly confused. To ward off this problem what is required is language exposure, adequate opportunities for both written and oral practice to drive home the confusing points.

The study reveals that uncertainty and confusion are serious problems in the use of a language. A staggering 82.80% agreed that they suffer from uncertainty and confusion regarding the right usage and correct expressions of the English language. In this way, the hypothesis that "Uncertainty and confusion as adverse psychological factors impede English language learning" has been validated by the study. Only a negligible percentage of 17.20% did not have such problems as is explicit in the following analysis and the diagram:

Question: 5. ***Do you suffer from uncertainty and confusion regarding the right usage and correct expressions of the English language?***

Sample	X	Y
No of items	12	12
Sum	231.0	48.0
Mean	19.25	4.0
Median	20.0	1.5
Variance	97.66	54.54
Standard Deviation	9.88	5.87

Diagrammatic Representation:

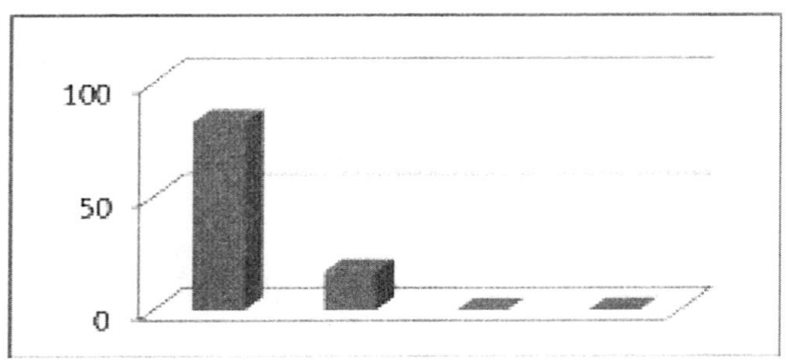

YES=82.80% NO=17.20%

6. Anxiety

A good number of students suffer from high level of anxiety when they confront situations where they have either to speak English or to write English. During learning process also many students suffer from anxiety caused by the inability to learn the language well or the complexity posed by the language itself. A pass in English is a cause of deep concern for many students. Their failures of the past attempts strengthen their anxiety. Such students should give close attention to their study process and get the required academic counselling and remediation from teachers.

The percentage of students who suffer from anxiety is 78.85% as the study points out, a quite bewildering percentage. Here also the hypothesis "anxiety as a negative psychological factor hinders English language learning" stands validated. Only a small percentage of just 21.15% did not have much anxiety. This is illustrated as follows:

Question: 6. ***Do you suffer from anxiety whenever you begin to learn English?***

Sample	X	Y
No of items	12	12
Sum	220.0	59.0
Mean	18.33	4.91
Median	20.0	4.0
Variance	69.88	19.17
Standard Deviation	8.36	4.38

Diagrammatic Representation:

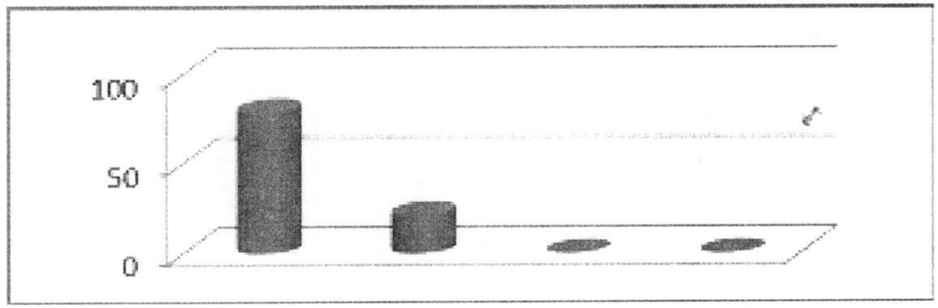

YES=78.85% NO=21.15%

7. Inferiority Complex

There are students who suffer from inferiority complex when they confront English situations or learning English language. It is due to the feeling developed in them that English is a language of the elite class and that hailing from a poor tribal background they do not possess the ability to learn an international language like English. They tend to associate English with their one-time supposedly superior white bosses in India and also with the language of the high society, the upper educated class. This inferiority born of reverence to English or attributing to it greater difficulties than it actually has, affects their learning process adversely. Only proper guidance and effective classes can cure them of this problem.

As the study reveals, more than a quarter of the total number of students suffered from inferiority complex, namely, 26.16%, which fairly supports the hypothesis.

Question: 7. ***Do you feel that since you are from a poor tribal background, you cannot learn English well?***

Sample	X	Y
No of items	12	12
Sum	73.0	206.0
Mean	6.08	17.16
Median	5.0	18.05
Variance	10.08	76.33
Standard Deviation	3.17	8.74

Diagrammatic Representation:

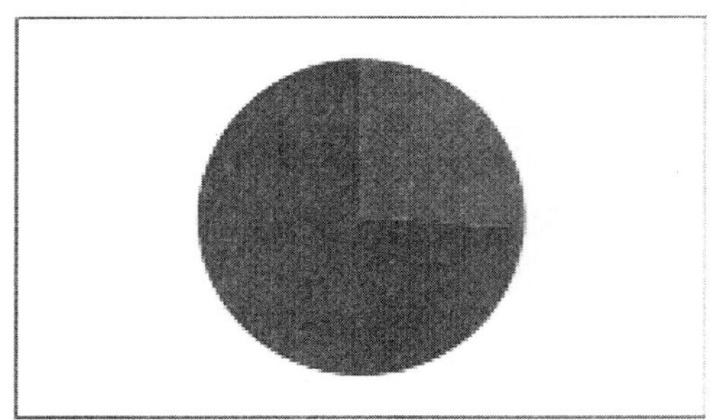

YES=26.16% NO=73.84

8. Indolence and Lack of Interest

Majority of students in the tribal belt are indolent in academic matters and it is more so in the case of English because it pauses greater difficulties being a foreign language. If students strain a little or put in a little more effort English can easily be learned. But their inactive nature, engendered by some indeterminate factors, either historical or cultural (or whatever they might be), deprives them of a large number of benefits from knowledge and job perspectives.

To learn and remember anything, one needs the required level of interest and attention. The tribal students generally are not that interested in English. Had they evinced sufficient degrees of interest, learning English would have been quite easy, as English is a comparatively easy language with very few inflections. It is either the lack of awareness of the benefits of English or the bad experiences in the past while learning English that could be at the root of this kind of lack of interest in English. It is also possible that a set of factors may be at work in creating this unhealthy tendency. Indolence and lack of interest are major obstacles in mastering the English language as the study reveals.

A staggering 82.08% suffered from laziness and lack of interest and only 17.02% did not have these problems. It attests to the veracity of the hypothesis and validates it beyond doubt. The study is as shown below:

Question: 8. ***Do you realize that it may be your own indolence and lack of interest in English that hinder your progress in English?***

Sample	X	Y
No of items	12	12
Sum	229.0	50.0
Mean	19.08	4.16
Median	17.5	4.0
Variance	73.90	11.06
Standard Deviation	8.59	3.32

Diagrammatic Representation:

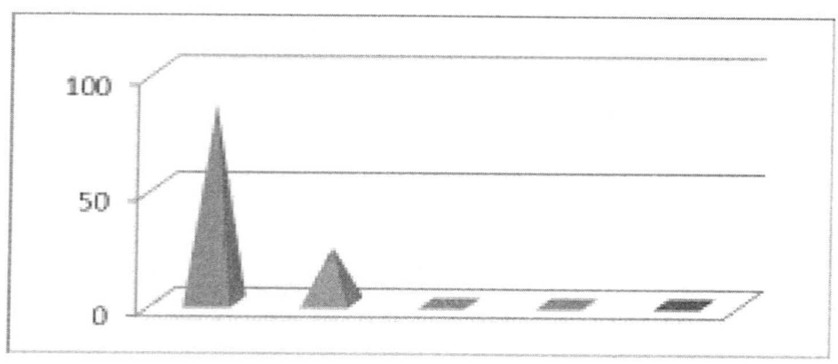

YES= 82.08% NO= 17.92%

9. Shyness, Hesitation and Lack of Confidence

These factors are interrelated. There are a good number of students who are very shy and hesitant to open their mouth to speak English. They feel shy to speak a different language other than their own. It could also be that they feel uncomfortable in speaking English. Being ill at ease is the outcome of lack of practice and inadequacy of language exposure. They are hesitant because they are unsure of the grammaticality and acceptability of what they are going to speak. It is equally possible that they are keenly aware that they lack knowledge and practice of the language. This is at the root of their lacking confidence.

Nearly 47% students suffer from the above-mentioned psychological problems, adequately validating the hypothesis.

Question: 9. ***Are you shy and hesitant to read/speak English in public?***

Sample	X	Y
No of items	12	12
Sum	131.0	148.0
Mean	10.92	12.33
Median	11.0	12.5
Variance	59.72	42.42
Standard Deviation	7.73	6.51

Diagrammatic Representation:

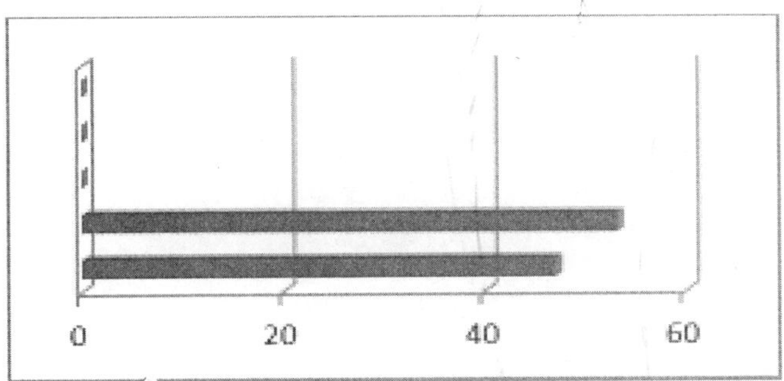

YES= 46.95% NO=53.05%

10. Lack of Motivation

Motivation is needed for any sort of activities to be accomplished well. This is particularly so in intellectual pursuits like learning a language. Motivation can be either internal or external motivation. If both kinds of motivation are easily available, learning becomes all the more effective. Students in the tribal areas generally lack both these types. Their non-intellectual tradition has deprived them of any internal or intellectual motivation; their un-educated parents and the ignorant and illiterate ambience around them do not provide them any external motivation. So a good number of students come to college without adequate motivation and involve in intellectual activities of learning quite mechanically and listlessly. Teachers have limitations in this regard but persistently strive to motivate them. Students admit the positive role played by their teachers.

The study reveals that 89.59%students get external motivation from teachers. But how far the students are spurred by internal motivation is a dubious proposition. The hypothesis is not adequately validated in this case.

Question: 10. ***Do you think your teachers properly motivated you (through their advice/guidance/own example) to learn English properly?***

Sample	X	Y
No of items	12	12
Sum	236.0	43.0
Mean	19.67	3.58
Median	19.5	3.0
Variance	73.70	16.08
Standard Deviation	8.58	4.01

Diagrammatic Representation:

YES= 84.59 No=15.41%

Conclusion

The study clearly reveals that several psychological factors like the ones chosen here for study have their deep impact on the minds of the learners especially the English language learners. The practitioners of education and particularly the English language teachers should know how various psychological factors adversely affect the learning process of their students especially the tribal students. This study is intended to help the teachers and policy makers have reliable insight into the working of the student psyche in relation to the English language learning process. Although the study is specifically related to the tribal students of Gadchiroli district in Maharashtra, it is likely to have a bearing on the rural students in general.

References

1. Passer Michael, Ronald Smith, Nigel Holt, Andy Bremner, Ed. Sutherland, Michael L W. Vliek, (2009), *Psychology: The Science of Mind and Behaviour* (European edition), Berkshire: McGraw-Hill..
2. Woodworth, R. S (2001), *Basic Facts in Psychology*, Delhi: Sports Publication.
3. Prabhu, N. S. (2002) Ideation and Ideology. *Teaching English in Non-Native Contexts: Essays presented to V. Saraswathi*, S. C Choudhary (Editor), Chennai: Chennai Orient Longman
4. Cruickshank, D. R, Deborah. B. J, Kim. K. M (2009) *The Act of Teaching (Fifth Ed.)* New York: McGraw-Hill.
5. Singer, M. R. (1987). *Intercultural communication: A Perceptual Approach*, Eaglewood Cliffs, NJ: Prentice-Hall.
6. Geertz, L, (1973). *The Interpretation of Culture*, New York: Basic Books.
7. Lyons, John (2007) *Language and Linguistics: An introduction*, United Kingdom: Cambridge University Press
8. Sperber, D, and D. Wilson (1986), *Relevance: Communication and Cognition*, London: Blackwell.
9. Gregg, K.R. (1989) Second language acquisition theory: The Case for a Generative Perspective. *Linguistic Perspectives on Second language Acquisition*, Susan M. Gass & Jacquelin Schachter (eds.), Cambridge, UK: Cambridge University Press.

6

Role of English in Travel, Tourism and Hospitality Industry

Joseph. T. C. &. R. G. Munghate

Introduction

Being the most widely used global language, English has been exerting a tremendous influence on all walks of modern man's life and playing an unsurpassed role in various spheres of his life. These comprise, among others, travel, tourism, and hospitality industry, in all of which the use of English has become an imperative need and much more than mere ostentation. The reverberations of the impact of English are being felt in the newly emerged knowledge economy as also in the traditional scientific, engineering, academic, and technological arenas. Besides, mass-media, library, banking, computer, internet, and a host of other fields also make vast use of English. With its ever-growing importance, the role of English in travel, tourism and hospitality industry has been assuming greater significance, and also undergoing some functional changes.

The Multi-faceted Role of English

It is not easy to enlist the numerous roles English is currently playing. Within the constraints of a paper like this, we are constricted only to dwell on its tangible and conspicuous roles. The more remarkable functional roles English plays, from among the complex matrix of its manifold roles, can be identified as follows:

S G M Arts & Science College, Kurkheda

1 Communicative/Interactive Role

When people travel from place to place or embark on a tour, they come across people of different linguistic backgrounds and naturally they have to communicate with these people, if the purpose of their travelling, or touring activities has to be fructified. Although communication can take place through written language yet, it is the spoken form aided by the body language that is used more frequently for communicative purposes than any other modes. But the problem arises when the tourists and travellers are ignorant of the languages used by the natives of the places visited.

In such cases, there is only one option left, and that is but using a common linguistic medium known to both the parties—the visitors and the visited. That medium, in all likelihood, in the present world situation, is none other than English, because among the numerous languages used in the different parts of the world, it is English that is most extensively used in the world presently. Its coverage is so vast that not many countries are ignorant of, and illiterate in English. So when English comes handy, it can be used for easy and effective communication or interaction in a multi-lingual situation. Hence, it has to be learned as best as possible so that proper oral and written communication can be carried on without any disconcerting hitch. And learning English, in the true sense, calls for commitment and hard work.

2. Integrative Role

Since the global situation is a medley of numerous races, languages, cultures, classes, religions, castes, geographical divisions, ideologies, etc, realizing world unity is extremely difficult. Mistrust, suspicion, misunderstanding, rivalry and jealousy are highly insidious forces surreptitiously at work and occasionally stupefying us when they rear their ugly, Hydra-like heads in such palpable forms as cross-border terrorism, economic sanctions, violence, cold war, disputes and dissensions, nuclear arms-race, the never-quenching avarice of the developed and developing countries to pile-up huge stores of lethal weapons targeting at the potential and real enemy countries. These are global menaces threatening our very existence and point to the sombre possibility of a potential annihilation of human race when we are counting our days here on our beautiful but seemingly ill-fated planet, under the ever-growing dangers of a nuclear holocaust looming large. All these damage beyond repair the fine fabric of world social order, global unity and universal security. Common unifying factors are crucial in such situations to strengthen the bonds of humanity among people and foster amity. 'A single language for all' is a noble idea which can enfold the peoples of the world under a single bower and integrate them into a unified community. All the differences can be sorted out, ideas can be shared and activities chalked out for a better future under the magic spell of a common language. English has been playing this integrative role for a long time now and that, too, much more than any other language in the world. When people set out on travels and tours, they confront with these diversities but English helps integrate all into a single family, aids free mingling, and bring about the much-desired solidarity.

Again those employed in hospitality industry such as air hostesses, those personnel in standard and star hotels receiving and entertaining tourists and travellers from distant places, those employed in the foreign embassy such as diplomats and ambassadors, Foreign Secretaries of nations, and all those officials associated with travel, tourism and other hospitality activities find English the most convenient medium to interact with foreigners and many natives belonging to different linguistic communities. English enables them to engage in polite exchanges and come closer to one another effecting national and international integration. But what is required is to learn and use with facility all those English formulaic expressions which are indicative of politeness and good manners. In other words, the functional knowledge of English and its contextual usages should be mastered well by all those in cross-border mobility, and also associated with hospitality industry. Language functions like: making polite requests, offering help etc are very crucial in hospitality industry. For, the personnel in such industries have to be extremely polite, tactful, warm, and profuse in their expressions exhibiting the least indifference and annoyance. Their language should be the least offensive and the most pleasing. Knowledge of Pragmatics is highly useful for such people. Pragmatics, which is an emerging branch of language study, focuses on language use in particular contexts in linguistic communities. It examines the meanings based on contextual usages, intonation, relationship between the speaker and the listener, their attitudes, hidden meanings etc.

3. Lingua-franca Role

Different linguistic states have different languages and so it is not easy for the travellers and tourists to learn all these languages and engage in easy communicative activities. A common link-language/lingua-franca can be beneficially used by those in mobility to communicate with one another and disburden themselves of the herculean task of learning a large number of languages. Here English comes to the rescue and facilitates easy and effective communication, because it is taught in most universities and institutions the world over. Today, Ancient Greek and Latin, as well as French, still retain some of their elite status, but "English is the de facto language of international communication" (Tsuda, 1999, p. 153). The advantage of this situation is particularly for the English people and the Americans. But it has serious drawbacks, too, as they don't have to learn another language, and learning another language in addition to one's own language is a healthy mental exercise and one that helps a person to have deeper insights into one's own language as well as effecting better intercultural communication.

Despite the obvious advantages and positive aspects of English as a lingua-franca, Judith and Nakayama are wary of the lingua franca role of English: "Learning a foreign language is never easy, of course, but the dominance of English as the lingua franca raises important issues for intercultural communication:

What is the relationship between our four touchstones and this contemporary linguistic situation? That is, how do culture, communication, power, and context play out in the domination of English? First, the intimate connections between language and culture mean that the diffusion of English is tied to the spread of U.S American culture around the world. Is this a new form of colonialism? If we consider issues of power, what role does the Unites States play in the domination of English on the world scene? How does this marginalize or disempower those who are not fluent in English in intercultural communication? What kinds of resentment might be fostered by forcing people to recognize their disempowerment?

In what intercultural contexts is it appropriate to assume that others speak English? For English speakers, this is a particularly unique context. Latvians, for example, cannot attend international meetings and assume that others will speak Latvian; and Albanians will have difficulty transacting international trade if they assume that others know their language." (Judith & Nakayama, 2004, p. 228) Thus, this lingua franca role of English cannot be said to be an unadulterated blessing, but one with possible lurking dangers, whose verity time will disclose eventually.

4. Relation-Fostering Role

English language can strengthen relationships globally through its unifying power. Language, through its power of communication brings people on a common platform of humanity. People begin to feel that they belong to the common family of mankind despite the peripheral and superficial differences. It enables them sacrifice their narrow, parochial interests on the altar of humanity. It prompts them open up their hearts and pour forth their pent-up emotions and finally iron out their differences, if any , and share emotions of joy, wonder, satisfaction, disgust, anger, frustration, resentment, admiration, love, fear, etc., while on a tour and coming across diverse groups of people and in strikingly different situations. Further, thoughtful sharing of ideas and concerns through the common medium of English can cement their relationships and dispel unwarranted fears. This builds up their reciprocal faith which boosts good relationships. When people of hostile linguistic communities chance to meet one another, English can be a welcome relief to enter into easy communication activities and forget their differences, at least for a while. It opens up new vistas of understanding and more such meetings of more members of the same states promote mutual respect and bring about better perceptional changes, finally resulting in healthier relationships. In the multi-cultural global set-up a common language like English can bring together people of all cultural groups and strengthen their relationships through dialogue and discussions. Hence English can build healthy relations on a global level through English which other languages are incapacitated to.

5. Economic/Business Role

It is not merely during travel, tourism and hospitality that English language seems to be of assistance but during economic and business transactions as well. Those on the move, either propelled by entertainment purposes or profit motives, naturally have economic matters of grave import. Through its global communicability, intelligibility and universal acceptability, English helps not only international trade and other economic transactions to be conducted in an easier manner but inter personal economic dealings as well. Even internal trade is also smoothly carried out in a multi-linguistic set-up with the help of English. Businessmen occasionally travel on business purposes to different states. Under linguistic plurality, it is mainly through English that they have their contracts, agreements, and transactions drafted and fulfilled without confusion. Even tourists buy many things while they are on tours. It is English that facilitates their dealings. Again, most banking activities are also carried out through English. This makes financial and business dealings much smoother, too.

6. Functional Roles

When a person moves about in strange and unknown lands, he/she has to seek information, every now and then, of various matters such as accommodation, food, destinations, shopping items, places of interest, historical backgrounds of the places visited, facilities available at different places, people to contact, etc. Being ignorant of the foreign tongue/s of the place, seeking information can be realized only through the common medium of English. Not only seeking information, but also giving information is also through English, thus, bringing a lot of relief and solace to the travellers in unknown countries. If travel is for a given purpose, tour is for entertainment and fun; hospitality is extended from cultural point of view and sometimes shown with the ulterior motive of mere expediency. But it is essentially a manifestation of civilization and goodwill. And in all these cases, English has a major role to play as the international language.

Various contextualized language functions such as 'offering help, seeking information, asking for advice, seeking permission, making requests, asking for directions, making inquiries, greeting, introducing, making complaints', etc., all can be effectively carried out through the common medium called English. In the absence of such a medium, only chaos and confusion would prevail in the word and very few would venture to undertake long, tedious and risky journeys outside their own countries. For in the absence of linguistic exchanges, rather than resorting to gestures and facial expressions, civilized persons are likely to prefer silence, but silence is painful and frightening after a point.

In such cases, the remedy is to be braced up with adequate mastery of English and through that glean information, and engage in free conversation reasserting one's gregariousness.

Conclusion

To conclude, in the global era, playing its multifarious roles, English has been reasserting its 'World Language' status which no other language as yet could command, nor lay claim to. Beyond doubt, the impact of English is all-pervasive now. Some of the important roles played by English, as discussed in the foregoing analysis, point to the ever-growing relevance and importance of English. Good working knowledge of English signals a much brighter future and ensures easy mobility and suave communication skills for travellers, tourists, and for all those engaged in hospitality industry. But in our unqualified admiration for the greatness of English, we should not be blind to the possibility of a hidden, neo-colonial agenda, and an ulterior neo-imperialistic political motive as adumbrated by writers like Judith, Nakayama and Tsuda, not to mention the genuine fears of the advocates of Post-Colonialism!

References

1. Tsuda, Y. (1999). The Hegemony of English and Strategies for Linguistic Pluralism: Proposing the Ecology of Language Paradigm. In M. Tehranian (Ed.), *Worlds Apart: Human Security and Global Governance* (pp. 153-167). New York: Tauris.
2. Martin, Judith. N and Thomas K. Nakayama. (2004). *Intercultural Communication in Contexts*. New York: McGraw-Hill.
3. Taylor Victor, E & Charles E. Winquist (Editors) (2001). London and New York: *Encyclopedia of Postmodernism*, Routledge,
4. Whorf, B. L. (1956). *Language, thought and Reality*, Cambridge, M. A.: MIT Press.
5. West, F. (1975). *The Way of Language: An Introduction*. New York Harcourt Brace Jovanovich.
6. Gudykunst, W. B., & Ting Toomey, S. (2003). *Communicating with Strangers: An Approach to Intercultural Communication*. (4th Edition). New York: McGraw-Hill.
7. Bhatnagar and Bell (2004), *Communication in English*. New Delhi: Orient Longman Pvt. Ltd.

7

Role of Proper English Pronunciation in Projecting a Better Personality

T. C. Joseph &. R. G. Munghate

Abstract

Good pronunciation has always been insisted on by the language scholars and educated people of every cultured society as an integral part of good oral language. The educated English were very particular about it. A successful and charismatic personality among them has generally been the one who pronounced English well. Good pronunciation has been thought to be a sign of good culture in any language community and so held in high esteem. Hence it adds to the charisma of an individual's personality. Since English is the major international language, standard pronunciation facilitates greater international intelligibility and acceptability. Language is an art and so has its own artistic aspects. Proper pronunciation is an indispensable aspect of that art ideally fusing correct articulation of sounds, right accentuation, proper rhythm, correct intonation patterns, and other finer nuances. All these give a charming musical quality to the English language and that is the artistic aspect about it. It adds to fluency and communicative skills and creates a better impression about a person. Therefore, one who pronounces English properly is like a good artist. Mastery of pronunciation necessitates considerable perceptive listening to standard models of oral English presentations and an equal degree of strenuous practice to emulate them. But many are lured by the one or the other aspect of English, like its literature or its grammar or its vocabulary, and overlook the phonetic side and in effect seriously handicapping themselves linguistically. Those who pronounce well are thought to be the

S G M College, Kurkheda

true masters of the language. In short, proper pronunciation plays a crucial role in projecting a better personality. This paper examines the various aspects of this issue and proffers the ESL/EFL students some suggestions for improving their pronunciation.

Introduction

One of the pre-requisites of an attractive and successful personality is the ability to pronounce a language well. This ability is more rewarding in the case of an international language like English. The mastery of its pronunciation turns out to be a glittering gem on the crown of a successful personality. Whatever may be the controversies centering round the universal adoption of English, or its colonial stigma, it has been an integral part of the education in a large number of countries of the world for long. The world language status accorded to English is grounded on this universal use of the language in the interactional and knowledge dissemination areas for which no suitable substitute language has so far been singled out. And it is highly unlikely that any other language will replace it in the imminent future. Hence no wonder the educated and the uneducated alike view knowledge of English as an enviable asset that enhances the academic quality of an individual's personality and its market value. Further, a large number of people consider English as the key to open the doors of the mighty, mysterious treasure-vault of knowledge itself, because English is the major library language, the language of the internet, of the natural sciences, of technology, and that of many others. Precisely because of this people hanker after sound knowledge of English, and many millions view its working-knowledge as an invaluable asset. It is not merely written English (that uses the graphic substance) which is widely used, but spoken English (that uses the phonic substance) as well. If a good style and syntactically impeccable expression is at the core of the written form, the beauty and the lure of the spoken form are conditional upon standard pronunciation and an acceptable style. However, many ESL/ EFL aspirants overlook the importance of pronunciation for one reason or another. This neglect deprives them of many possible benefits since proper pronunciation always helps to project a better personality.

The spoken form, as is well-known, is used much more frequently than the written form. Therefore, it is not a person who is proficient in writing but one who is proficient in speaking who has the greater chance to shine and to be in the limelight. If a person has a sensible mastery of practical phonology and pronounces English well, then s/he will no doubt be the centre of attention and will be listened to with rapt attention and admired wherever s/he goes. This implies that her/his good pronunciation has added to the charisma of the personality. S/he will be thought of as a well-refined, well-educated person trained in some standard institutions. This impression augments the chances of her/his employability. In today's globalized era when communication (particularly oral communication) has assumed serious significance, it is natural that a person who speaks English with a fine pronunciation is highly looked up to as an important personality. It creates for her/him an aura of importance, for it suggests an intellectual, academic, cultured background behind such a person. Numerous are the institutions that are looking for such candidates. They are ideally thought of as the best to handle situations which require communication skills, particularly oral communication. Standard educational institutions, travel and tourism industry, medical profession, management profession, legal profession, the entire business world, the export-import sectors, telephone operators' job, that of receptionists and computer operator's job, scientific profession, engineering profession, diplomatic and ambassadors' profession, the public administration arena—all expect personnel of proper English pronunciation. But mastery of good pronunciation is not all that easy. It is hemmed in by numerous problems or difficulties and so is generally dismissed as something inaccessible and superfluous by the frustrated aspirants. A proper examination of these problems and an attempt to devise some effective steps will be quite rewarding to the aspiring students of English.

Problems/Difficulties in Mastering Pronunciation:

Although there are two dominant models of pronunciation to be emulated in the global situation, namely, the English R.P and the American Pronunciation, most people in the world are more acquainted with the R.P model which is the pronunciation of that variety of English known as the Standard English/ King's /Queen's English/ BBC English etc. Rather than revolting against the existing models, it would be wiser to follow that model which is widely used, and excel in it because it has great currency, acceptability, and intelligibility. In this regard, English RP has an upper hand over the American variety. Some of the more important problems related to mastering English pronunciation can be identified as the following:-

1. Phonological Problems:

Of the phonological problems, the most thwarting one is what is generally known as the **"Mother Tongue Interference".** For the ESL/EFL students, the constant use of, and exposure to, their own native language cause the limited sounds of their own mother tongue to be deeply engrained on their minds to the extent that they are unable to realize the existence of any sounds which are at variance with the sounds of their own mother tongue. When they later learn another language like English, they naturally tend to find equivalents of the sounds of such a language in their own mother tongue. Instead of learning the new sounds of English as they are, they substitute the mother tongue equivalents and wrongly believe them to be correct. This deprives their speech of **"Englishness"** which is the peculiar beauty of English. This "Englishness" is what every foreign learner should strive to achieve. "The main problem of English pronunciation is to build a new set of boxes (in the mind) corresponding to the sounds of English, and to break down the arrangement of boxes which the habits of our native language have so strongly built up."(J. D. O'Connor, 2008). Majority of ESL/EFL learners find it difficult to articulate certain consonants and several vowels, particularly the diphthongs. They are ignorant of the correct **'points of articulation', 'manner of articulation', proper 'lip positions' to be assumed, the 'tongue heights' to be effected, the 'part of the tongue' to be used** etc, during articulation of these consonant and vowel sounds. This ignorance and lack of training mar their prospects of achieving fine English pronunciation.

2. Articulation Problems

Some of the main articulation problems are: a). **Lack of resonance, b). Nasality, c) Indistinct Articulation, and d). Haste and Indifference.** The quality of the voice is very much dependent on **resonance**. Voice is produced by the vibration of the vocal cords, but it is enriched and amplified by the cavities of the chest, pockets of larynx, the pharynx, the mouth, the nasal cavity, and the sinuses. This amplification is called resonance, but this is not effectively done by many foreign speakers of English to the extent required for the English sounds. **Nasality** is speaking through the nose. Though some nasal resonance is tolerated, too much nasality spoils the beauty of articulation. Nasal sounds do need nasality but if nasality is applied to vowels unconsciously, as is done by many foreign speakers of English, the beauty of English is adversely affected. **Indistinct articulation** is the offshoot of inadequate use of the movements of jaw, lips, and tongue. If speech muscles move sluggishly, then articulation is blurred and indistinct. This might be either the outcome of laziness or inability. Another articulation problem is caused by **haste and indifference**. Many foreign speakers of English, both students and grown-ups, **speak very fast, tripping and slurring over words** making the listeners strain for the messages being communicated, and making them weary of listening. There are also good many people who are simply nonchalant about pronouncing words well and correctly. Laziness is at the root of their utterances. This results in several speech blemishes and repels the listeners from such people. All these create a bad impression on the personality of the speaker.

3. Lack of Proper Phonation:

Our voice signals a good or bad personality. It reveals our personality hinting at our prevailing mood, our elation or blues. At best, our voice sounds pleasant and melodious, and produces the finest music; at worst, it sounds raucous, raspy, harsh, muffled, husky, metallic, squeaky, monotonous, shrill, jerky, and gruff. It can attract people towards us or repel them from us. Under healthy conditions, a little care shown, sounds can be properly 'voiced' whenever they have to be. Of the 44 speech sounds/phonemes of the sound system of the English R. P., only nine sounds are voiceless (produced without any vibration of the vocal cords) and the rest, i.e. 35 sounds are voiced (produced with the vibration of the vocal cords). In other words, 15 consonants and all the 20 vowels are voiced, forming a large majority of voiced sounds in English requiring proper voicing/ phonation and the accompanying resonance. But most foreign learners do not properly voice the sounds resulting in lack of phonation highly affecting the quality of English sounds.

4. Ignorance of Proper Intonation Patterns:

Intonation refers to the pattern of changes in the pitch of the voice when we speak and the terminal contour. The use of proper intonation is an integral part of good oral communication in English. The use of wrong intonation can change the meaning of the speaker's words and larger utterances. Intonation is determined by the pitch of the voice and pitch itself is determined by the frequency of the vibration of the vocal cords. A high pitch is the result of a high frequency of the vibration of the vocal cords and a low pitch that of a low frequency. A rising intonation is a change in the pitch of the voice from a low to a high pitch; a falling intonation is one from a high to a low pitch. Other intonation patterns like fall-rise and rise-fall etc are also occasionally used by the English people. Knowledge of the contexts and kinds of sentences in which these are varyingly used is quite inadequate on the part of the ESL/EFL students of English. It is imperative that one should know, for effective communication, the type of intonation pattern used in statements, Yes-No questions, Wh-questions, Tag-questions, exclamatory sentences, commands and polite requests. Again, one should know the type of intonation to be used for incomplete utterances, counting numbers, listing items, clause-final positions, and the sentence-terminal positions. These are the common contexts and types of utterances we usually come across, although numerous other variations are also possible. But many are unsure as to the type of intonation to be used in diverse contexts. Tonality, tonicity, and tonic have also to be decided for proper intonation use.

5. Spelling-Sound Disparity:

English is one of the least phonetic languages. In English, there is no one-to-one correspondence between the spellings and the sounds representing them. Although there are only 26 letters in the English Alphabet, there are as many as 44 sounds used while speaking English. In order to remedy this defect English phoneticians have devised 44 phonemic symbols representing the **44 speech sounds** or phonemes, on a one-symbol one-sound basis. These phonemes are defined as the smallest distinctive units of speech sounds in the sound system of the English language. A single letter in English has often more than one phonetic realization, too. For example, the letter 'a' is differently pronounced in such words as—***an, art, all, ate, aim, passage, away,*** etc. Occasionally, we come across some words with one or more letters silent or not pronounced at all. **Double letters are to be pronounced as a single lette**r. When a given sound is represented by different letters the matter becomes all the more complex. All these pose great difficulties to the ESL/EFL students. Generally the learners of English pronounce English as it is graphically represented through spellings, unless they are fortunate to get some excellent English teachers who pronounce English well, and have considerable knowledge of Phonetics to nip their errors in the bud.

6. Allophonic, Morpho-Phonemic and Phonotactic Problems:

Many ESL students are unaware of the allophonic variations. They are in no way to make a difference between the /p/ in *president* and *couple*, or the /t/ in *touch* and *cattle*, or the /k/ in *kite* and *sky*, etc. Further, they can not in some cases, at least, make any distinction between the /l/ in *love* and *help* where there are clear-cut allophonic differences. Although phonemic realizations of the past tense morpheme *-ed* in the words like *jumped, faded,* and *robb*ed are all different, not many are aware of such differences because graphically they look alike. Further, the plural morpheme –s/es of nouns, and the third person singular morpheme –s/-es of verbs are differently realized in different phonetic environments such as *cats, girls, buses* (all plural nouns), and *looks, begs*, and *realizes* (all third person singular verbs). In the same way, the distributional or phonotactic problems of some consonants and a few vowels also vex the ESL students, to a great extent. Those who do not know that /w/ is not phonetically realizable at word-final position even when spelling permits it, are likely to pronounce it at word-final position. Similarly, /j/, /r/, /e/, /o/, /u/, etc, have similar problems of which many learners are not conscious. These are phonotactic problems that adversely affect good pronunciation.

7. Accentuation/ Stress Related Problems:

Most ESL students lack knowledge of syllable structure of words and are equally at a loss as to which all monosyllabic words are stressed. Most of them do not know that content/form class words are normally stressed and that function class words are not. Another problem faced by them is the inability to decide which syllable of disyllabic, tri-syllabic and poly-syllabic words are stressed. English, which is a stress-timed language, gets the characteristic rhythm in larger utterances from the fact that stressed syllables tend to occur at regular intervals of time and irrespective of the number of unstressed syllables occurring between two stressed syllables. The time taken between any two stressed syllables is approximately the same. This feature is isochronous, but many are ignorant of such aspects and as a result unable to capture the musical quality of English. Stress, rhythm, and intonation are supra-segmental/prosodic features and are highly inter-dependent. Mastery of one thing necessitates the mastery of another. Even those who know about these can not considerably improve their pronunciation in the absence of strenuous practice, and that itself is another problem for the indolent and the less-aspiring.

8. Strong & Weak Forms:

Many functional words in English have one or more weak forms in addition to their normal strong forms. In connected speech, when these function class words which are unstressed are uttered rapidly to bring about the rhythm of sentences, only their weak forms are used. Personal pronouns, prepositions, conjunctions, articles, auxiliaries, etc have these strong and one or more weak forms. Many learners neither know about it nor take pains to master them so that speedier, fluent and typically English pronunciation becomes possible.

9. **Assimilation and Elision:**

Sounds are affected by their phonetic environments. "The shape of a word may also be altered by nearby sounds" (J. D. O'Connor, 2008). '**Assimilation**' refers to the way sounds influence each other in given phonetic environments. A given sound under the influence of another sound may become an entirely different sound. For example, in the phrase, '*that girl*' the second /t/ becomes /k/ under the influence of the next /g/. Imitation of such assimilatory changes is not easy for foreign learners of English, nor necessary. But knowledge of such changing word shapes helps understand the native speakers of English when they speak. In the absence of this knowledge it is difficult to make out what an Englishman says. Omission of sounds in certain phrases or word combinations is called **elision**. Knowledge of elision is good to improve pronunciation. For instance, the first /t/ in the combination *'last time'* is dropped. The ESL learners should learn such instances, though not an easy task.

Suggestions for Improving Pronunciation:

1. The most important phonological problem, namely, the habit of substituting the phonemes of one's own mother tongue for the English phonemes, can be overcome by **rigorous practice of repeating several times the correct sounds of the RP** either under the guidance of an expert English language teacher or by constant listening to the sounds and longer utterances from a standard CD. By careful listening, the 'Englishness' of the sounds should be captured and repeated as many times as required till one is fully sure that the sound produced approximates to the sound heard.

2. Through **proper breathing exercises**, particularly, breathing from the diaphragm and also considerable breath control, the drawbacks related to Breathing, Phonation, Resonation and Articulation can be overcome. Pranayama, the well-known yogic breathing practice, is excellent for this purpose. Nasal resonance can be gained through light humming. Similarly, nasality can be reduced by sending more air through the mouth rather than the nose. Proper exercises of the tongue, lips, and jaws help distinct articulation. Similarly speaking quite deliberately in moderate speed helps overcoming the problem of haste. *The Power of Spoken English,* by Cedric M. Kenny (2006) is an ideal book that mentions several such exercises.

3. There are numerous books available currently that contain various intonation patterns and plenty of exercises to master them. Such books can help solve the problems related to inadequate knowledge of intonation

patterns. The series of three books published by the CIEFL (Hyderabad) titled *'Spoken English'* deal practically with most problems related to pronunciation. Numerous exercises are given in book-I of this series on different intonation patterns. Also *Better English Pronunciation* by J. D. O'Connor is of considerable help in this regard. Another useful book is *'A Course in Phonetics and Spoken English'* by J. Sethi & P. V. Dhamija. Since such books contain plenty of practical work doing the exercises mentioned in them will be of immense help.

4. **Learning the phonetic symbols of English R.P** and **looking up either Daniel Jones'** ***English Pronouncing Dictionary*** or *The Advanced Learners' Oxford Dictionary* to find out the pronunciation of each and every word, when in doubt, will remedy the confusion caused by the spelling-sounds disparity. Everyday some time should be spent with the dictionary to acquaint oneself with the pronunciation of words, and that too, accompanied by rigorous practice!

5. Learning "**tongue twisters**" is both a useful and interesting activity for learners. Since these are difficult to pronounce fast, with repetition of some difficult sounds, practising them is a good exercise for the flexibility of the tongue. The following are some such samples: 1. *Peter Piper picked a peck of pickled pepper.* 2. *She sells sea-shells on the sea shore.* 3. *Around the rugged rock the ragged rascal ran.* 4. *Bettie bought some butter which was bitter, and to make the bitter butter better she bought some better butter.* 5. *A big black bug bit a big black bear.* 6. *I saw a sawyer sawing with a saw.* 7. *How much wood would a wood-chuck chuck if a wood-chuck could chuck wood?* 8. *How high holds his highness' haughty head!*

6. For all the rest of the problems, **studying a good phonetic text book** like *Gimson's Pronunciation of English* will be of invaluable help and any English learner committed to learning the language well should have a try at it. Then, practise the sounds as loudly as possible for maximum effect!

References

1. Gimson, A. C. & Alan Cruttenden (1994), *Gimson's Pronunciation of English* (Revised Edition), Oxford University Press, New York.
2. O'Connor, J. D (2008), *Better English Pronunciation*, (with 2 Audio C.Ds), (Second Edition), Replika Press Pvt. Ltd, India.
3. Sethi, J. & P.V. Dhamija (2003), *A Course in Phonetics and Spoken English* (Second Edition), Prentice-Hall of India Pvt. Ltd, New Delhi.
4. Tucker, W. Victor, S.J (1987), *Improve Your Pronunciation*, Sathya Bharati Press, Ranchi.
5. Bansal, R. K. & J. B. Harrison (1995), *Spoken English*, Orient Longman Limited, Hyderabad.
6. Sethi, J. & D. V. Jindal (1993), *A Handbook of Pronunciation of English words* (with two 90-minute Audio cassettes), Prentice-Hall of India Pvt. Ltd., New Delhi.
7. Dr. Syamala, V (1994), *A Textbook of English Phonetics and Structure for Indian Students*, Sharath Ganga Publications, Trivandrum.
8. Sasikumar, V., P. Kiranmai Dutt., Geetha Rajeevan (2006), *A Course in Listening and Speaking-I*, Foundation Books, New Delhi.
9. Kenny, Cedric M (2006), *The Power of Spoken English*, Sterling Publishers Pvt. Ltd, New Delhi.
10. Daniel Jones, *English Pronouncing Dictionary* (15th Edition), Cambridge University Press, U. K.

8

Socio-Cultural Factors in Teaching English Language to Tribal Area Students

Abstract

Teaching English language to tribal students is a vexatious proposition. Even the most brilliant teacher with all his/her resources and methodology fails to bring about desirable changes and praiseworthy teaching outcomes in the tribal areas. The main reason is that students lack motivation and are averse to learning English or studies in general. Their apathy and the intellectual inability is the result of exploitation they suffered over a millennium or so under the caste system or other historical, cultural and social forces. These students are very slow responding to intellectual matters like learning English language and they often sit listlessly in the classroom as though suspicious of everything and wary of subjecting themselves to the influences of the classroom experience. The society they come from and the culture they have inherited have conditioned and programmed them in the way they are now. A study of these matters will shed light to their present plight and help the English teacher to approach them with greater empathy. This will improve in all probability their performance in English language classes.

Introduction

English language teaching in tribal areas is highly constrained by such factors as the peculiar social, cultural, historical, economic, and psychological conditions prevailing there. Of all these variables, socio-cultural factors seem to be more crucial than the others. Social set-up and culture of these areas are such that they impede teaching and learning of English. Students of the tribal areas like Gadchiroli are generally nonchalant to learning English. Somehow they are not lured by the charm of English, nor are they deeply convinced by the numerous advantages of learning the English language. They do not seem to be convinced by the prospect of a brighter future through the mastery of English language which holds in its womb tremendous job potential in the globalized era and incredible access to knowledge. Either they underestimate their capacity to learn English or they are laze in learning it. It is equally possible that they are not fully convinced by the argument in favour of learning English. The possibility that they lack awareness of the great advantages of learning English cannot be ruled out. Despite the genuine efforts of a good number of teachers, their performance is abysmally poor. Neither techniques nor any methodologies prove effective for them. It is as though they suffer from some intellectual impotency. Their present condition, both mental and physical, is the outcome of certain factors at work. These bring about this deplorable situation and they are, in all likelihood, the socio-cultural factors peculiar to these regions. Closely allied to this set of factors are the psycho-linguistic variables which also baulk the progress of students in English. Hence even the most genuine teaching effort proves futile and abortive. Both the social set-up and its culture do condition the minds of the people and form their attitude towards life and everything in life. It appears their minds are so programmed as to be insular to the halcyon influence of English, though the post-colonial detractors of English look askance at it.

Sociological Factors

One of the prime causes why they are not inclined to intellectual pursuits including the learning of languages like English could be that they suffered terrible intellectual deprivation for thousands of years under the debilitating influence of caste system which has been a blight on the Indian society for centuries. Pushed to the lowest rung of the caste ladder, these tribal people, treated as the scum of the society, were driven home the idea that knowledge is not for them. They had been scared away from academic activities and pursuits involving subtle mental operations. This stunted their mental growth and these mental streaks are running through their future generations as are evident in the current generations. It will in all probability take a lot of time for these people to come out of the quick-sand of this problem. Once they develop their aptitude for learning and are intrinsically motivated, they will be on the trajectory of mental growth. But time factor plays a decisive role among other things for their enlightenment. In the current situation they are in no mood to take to abstract thinking as they had from times immemorial been given to a life of mere physical activities and very little guided inner activities such as high, and critical thinking as developed through formal education. Hence they find it difficult to digest the abstract ideas and concepts as are imparted in colleges presently, and no doubt, higher education has much to deal with abstract ideas.

When teaching English to the rural tribal students their social background and the various social factors, that encumber learning, have to be considered. From the social point of view, most tribal students are first generation students. Their parents being mostly illiterate and uneducated ones are in no position to guide their children in educational matters and especially in English. This deprives children of getting the basic external motivation from parents. Involving mostly in agricultural and allied activities the tribal people lack the positive economical condition supportive to academic pursuits. Dire poverty robs them of their interest in learning, particularly a foreign language like English with all its cultural peculiarities to which these people are alien. A good number of students come to the classes in either empty or half-hungry stomachs. When hunger haunts them they find it difficult to remain in classes for long. So after a few periods they bunk classes and go back home with barely sufficient energy to reach back their homes in far off places. The long and risky journey to reach educational institutions and back home always causes fear and anxiety in the minds of many students. This acts as a distraction to their study. Joint family system, the small shanty-like, dilapidated houses lacking the basic facilities for silent and lonely pursuit of study, non-availability of electricity, dearth of good schools in the vicinity to lay sound foundation for the initial English classes, non-availability of good libraries, inspired and devoted teachers, the intricacies and implications of their peculiar culture, etc, all affect their English learning. This implies that teaching to such students is less productive of the desired result.

Cultural Variables

A more decisive factor that affects teaching and learning of English is culture. 'Culture functions mainly at the subconscious level because it is something that we live.' Our life and personality are instinct with culture. In a sense, culture is 'traditional pattern of living' and also 'a pattern of perceptions.' Wen Shu Lee identifies different common uses of the term 'culture': culture means 1. unique human efforts 2. refinement, mannerism 3. civilization (as different from backward barbaric people) 4. shared language, beliefs, values 5. dominant or hegemonic culture as different from marginal culture 6. the shifting tension between the shared and the unshared. Though none of these definitions captures the full meaning of the term culture, they all hit at some main aspects of it.

There are anthropological and psychological definitions of culture. Some anthropologists view culture as a set of patterns of thought and beliefs; others view it in terms of a set of behaviours; a few on the non-material aspects of human life or the material aspects of societies. According to Anthropologist Clifford Geertz culture "denotes a historically transmitted pattern of meaning embodied in symbols, a system of inherited conceptions expressed in symbolic forms by means of which men communicate, perpetuate and develop their knowledge about and attitudes toward life." A psychological definition of culture as put forward by Geert Hofstede (1984), defines culture as the "programming of the mind and the interactive aggregate of common characteristics that influence a human group's response to its environment" (p.21). Social scientists emphasize the role of perception in cultural patterns. "Culture is defined as a pattern of learned, group-related perception – including both verbal and non-verbal language, attitudes, values, belief systems, and behavior" (Singer, 1987, p. 34).

It is customary to draw a distinction between cultural and biological (i.e. genetic) transmission. As far as language is concerned, it is possible that there is an innate language-acquisition faculty. Whether or not this is so, there is no doubt that one's knowledge of one's native language is culturally transmitted: it is acquired, though not necessarily learned, by virtue of one's membership of a particular society. Moreover, even if there is a genetically transmitted language-faculty, this cannot result in the acquisition and knowledge of a language unless the data upon which the language-faculty operates are supplied by the society in which the child is growing up and, arguably, in conditions which do not seriously affect the child's cognitive and emotional development. This means that the cultural and the biological in language are interdependent (John Lyons, p. 303).

When students of a particular culture (for e.g. tribal culture) try to learn a language like English, which is of an entirely different culture these students who are ignorant of the various aspects of the English culture, naturally find it very difficult to assimilate what is given in the English syllabus. The cultural factors operating in the students are so strong that they cannot easily modify them to accommodate English. The students, who are very much used to the tribal dance, tribal songs, tribal food habits, tribal mode of agriculture, with their peculiar musical instruments and various utensils, with their specific day to-day experience, perceptions and beliefs, with their unique customs, conventions, habits, norms and mores, do not find equivalents in the English syllabus to absorb matters easily. It is not only a matter of structural differences and sign differences between the tribal languages and English, but much more than that the experience encoded in the lessons is quite alien to their daily experience. There is a lot of difference between what they encounter daily and what they hear in the English classes. This baffles them and makes them feel like fish out of water.

When a teacher teaches English in the tribal background he has to take into account all these factors and try to use words and examples which bring to the minds of the students their familiar world with all the familiar things. Then they will feel at home with English. English lessons which deal with more jungle descriptions, animals, rural background, agricultural operations, rivers, rocks, hills, trees and plants, and all that deals with nature will interest these students. If the syllabus is not of this kind the teacher should take examples from such rural backgrounds in teaching them grammar and spoken English. Then the tribal students are likely to take to serious study and English learning will become more interesting and rewarding for them. Socio-cultural factors have to be considered properly before even devising the syllabus for the Indian background or for the ESL students in general. Although there are differences between cultures and social conditions of different tribes, there are some common features based on which the English syllabus can be drafted. Since we have in all cultures several sub-cultures operating, expecting a uniform culture is sheer folly.

Conclusion

To conclude, sociological and cultural factors do affect teaching English language to tribal students. The type of society from which the student comes to learn a second language like English is an important factor, so also the kind of culture that has conditioned the psychic world of the learner. The tribal learners are slow at learning English because of their peculiar socio-cultural backgrounds with all their peculiarities. A study of these factors will enhance the awareness of teachers regarding the obstacles which render ineffective the genuine efforts of English language teachers. Insight into the tribal realities is a precondition for better English language teaching in tribal areas. The greater the insights into the tribal culture and finer the adaptation of the syllabus to it, the better will be prospects for more effective English language teaching in tribal areas.

References

1. Geertz, L, (1973). *The Interpretation of Culture,* New York: Basic Books.
2. Hofstede, G. (1984). *Culture's Consequences,* Beverly Hills, CA: Sage.
3. Hofstede, G. (1997). *Cultures and Organizations: Software of the mind* (Revised ed.), New York: McGraw-Hill.
4. Singer, M. R. (1987). *Intercultural communication: A Perceptual Approach,* Eaglewood Cliffs, NJ: Prentice-Hall.
5. Lyons, John, *Language and Linguistics: An introduction* (2007). United Kingdom: CUP.
6. Yule, George (2004). *The Study of Language* (Second ed.). U.K: CUP

9

English Language Teaching in Rural Areas: Problems and Solutions

Introduction

English Language Teaching in rural areas is no less than a challenging task. Numerous psychological, linguistic, institutional and other factors converge to render English language teaching in rural areas a virtual Gordian knot, and English learning a bleak experience. Historical and economic factors obfuscate the sombre scene. The remoteness of geographical location from the great centers of learning in metropolitan cities and urban sprawls deprive the rural areas of several developmental and academic benefits. The non-availability of enlightened and proficient English teachers in villages dampens the prospects of effective curricular transaction to make learning a pleasant and rewarding experience. The non–job orientation of the Arts subjects dissuades the students from being assiduous to master a complex language like English. They dilly-dally their time in a lackadaisical manner. None of the educational stakeholders (the teachers, the students, the management, the parents, the government) is perfectly fit in rural areas to help students master the labyrinthine nature of the English language with its bizarre idioms, notorious spelling systems and queer pronunciation (because there is hardly any one-to-one correspondence between the letters of the alphabet and their pronunciation). Prepositions and their word collocations now and then vex even the most erudite language scholar. Hardly do we find anyone equally at ease with the four language skills, namely, listening, speaking reading and writing, and having a laudable mastery of all these four. Some write well, but lack fluency in speaking; some speak, but lack good pronunciation. Those who speak fluently often turn out to be poor at writing, and many lack proper listening skill to discern the nuances of the phonic substance and grasp the semantic import, or rather the message being conveyed. Good English teaching should harmoniously blend the mastery of these four skills. But it seems to be a distant prospect for the rural aspirants of English.

This paper attempts to have a closer look at the numerous problems which the rural ELT scenario is engulfed in, and ventures to suggest a few feasible solutions to disentangle it and turn it a vivifying force to brighten up the rural educational set-up.

A. Problems

The main problems that cripple ELT in rural areas seem to be the following:

(1) Faulty Pedagogy

The pedagogy adopted in teaching English, alike in rural and urban areas, displays serious flaws. It has so far focused on the written form and neglected the spoken skill. Similarly listening and reading skills were also not properly and simultaneously taken care of. Any language learning should be spoken-oriented (in the initial stages, at least). Listening, speaking, reading and writing—that should be the natural order. To have the real language experience, spoken-based classes - questions, answers, discussions, descriptions, elaborations, interactions, free sharing of thoughts and feelings in the target language, critical opinions freely expressed, etc - are imperative. But this was not the case. Nor was there sufficient oral drills, and oral production of a pretty good number of sentences or phrases for better pattern-grasp. What went on in the classrooms was sheer written English training, to the serious neglect of other skills.

Excessive focus on grammar rules thwarted the creative and spontaneous impulses of students to make free expressions. The fear of committing grammar mistakes has been a constant obsessive impediment even to the brightest. Of course, grammar mastery is a must in written English. But Spoken English does not need to be constricted by an adamant adherence to it. Many elliptical and shortened expressions are permitted in the colloquial mode, not to mention the numerous informal uses/slang. Grammatical niceties are ignored in actual speech experience. But these factors were overlooked by the academicians either out of ignorance or servile imitation of the classic models.

As the National Knowledge Commission (2006) rightly pointed out, "lack of contextualization of the pedagogy of English" was a chief reason for the failure of learners to acquire proper mastery of English. Contextualized language as in stories, plays, etc, could be checked through gestures, single-word answers, or even through the mother-tongue. Adequate exposure to such contextualized language strengthens students' mastery of English. Throughout the class oral communication in English is to be encouraged rather than mere written work.

Teacher-centred methodology without adequate chances for students to express themselves through speech, activities, etc also has crippled the English language acquisition of students in general and rural students in particular. The 'Chalk and talk' methodology of a dictatorial teacher or a lecturer was a suffocating experience for students. If teacher is an excellent communicator, the lecture-method cannot be faulted, but the case is often different. This creates, as a consequence, a helpless aversion in the students who suffer the burden of monotony and incomprehension.

(2) Incompetent Teachers

Teachers who have to be models of good language through their fluency, felicity and facility often prove otherwise and turn abject objects to be pitied. Many of them speak in husky voices, in a broken manner, fumbling for words and the right expressions and often faltering. Some are too fast (in speaking) to be easily understood; yet others too slow to excite any interest in the listeners. If some affect a foreign accent, some others err on the other side by speaking with gross regional peculiarities making English less intelligible. After the minimal educational requirements for appointment, a good number of teachers steal into the sublime field of teaching, often after paying the management huge sums as donations. This cannot in itself be held to be the prime cause of decline in standards. What happens in reality is the degeneration of the teacher into one that turns teaching into a routine activity without adequate preparation for the class and sufficient related reading. The moment he stops reading books and periodicals, his mental horizon begins to shrink and the furthering of knowledge becomes impossible. Quality teachers read plenty of books to whet their skills and keep alive their intellectual curiosity. Those who merely look to teaching as a secure job and hug the philosophy of life: 'eat, drink, and be merry', ruin it irredeemably. If teaching is 'a life-long learning process', teachers have to strive after learning. What really matters is the actual quality of the teachers and their passion for better teaching. It is their knowledge and effective mode of delivery that actually counts. Mere literature-addicted teachers cannot train the students in skills.

(3) Lop-sided curricula

The curricula generally do not offer the materials for all-round development of the skills. They are weighty with and biased in favor of the written form and crammed in ill-chosen teaching materials. They insist on only written examination and so turn out to be the bane of students rather than a blessing. Sub-standard teaching materials prescribed in the syllabus do not help the mastery of English. Teaching materials should be student-friendly, communication focused, and function-oriented. These should be simple enough and attractive for students. Rural students are often repelled by the very exacting and tedious nature of the currently prescribed syllabi followed in most Indian

Universities. Besides, it is literature-laden and void of actual language experience.

(4) The Psychological Constraints

A good number of rural students in colleges are "first generation students". They lack any academic and intellectual precedent to draw inspiration from. They are simply bewildered and lack any serious academic motivation to pursue deeper language studies and higher intellectual pursuits. Their ignorant parents and siblings do not furnish them any intellectual background and the necessary spur. Hence they remain apathetic towards their studies. English language learning is no pleasant an exercise from their cultural point of view. They are alien to the ethos of English language as well. Again, many students are the famished children of the poor farmers. They suffer physically from poverty and mentally from inferiority complex. The Indian students reach colleges with prejudices against English as the language of their one-time oppressors, the British people. Some students fear English is a difficult language and beyond their comprehension. Most students reach colleges with poor English knowledge and scanty language experience hailing from sub-standard schools. All these adversely affect ELT in rural areas and make it no less than a nightmarish experience.

(5) Remoteness of the Geographical Location

Villages are generally located far from cities and towns. This remoteness is repulsive to many an aspiring teacher to settle in villages. Thus, most quality teachers are chary of serving in villages and hail to urban areas for convenience and career prospects. This leaves the villages to be satisfied with the mediocre teachers who fail to improve the English standard of rural students. Again, cities are blessed with a copious supply of all sorts of teaching-learning materials and modern articles of teaching equipment such as the computers, LCD projectors whereas the villages lack all these, along with the periodicals and even the English news papers. Besides, the numerous job opportunities in cities goad urban students into learning

English properly so as to secure well-paid jobs. The rural students are mostly ignorant of these, and feel quite helpless economically to hunt for jobs in the cities. The chances of exposure to English in cities are galore where as it is scanty in rural areas. All these militate against the chances of rural students gaining good English language mastery, and pose as stumbling blocks to English Language Teaching.

(6) Infrastructural Constraints and Overcrowded Class Rooms

English Language Teaching and effective learning presupposes not only a good teacher and his /her resort to an effective methodology but also the existence of standard infrastructural facilities such as sufficiently large buildings, a sizeable campus, well-furnished classrooms, copious learning materials, large libraries and a language lab. These are but non-existent in rural areas which make ELT further difficult. Besides, over-crowded classrooms also render language teaching ineffective. The teachers find it humanly impossible to make their teaching effective when they are lecturing to huge classes of more than a hundred or more students. In such cases, paying individual attention to students is next to impossible. Besides, handling mixed ability classes is a daunting task. Learner differences pose serious problems even to the most enlightened teachers.

(7) Linguistic Impediments

Language mastery posits mastery of all four skills— listening, speaking, reading, and writing. English language itself has some odd peculiarities which impede the mastery of these four skills. Some of these problematic peculiarities are the strange spelling system where the same letter is pronounced differently in different words. For example, the '*a*' in c*a*rt, c*a*t, c*a*ll mess*a*ge, *a*te, s*a*le, and *a*rea, are all pronounced differently. Again, English which has only **26** letters in its alphabet has **44** sounds! So there is no one-to-one agreement between the letters and sounds as we have in the Indian languages. Hence, English is one of the least phonetic languages causing great difficulty to the students. In some words, there is the redundancy of spelling compared to the sounds. For example, '*caught*' has ***six*** letters but only ***three*** sounds!

Moreover, the morphophonemic realizations of inflectional morphemes like '*-s*' or '*-es*' and '*-d*' or '*-ed*' pose great problems for English students. These are 'phonologically conditioned' and the teacher (if he has the knowledge of it) has to train the students through sufficient oral drills. *Homophones* and *homonyms* also further confound the situation. Syntactically, the Indian students who are used to the **SOV** word order or the sentence pattern of the Indian languages, when confront the **SVO** English pattern, they have to use a lot of brain energy to change the habitual pattern of presentation of ideas and feelings from **SOV** to **SVO** in English. This is quite strenuous for a long period of time. Besides, mastery of the vast repertoire of English phrases (noun phrases, adjective phrases, verb-phrases, prepositional phrases, phrasal verbs, adverbial phrases, etc), idioms, and peculiar word-collocations, and so on, is quite a daunting task. These general problems are more easily overcome in the urban areas (where they have better language exposure, better teachers and better study materials) than in rural areas.

In short, every favorable factor to help rural students pick up English and render ELT easier in rural areas is conspicuous through its absence. The problems mentioned above are some of the major causative factors and point to why English is at a low ebb in villages and explain why English still remains a cause of perpetual dread and constant shudder !

B. Solutions/Suggestions for Improvement:

1. Teachers should focus on ***skills development*** and shift in favour of ***oral*** rather than written practices in the class room.

2. When grammar is taught, importance should be given to the ***functional aspects*** rather than the formal.

3. Switch over to ***learner-centred, communicative approaches*** from the obsolete teacher-centered learning based on the unmodified lecture-method.
4. Conduct ***discussions, brain-storming sessions, role plays, mock-interviews, Quiz contests, public speaking, debates,*** etc.
5. Teachers should be trained in ***Phonetics*** and Spoken English; they should help students acquire an ***acceptable pronunciation*** and a fair degree of fluency.
6. Introduce ***Spoken English Course*** for the interested students.
7. Arrange ***remedial teaching*** and conduct ***Bridge Courses*** for the students of low English standard and poor schooling background
8. Make use of ***modern technology*** such as computers, OHP, LCD projectors and establish language labs in rural areas.
9. Help students develop a neutral accent, purging their English of M.T Interference (especially syllable-timed rhythm), and train them acquire the ***stress-timed rhythm*** peculiar to the English language.
10. The teacher should ***speak English at a moderated pace*** uttering every word clearly. He should not be too fast, inaudible, incoherent or inarticulate. What he speaks should ***be clear***; his pronunciation should be exemplary and verbal mastery commendable.
11. ***Radio/TV*** can be used effectively to listen to news or any other English programme. Tape recorders are excellent for listening to ***Spoken English Cassettes of the BBC/CIEFL***. This is quite practical in rural areas where computers are not easily available. ***CDs/ DVDs*** can be effectively used wherever computers and CD/ DVD players available. Frequent listening by students to such cassettes/CDs helps them identify and acquire the correct English sounds.

12. The management should be sensible enough to ***appoint quality faculty*** rather than making a flourishing business out of educational institutions by taking huge donations from newly appointed members of the staff who have neither aptitude for teaching nor the required quality. ***Only committed and quality faculty*** can improve the standard of the students. There is no other panacea.

13. Give plenty **of *loud reading and silent reading training***. Encourage ***library work*** and ***give assignments.*** Help students develop ***metacognition.***

14. ***Relate teaching to the natural rural surroundings***. Use examples from this background, which they easily understand and enjoy.

All these practical steps along with a regular dose of *academic counseling* are sure to motivate the students, and English language teaching will bear marvellous fruits in the rural set-up with all its inhibiting factors. What is required is the strong ***will*** to execute these ideas!

References

1. Sharma, R. A., (2014), *Teaching of English*, Meerut: Vinay Rakheja c/o R. Lall Book Depot.
2. Adinarayana, L, (2008), *Spoken English*, Hyderabad: Neelkamal Publications Pvt. Ltd.
3. Subhash Lata Morey, ((2008), *Methods and Techniques of English Teaching* Nagpur: Pimplapure & Co. Publishers.
4. Baruch T. C., (2006) *The English Teacher's Handbook*, New Delhi: sterling Publishers Pvt. Ltd.
5. Diane Larsen-Freeman (2004), Techniques and Principles in Language Teaching (Second Ed.), OUP
6. S.C. Chaudhary (2002), *Teaching English in Non-native Contexts*, Orient Longman, Chennai.
7. Dr. Syamala, V (1994), *A Textbook of English Phonetics and Structure for Indian Students*, Sharath Ganga Publications, Trivandrum.

10

Language Mastery through Vocabulary, Grammar, and Phonetics

Introduction

There is no consensus among linguists, educationists, and policy makers regarding the easiest and the most effective way a second language can be mastered by a non-native learner. The hitherto history of English language teaching has witnessed the birth, short-living application and the evanescent petering out of a plethora of methods, techniques, and approaches. No sooner did a technique/method/approach win acclaim, than the adherents of it kept making high claims about its efficacy. But the passage of time proved all these methods to be less effective than the practitioners of these had once claimed. Something was lacking in all these. After the initial rhapsodies subsided and the interest waned, generally a gloom of disillusionment set in, spurring further quest for a better method. These went on and on breeding theories and methods, but not of much avail, as language learning process proved sluggish as ever.

The much-hyped Grammar-Translation Method had to give way to the novel Direct Method. This method too had its own day and was in its turn soon eclipsed by the one-time revolutionary Audio-lingual Method in the 1950's, much to the chagrin of the advocates of the former. And much time did not elapse when by 1970's Audio-lingualism was submerged by the mighty billows of the guru-led methods like the Silent Way, Total Physical Response and Suggestopedia. When these fell out of favour by 1990's, still more new approaches cropped up such as the Task Based

Instruction, Neuro-linguistic Programming, Multiple Intelligences, etc. On the other hand, a powerful trend setter - Communicative Language Teaching - began to reign in the language teaching domain and which, to this day, has not been dethroned, although discontent murmurs against it is being raised currently. No doubt, this approach is also not free from flaws and sooner or later it too will be relegated to the background when another approach or method catches the fancy of the academic circles. The history of ELT proves that language has been approached so far from different angles like the well-known blind men who adamantly stuck to their views of the elephant when felt from different sides, yet all of them gave only partial views distorting reality. The mires of controversies only serve to complicate the matter further. Whether we learn a language following one method or another is a matter of mere convenience and choice. The essential facts about language remain as they are, forever, a riddle. These essential facts are: Vocabulary, Grammar, Phonetics and the four language skills.

In this paper, effort is made to show how their mastery leads to the mastery of language especially the English language. No panacea is suggested but their mastery through sincere efforts.

Language mastery presupposes the mastery of lexis, structure, and the sound system. Some can achieve mastery of these without much labour, but others have to 'sweat' for it because language has in it an intricate system, quite challenging and exacting— a time consuming commitment. The length of the time for its mastery is quite relative - less time for the brilliant and the ones blessed with the required aptitude, and more time for the less aspiring and the mentally feeble. When language learning affords great pleasure for some, it turns out to be an anguishing experience for many. Following the communicative methods, it is easy to develop a certain level of oral fluency within a brief period of time but mastery in the true sense of a strong vocabulary, laudable command of grammar and deep knowledge of phonetics requires time. 'Mastery' is not peripheral knowledge but it is deep knowledge that enables one to write admirably well, listen and understand thoroughly, read and perceive fully, and speak with fluency and facility. Such a speaker sounds a near-native accent and articulates the sounds as the rules of the sound system demands. This process of language acquisition is time consuming indeed, and produces excellent language scholars. They plunge easily into scholarly pursuits and absorb the textual knowledge to generate more knowledge. Language mastery should lead to this level. A mere job is not its aim but acquisition of knowledge and its dissemination. Lecturers have to grow into this level so that the millions of students stand to benefit. Quality students will brighten India's future and teachers will enjoy job satisfaction, too.

Why Is Vocabulary Vital?

Whether we write or speak, the building blocks of the mighty edifice of language are none other than words! No words? Then, silence is the dreadful outcome, if not gestures are not resorted to. The more words we learn, and keep in our active memory, the easier it will be to tame the language horse. With more words at our disposal we can construct sentences and make utterances to convey meanings. This leads to effective communication, provided it is supplemented by non-verbal aspects like suitable facial expressions, gestures and helpful body movements. A person who has a powerful vocabulary does not need to fumble after words or falter for the right expressions. Vocabulary comprises words, phrases and idioms which armour us with a ready stock of these to rush for a communicative encounter with anyone, anytime, anywhere. The felicitous and easy usage of these comes from constant practice. Such a practice is an act of the will. It depends on the individual whether he has in him a consuming passion for vocabulary and its right usage. After garnering a commendable vocabulary scattered over different subjects, and professions, the learner must use them judiciously whenever the occasion demands, or learn them by creating artificial or imaginary situations. Every word has to be used in sentences to make sure of their syntactic context of occurrence and collocation environment.

But, how can vocabulary be strengthened? The basic principle is that the meaning of every common, ordinary, simple word should be studied first. Then move over to the study of new and less common words. A good learner always learns the meanings of any new word that he happens to encounter. Imagining that the meaning of every new word will be asked by someone and so necessarily to be learnt impels a person to remember words because he has a purpose. Imagining that you would use it in some imminent context as the one you used may also help to remember it. Keep thinking about the new word for sometime till the brain accommodates it well. Occasional recall further makes it deep-seated. Another good practice would be to keep a notebook exclusively for vocabulary. Note down in it the meaning/s of the newly come across words. The very act of writing the meaning facilitates memorizing it. Then put heart and soul into it and mentally play with it in such a way that the words are used in different syntactic contexts, applying them to different animates and in-animates and places or even abstract entities. Associating the unknown with the known will ease the strain of remembering. When one note book is full, turn over the pages and have a quick revision. This fixes them firmly in the mind. Keep more books and continue the process never to stop, for learning is a life-long process. Keep the mind receptive to the newly born words. Like stamp collection, words collection is also an engrossing and rewarding hobby. Some time should be set aside for this process. One should hunt for new words in the dictionary, newspapers, magazines and books. Listening to erudite discourses will also prove beneficial. The moment a new word is seen a good dictionary should be looked up. Collocations, phrases, idiomatic usages have to be specially noted down. It is not only synonyms but antonyms must also be learnt, for contrast and quick communication. Eloquence demands it. Through interface with images, words will come handy in the memory. But with development of the abstract thinking power this process is not necessary. Our human brain has the amazing power of linguistic imaging not merely linguistic symbols but even ideas too. This power is highly advanced in good thinkers and researchers. All should aspire to reach this level for transcendental experience. Both "located memory" and "photographic memory" assist in this process, so that we remember spellings, words, paragraphs, or even the entire discourse. In that mysterious psychic experience our consciousness is very high and like Plato we, too, begin to feel that "Thinking is a dialogue with one's own self."

Vocabulary can also be learned through the morphological rules of derivation and other word-formations. Also knowledge of the foreign and native prefixes and suffixes and root meanings helps verbal mastery considerably. Etymological search also makes word-learning quite interesting. A good dictionary and spending a lot of time with it, going through different word entries and examples will prove to be a great aid in the accuracy of usage. It develops confidence while making oral and written expressions. An autonomous learner follows all these techniques and has fully developed "meta-cognition" — the way he self-regulates and organizes his studies. Every learner should grow to this level so that he becomes a word-hunter. A feel for words and their musical, alliterative, assonant aspects will lure a person to the charm of words and their magical potential. A good learner becomes aware of the metaphoric, connotative significance of words besides the literal meanings. That transcends him to another level of linguistic experience. The suggestive, associative, allusive aspects of words have a high evocative power and a fine transporting potential. It is this knowledge that makes literary reading quite enriching. Logicians classify words into referential words, abstract words, emotionally-toned words, neutral words etc. Knowledge of vocabulary can thus help plump a new world of experience. With the help of these words that experience can be communicated provided the rules to order them are known, namely, grammar.

How about Grammar?

Mastery of grammar is a necessary but not a sufficient condition for language mastery. "Grammar is the set of rules that governs the right usage of a language". Mastery of these rules helps a person write and speak correct English. But grammatical mastery need not ensure fluent speech in the absence of the mastery of the spoken form and its specific requirements. Learning the formulaic expressions, colloquialisms, and informal expressions are essential in spoken English. Nevertheless, the basic grammar rules are more or less followed in the oral manifestation of the language. Grammar mistakes need not obstruct communication, but polished and sophisticated speech requires accuracy and appropriateness of expression as well as grammatical niceties. It is a part of good education and culture. A good speaker does not make grammatical mistakes. For instance, 'He go there' is not grammatically acceptable in either version -spoken or written. Such errors create a bad impression in the minds of the listeners. Hence grammatical knowledge equips one with the right expressions and correct sentence constructions leaving no room for ambiguity.

There is generally an unfounded dread of grammar, a kind of phobia, an irrational fear in the minds of most ESL learners. But that is the outcome of either indolence on the part of the learners or a pedagogical failure on the part of the teachers. A little effort sincerely put in can ensure grammatical mastery. An efficient teacher's handling of grammar classes will excite the curiosity and interest of the learners. Grammar classes should be quite interesting with plenty of easy examples and adequate drills, both written and oral. If the teacher himself is not good at grammar how can the students be? Where does the fault lie? Is it in the subject or in the learner or in the teacher? Probably, the syllabus was not drafted well incorporating the fundamental grammar items which are practically essential. Some syllabi go too much after theoretical grammar which is not of much practical relevance and induces weariness in the minds of learners. Hence, students feel grammar quite repugnant to their tastes and an insult to their imagination.

Some important grammar topics which will prove highly beneficial to learners in general are: 1) Form Class words and Function Class words (parts of speech) 2) Basic sentence patterns 3) Kinds of sentences 4) Voice 5) Tense 6 Direct and Indirect speech 7) Elementary forms of the verb 8) Anomalous Finites (Auxiliaries) 9) Embedded Questions 10) Concord/Subject-Verb Agreement 11) Articles 12) Tag Questions 13) Interrogatives 14) Negatives 15) Clauses, etc. An aspiring student goes after many more grammatical topics, and gets properly drilled in them so as to use them effortlessly

If Students are taught the English sentence patterns well, it will increase their speed of sentence construction. Some training in Patterns like SV, SVO, SVC, SVOO, SVOA, and ASVO, will prove highly beneficial to them. There is no meaning in instant speech by the learners. It requires some time for proper assimilation of these patterns and when the ripe time comes, they will use them well, provided they have been taught well.

A generally neglected area is the teaching of the auxiliary verbs. Their importance in spoken English and written English is paramount. The reason is that they perform some six important functions, namely

1) *Framing Questions*

   Will you come tomorrow? Do you know English?

2) *Making Tenses*

   She is coming

3) *Making sentences Negative*

They speak English.

They do not speak English.

4) *To frame tag Questions.*

They read news papers, don' they?

5) *To make Passive Voice.*

She kills a snake.

A snake is killed by her.

6) *To make short replies.*

Do you pray every day?

Yes I do.

Such functionally important grammar topics should be taught first. Properly understanding the grammar topics and mastering them through adequate drills and practice will disabuse one of the irrational fears of grammar.

Why is Phonetics Important?

Sound Theoretical and practical knowledge of Phonetics increases the communicative skill of a person through better intelligibility and Englishness of the language. Very often Mother Tongue Interference renders one's pronunciation less intelligible, and proper communication is affected. In India, there are as many varieties of English as there are languages. A person's speech may be easily understood within his own state. But the mother tongue-affected, distorted pronunciation hinders his being understood well by the people of another state. Hence for national level and international intelligibility the variety of English pronunciation called the R.P. which has wide currency should be approximated as far as possible. The American variety will also prove beneficial when dealing with the Americans.

When learning Phonetics the 44 phonemes of English should be properly learnt. These comprise 20 vowel sounds and 24 consonants. Vowels are further classified into 12 monophthongs and 08 diphthongs. How these sounds are classified and described should be studied with proper attention. Then how each sound is produced by the native speaker should be noted and repeated until one comes closest to the native-like sound production.

Some important points should be noted for better pronunciation:

1. 'r' is not pronounced in word final positions. In sentence context a linking 'r' is possible, if the 'r' in the word final is followed by another word beginning with a vowel sound.
2. 'r' is not pronounced if followed by a consonant sound.
3. There are no retroflex sounds in English, but there are many in the Indian languages.
4. Double letters in English are pronounced only as single letters.
5. Consonant clusters have to be specially practised.
6. Incomplete plosives, nasal plosives, and lateral plosives have to be specially practiced.
7. There are aspirated and unaspirated varieties for /p/, /t/, and /k/.
8. Allophonic variations have to be specially noted.
9. Morphophonological realizations of past tense morphemes and plural morphemes have to be specially practised.
10. Stress - both word stress and sentence stress - should be learned with a lot of care.
11. Rhythm of the English sentences should be learnt.
12. Intonation - rising, falling, and fall-rise - should be closely studied, because it is very important in English.

14. Loud practice under the guidance of a teacher through repetition is a pre-requisite for good pronunciation.

15. Practise with tongue-twisters.

Conclusion

In brief, considerable mastery of the vocabulary, grammar, and phonetics ensures mastery of the English language although the process is a bit time-consuming. But then, there is no short cut to language mastery. What one can do at best is to speak a little English in a short time, but good writing as well as good speaking presupposes mastery of vocabulary, grammar, and phonetics whether or not much time is taken for their mastery.

References

1. Dr. Syamala, V (1994), *A Textbook of English Phonetics and Structure for Indian Students*, Sharath Ganga Publications, Trivandrum.

2. Lyons, John, *Language and Linguistics: An introduction* (2007). United Kingdom: CUP.

3. Yule, George (2004). *The Study of Language* (Second ed.). U.K: CUP

4. O' Connor, J. D (1980) *Better English Pronunciation* (Second Edition) London: Cambridge University Press, Reprint, 2008.

5. Jack C. Richards and Theodore S. Rodgers (2007) Approaches and Methods in Language Teaching (Second Ed.), Cambridge University Press.

6. Diane Larsen-Freeman (2004), Techniques and Principles in Language Teaching (Second Ed.), OUP.

11

Language Skills and Global Competitiveness

Abstract

In the prevailing capitalism-driven global world order, the job-market has become acutely competitive. Most well-paid jobs call for fairly good communication skills which in turn hinge mostly on fine language skills. Listening, speaking, reading and writing— the four language skills— have to be so developed as to meet global standards and ensure proficiency in languages (like English) which are internationally used. No doubt, English has the greatest job-potential presently. Educational institutions must focus on developing all the four language skills simultaneously and with more or less equal weightage, although the oral form seems to have more practical bearing than the others. The skill of listening leads to the development of the spoken form. Listening is not just passive hearing. It is hearing with rapt attention bringing all the mental powers into play and with perfect concentration. Listening act requires the suspension of all inner and outer distractions. It is a process involving 'thinking, analyzing, contrasting, filtering, classifying, inferring, synthesizing', and many more inner activities. Similarly, reading, whether loud or silent, is both a source of information-gleaning and communication. Silent reading to acquire knowledge is a great step towards self-education and language mastery. Loud reading requires the help of phonetics for fine articulation. The better the pronunciation, the better is the reading. Just as listening, so is silent reading highly dependent on all inner powers and requires almost perfect concentration for better absorption and perception of ideas. The oral or spoken skill is one achieved through direct language exposure and actual language experience. Here, too, pronunciation is of paramount significance. Training in articulation of speech sounds, stress, rhythm and intonation has much to do with the quality of oral, delivery. Body language, too, has to be exploited for better communication. One must learn to tackle the diverse spoken contexts to master the oral skill. The vocabulary and style used should be adequate, acceptable, and appropriate. Attending standard Spoken Courses can guide and improve the students greatly. Finally, the written skill, an invariably vital language skill, has always been helpful for candidates to get through competitive exams, academic exams, and in writing articles and books. For the research students this skill is of paramount significance, too. Mastery of grammar, vocabulary and style goes a long way in the mastery of the written skill. Of all skills, it is the spoken skill along with the written skill which helps the students to forge ahead in the present competitive world. Hence, the various training programme sessions should give required weightage to all the language skills. Finally, the skill of thinking clearly and systematically is a necessary corollary for language skills. This paper is an attempt to have a closer look at the language skills, and it proffers a few useful suggestions to develop them all simultaneously for better language mastery to be properly braced up to enhance competitiveness in the changed world of cut-throat competition.

Introduction

With the surge of the market forces, the unleashing of competition, the explosion of communication and the expansion of transportation facilities, life in the post-globalized world has become exceedingly complex, insecure and subject to erratic changes. In a world where neither the talented nor even the brilliant feel secure in any profession (on account of privatization), how risky and precarious the career-prospect of the unskilled and the mediocre citizens is! A horrid awareness has now gripped the general public like a haunting nightmare that if life is to be anywhere near the margin of security, there is no other choice than getting trained in skills and opting for highly job-oriented courses. Unlike the situation that prevailed a couple of decades ago when competition was more or less limited to the confines of one's own country, the present day competition is global, involving hundreds of countries and several millions of people. Only those with exceptional skills and talents can aspire to get at really well-paid jobs. But, with the widening of the employment horizon and the opening of new vistas of jobs, there is scope even for the ordinary people to get hold of one job or the other provided skills are developed and particularly language skills. Numerous are the chances awaiting those with proficiency in language skills, especially speaking and writing.

The educational institutions should, therefore, help students develop not just one or two language skills, ignoring the others, but all the language skills—listening, speaking, reading, writing, and even thinking which is common to all the other four skills. Marked changes in the curricula have to be effected to realize the synchronized development and mastery of these language skills. The existing curricula in many universities are biased in favour of the written skill, to the serious neglect of other skills, particularly the spoken skill. Language mastery presupposes the equal and simultaneous mastery of all the language skills. Only a smattering of these skills is sheer cold comfort. They might help communication, but the need of the day is first-rate communication skills, and other 'soft skills'. The language skills acquired should be of global standards, and tailored to meet the global requirements. Aiming at excellence in listening, reading, speaking, writing, and thinking skills is a great step towards job-assurance. The greater the quality and mastery of these skills, the better is the career prospect. Hence, a deeper look at these skills, their potentials, prospects, and implications is the dire need of the day.

a) Listening Skill

Listening is the first requirement for learning a language. Listening to a language helps a person sense and internalize the in-built mechanism of the language and perceive its semantic intricacies. But listening is not so simple an act as it is generally held to be. It is not just passive hearing or attending to someone speaking a language. Rather, it is an active, dynamic process spurring creativity. Listening is hearing accompanied by rapt attention during which all the psychic powers are brought into play with deep concentration. True listening is done with a high level of empathy and a fair level of sympathy. A true listener takes the aid of his intellect, intelligence, imagination, memory, thinking, emotion, perception, volition, and attention. In other words, even as a person is listening to somebody or something, he is simultaneously thinking, imagining, analyzing critically, understanding, taking decisions, and even feeling what is being said. Perhaps, more complex is the process involving still more mental powers and activities than I have just mentioned. Keeping at bay, or the warding off, of all inner and outer distractions is one of the prime conditions of listening. An attempt is to be constantly made to get at the core of the message or the content being transmitted. An effort to discern the spirit of the message being conveyed is also integral to effective listening. But such single-minded listening is not that easy, because mind wanders; distractions crop up; and the listener is persistently pestered. Eventually, a tendency to avoid listening creeps in; for true listening is the outcome of enormous mental energy, which the average brains lack. The implication is that much listening- training must be given to the learners of a language. This can surely sharpen and sustain their skill at listening for a considerable length of time.

However, listening can become really arduous for those who have had bitter childhood experiences. Traumatic experiences of the past recur to the mind and keep gnawing at it. It makes the psychic world highly turbulent, chaotic, full of conflicts, hurt feelings, and a negative attitude towards anything and everything. In the case of such learners, counselling is of utmost significance. This helps them re-establish their inner harmony, enabling them to become sensible learners with fairly unruffled minds. Encouraging learners to participate in frequent *conversational practice, discussions,* and *debates* in the target language can contribute to the development of the listening skill. Such activities are highly thought-provoking and whet the thinking skill greatly. That, in turn, causes much better linguistic effusion. Learners should frequently listen to the various programmes (in the target language) on the Radio, T.V, Tape Recorders,

CDs/DVDs and the internet. Such developed listening skill later helps a person in the global market to easily capture the meanings and messages of the interactions he is likely to engage in with the foreign employers, and other job-related personnel. This paves the way for smooth and easy communications making one successful in the global arena.

b) Speaking Skill

Next in the natural order comes a more serious language skill, namely, the speaking skill. Listening and reading are the inputs of language production, and speaking and writing are its outputs. If the inputs are well-supplied, the output will be of notable magnitude. Better listening and daily reading of varied materials can greatly contribute to improved speaking as well as writing skills. Of all the language skills which are of great demand globally, it is the oral or spoken skill which occupies the pride of place today. The reason is that communication revolution, especially through the telephone, the mobile, and the internet is of far- reaching effects and led to an unprecedented level of oral communication at the global level, in this era of communication. Numerous are the chances in the employment market for those proficient in the oral skill, especially in a global language like English. It may be, for instance, that of a telephone operator, a receptionist or a tourist guide. It is now, therefore, the bounden duty of educational institutions to give the due thrust on the oral skill, which had been virtually ignored in the curricula for long. It is high time the universities pondered over the most effective ways to help students master the spoken skill within the briefest time span possible to prepare them for the global job market.

It has been generally agreed that the easiest way to learn spoken English is to have adequate exposure to English. But such exposure is difficult in rural areas where there is considerable dearth of quality teachers who have any laudable language mastery. Nevertheless, the educational institutions should arrange *Spoken English* classes, conduct *dialogue practice sessions*, set up *language labs* (with tape recorders, computers, multi-media packages, etc), and encourage students to listen to standard Spoken English *cassettes, CDs/DVDs, Radio news, English T.V. Programmes* etc. Students should be properly trained in *conversation practice, public speaking, debates, group discussions, co-operative language learning* techniques (through language clubs, pair/group activities, etc). Teachers should guide the learners (a) to build up a rich *vocabulary* suitable for diverse speech contexts,(b) to master the minimum required *grammar* rules, and (c) to achieve a sound mastery of *phonetics*. The spoken mode when used at the international level has to be as free from gross regional peculiarities and mother tongue-interference as is possible. It has to be ensured that the learners get considerable practice in *stress, rhythm,* and *intonation patterns*. It is not only the right *articulation* of the English sounds, but also correct *accentuation*, proper use of intonation and the knowledge of the *stress-timed rhythm* of the English language, which are imperative for oral proficiency of the English language. Considerable practice in all these areas has to be given to the aspiring learners. Not only that, the teachers who lack expertise in these areas also should be persuaded to undergo necessary training so as to be able to help the students. It would also be desirable to encourage students resort to *Role Plays*, and face *Mock-Interviews*, and stage *plays* to exploit the dialogue potential of the *drama*. Active participation in *seminars, conferences, anchoring, announcements*, the various *activities of the literary association*, reading *newspapers*, reading *story books, periodicals, magazines*, etc. can also improve the spoken skill.

No doubt, oral proficiency, contributes greatly to an individual's personal and social development. A person's potential for learning is highly benefited by it, too. It can also affect his /her self- concept. Oral proficiency also aids leadership role and in becoming assertive individuals. Researches reveal an inter-relationship between oral proficiency and assertive personality. Contrariwise, shy and retiring personalities are often found to be hesitant to speak in public. They badly need counselling assistance and much group practice to become sufficiently social and freely interacting.

There are three notable characteristics of speech that deserve special attention. The first one is *'vocal control'*. Effective speech is pleasing to the ear, rhythmic, free from hesitations, repetitions, and interruptions. The tempo and volume of effective speech are suited to the context and the audience. All sounds are clearly articulated and distinctly pronounced in such speech. The second characteristic of speech is *'articulation of sounds'*. Learners must listen to, practice, and correctly reproduce the sounds of a language for being effective speakers of that language. Practical knowledge of the points of articulation/places of articulation, and manner of articulation/the stricture involved, the classification and description of speech sounds, etc, is a precondition for the correct production of speech sounds resulting in intelligibility, and acceptability of the language spoken. The third feature of speech is *'gestures and bodily expression'*. These are added advantages of speech over writing for effective communication and so, they have to be optimally used.

Spoken English also requires adequate knowledge of *'language functions'* such as 'greeting,' 'apologizing', 'seeking advice', 'offering help', etc. The *formulaic expressions/patterns* used during diverse functions must be mastered properly for acceptable, more effective, and better conversation. The various *space fillers* such as 'Er, well, right, now, so, etc., also have to be judiciously used for native-like natural speech.

c) Reading Skill

Both loud reading and silent reading have their own specific roles to play. On many occasions we have to read something loudly. Many papers are read aloud during conferences and seminars; during symposium also the prepared papers are read aloud. But very often such readings are very hasty, hazy and like babblings. They are repugnant to the taste of the educated listeners who expect the music of the language when something is read. Hence, reading should be in moderate speed, with pauses wherever there are tone groups. Here also *vocal control* is very important. Training in *Phonetics* will help students become good readers who read clearly, slowly, using the right tones and above all pronouncing well. Such loud reading will help the listeners understand the content well and enjoy the reading activity itself. Good communication is the outcome of this effort.

As for silent reading, which is done for delight and instruction, or for gathering information, the prerequisites are concentration or rather focusing of attention, displined and comfortable posture, and a quiet atmosphere. Mental discipline, getting rid of all distractions, quick settling down to intense reading, etc., is indispensable for effective reading activity. This prevents the leakage of time. Just as listening makes use of all mental powers, so does the reading act. This also stimulates creativity and can be held as an essential activity to activate the brain neurons making one more alert and intelligent.

Further, reading should be systematic, sufficiently speedy, well-planned. It should be based on a definite schedule and having chosen the right type of reading materials either from the library or from the internet. Reading should include books, magazines, periodicals, newspapers, reference books, etc. A good reader *previews the books, marks the books, makes notes*, and tries to *recall and remember* information frequently, and follow *effective learning strategies* if reading is for instruction. But reading done for pleasure is easier and more absorbing because of the very nature of the subject in question. However, in any reading activity, total absorption in the activity and activating all inner powers are necessary conditions. Bacon's aphorism: "Reading maketh a full man" points to the need for resorting to reading seriously for acquiring knowledge so as to become well- informed persons. Reading is the fountainhead of knowledge. Development of the reading skill, setting aside of all other concerns as secondary, will help students to be fully prepared with adequate knowledge to face the terrible competition today.

d) Writing Skill

In order to develop the writing skill students should be given insights into the process of writing. The different stages of this process —-*pre-writing, writing,* and *post-writing*—must be taught to them sensibly. In the prewriting stage, much preparation is to be done for actual writing by way of reading, talking to others, using of several resources, taking notes and possibly making an outline. Selecting a suitable topic which befits the powers of the writer and exploring that topic are two important activities in the prewriting stage.

In the writing stage the writer gets an organized text on paper so as to enable him to read it. Many writers go beyond this first draft and improve on it. That is the post writing stage. Here they learn about revision and engage in revising it, after due discussions with the teachers, peers, or scholarly people. Then, additional drafts are made before proper editing and publication of the final draft. It is good to bear in mind that organizing content well, developing sentence sense, remedying sentence faults, sentence combining activities, improving word choices, gleaning information regarding the form and conventions in writing (e.g.: punctuation, page appearance, capitalization and other agreed upon customs of putting language symbols on paper),are all part and parcel of good writing

In addition to the above, a series of mental activities such as observing, remembering, investigating, explaining, evaluating, problem solving, arguing, exploring, researching, etc., are integral to the writing process. The development of the writing skill helps students write not only commercial letters and drafts but more serious writing activities like dissertations, theses, and many other sorts of writing (like research projects),which help them grab the best jobs. Students should be given sufficient practice in all sorts of useful writing such as letters, drafts, notices, agendas, advertisements, reports, essays, dissertations, etc to enhance their global competitiveness. Repeated writing fine tunes their style, and activates their vocabulary.

e) Thinking Skill

Thinking skill is essential to master all the four language skills and so it has become currently fashionable to include thinking skill with other language skills. Thinking skill is imperative for numerous mental activities, and their products such as the sciences (natural and social), arts, logic, philosophy, and even literature. There is, in fact, hardly any branch of knowledge which is divorced of thinking skill. Thinking is productive of exuberant linguistic expression. It is a complex process implying comparisons, contrasts, classifying, predicting, identifying important ideas, making inferences, etc. It also involves finding correlation between diverse ideas, or rather, association of ideas. Thinking is a creative process generating plenty of ideas. It links facts, having detected the underlying similarity among them. Language is the main vehicle of the expression of thought. Thought-power stimulates linguistic skills of oral and written expressions. Thus, it is in proportion to the power of thinking that the other four skills also develop eventually.

The thoughtful people have inexhaustible funds of ideas to speak on, and write about. On the other hand, those people lacking thinking skill, for all their grammatical knowledge, and phonetic mastery, will find it very difficult to speak fluently and for any considerable length of time. A brain not trained in thinking fast and clearly, turns out to be quite dull and easily confused. His/her stream of thought will be turbid and often obstructed. A person with such a brain does not have anything substantial to expatiate on, nor does he/she have any sustained interest in speaking or writing. Hence, anyone who fondles the hope of a rich and fluent language should, of necessity, develop thinking skill, too, as an essential linguistic accompaniment. It develops systematic handling of matters, consistency, coherence, order, and clarity of perception and expression. All these are essential for good communication skills. When a person listens he/she is actively thinking too; when he/she speaks, simultaneously thinking also goes on in the mind; while doing reading and writing also thinking is inevitable so as to make any sense.

To conclude, all the above mentioned skills, combined with the skill of thinking, should properly be developed to achieve a high level of global competitiveness which ensures students rewarding jobs and a certain level of economic security in this world of cut- throat competition. For this purpose both the students and the teachers should work in unison and with concerted efforts. Skills development is not attained within a short period of time and through easy methods. On the contrary, it is a time consuming process demanding patience and hard work. But then, it is quite rewarding in this period of great perplexity and unprecedented change!

References

1. Reid, Stephen. *"The Prentice Hall Guide for College Writers"* Prentice Hall, Inc. New Jersey, 1989
2. Fernandez, Martin. *"Spoken English"*, Commonwealth Publishers Pvt. Ltd. 2009
3. O' Conner J.D. *"Better English Pronunciation"* (second edition) Cambridge University Press, 1980
4. Radhakrishna Pillai G. Rajeevan K. *"Spoken English for You'* (Level One), Emerald Publishers, 2006
5. Mohan, Krishna, Singh N.P *"Speaking English Effectively"* Macmillan India Limited, 2003
6. Petty Walter.T, Petty Dorothy.C, Salzer Richard.T. *"Experiences in Language – Tools and Techniques for Language Arts Methods"* Allyn and Bacon, Massachusetts, 1994
7. Shepherd James. F, *"College Study Skill,"* Houghton Mifflin Company, Boston, 1998
8. Stewart LTubbs, Sylvia Moss. *"Human Communications"*, McGraw Hill Higher Education, 2002

12

Pronunciation: Importance, Problems and Some Feasible Solutions

Abstract

For most ESL learners in India and elsewhere in the world pronunciation remains a hard nut to crack. There are several problems that baulk their effort to master English pronunciation. Pronunciation is the formal side of spoken English which is a sine qua non in the globalized era of increased and better communication. Unless the problems of pronunciation stemming from phonological, graphological, articulatory and supra-segmental areas are properly remedied, the non-native speakers cannot fare far in the realm of pronunciation. This paper looks into the importance and problems of pronunciation, and suggests some practical solutions to overcome the difficulties of English pronunciation.

Key words: Pronunciation, phonetics, communication, intelligibility, articulation, phonation.

Introduction

Pronouncing English well presupposes sufficient knowledge of and adequate practice in Phonetics, which is not everyone's cup of tea. Not all universities and colleges in India offer classes in Phonetics at the post-graduate and undergraduate levels. I do not know why it is so. It may be because of the dearth of quality teachers to teach it or may be because of the lack of awareness about the usefulness of the subject in question. Consequently, most students of a good number of educational institutions in our country stand to lose the salubrious effect of learning pronunciation which can prepare our students through better communication skills to face international competition in the job market. No doubt, mere theoretical knowledge will not help much unless accompanied by sufficient practice in articulatory phonetics.

Importance

It has now become a bad academic habit to underestimate the benefits of good pronunciation just because most of the educated people were deprived of the benefits of it. Merely because they were unfortunate to miss the phonetic course, most speakers of English in India justify the way they speak and say phonetics is not that important. In fact, it is easily obvious that those who have subject-knowledge and a good pronunciation always stand to have an upper hand whenever and wherever a programme is conducted in English. The general public expects that the educated people speak English with the right accent and good articulation. If this does not happen, it is natural that the type of education availed will be taken to be of inferior quality. Hence it is to be inferred that both teaching and learning of Phonetics not only at UG and PG levels but at every level from KG to PG is very important. There was a time when good pronunciation was not that important, but now in the globalized world good pronunciation is essential for better international intelligibility and naturally better communication. In their prefatory remarks Sethi and Dhamija point out:

> The need for learning spoken English has, over the last few decades, grown enormously all over the world. Time was when most learners of English in India, for example, could do reasonably well even without adequate proficiency in speaking the language. But this is no longer true. With the tremendous increase in the volume of international tourism, travel, and trade, and a bigger-than-ever exchange of experts in various fields and professions now, the demand for acquiring the spoken form of English has gone up considerably. People are no longer content with acquiring only the reading and writing skills of the language; they want to be able to speak it too - and speak it in a way that they are understood not only by the next-door neighbour...but also by the English-knowing inhabitant of a distant continent. (2012)

It has now become a truism that only better communication can command better jobs, too. One of the key requirements of good English is learning to pronounce it intelligibly and acceptably divested of 'gross regional accent', while speaking. The reason is that spoken English has not only 'content' but also 'form':

> A course in spoken English can take the form of either a course in 'what to say' or a course in 'how to say'. The former is usually a course in English conversation, and the latter a course in English pronunciation. The former is a situationally-governed course, which aims at training the learner in how to express greetings, farewells, thanks, apologies, regrets, and so on. The latter is a course in how to say English words, phrases, and sentences. Both these courses are important, and useful. (Sethi & Dhamija, p. vii)

Commenting on the intelligibility of Indian English and the Spoken English in India, Bansal and Harrison rightly remark:

> Even within India there are a large number of regional varieties, each different from the other in certain ways, and retaining to some extent the phonetic patterns of the Indian language spoken in that particular region. These regional varieties of English are sometimes not even mutually intelligible. In every region, however, there are people who have shaken off the gross features of regional accent and speak a more 'neutral' form of Indian English. It is also true that in every region there are good speakers of English and bad speakers of English, the terms 'good' and 'bad' referring to the degrees of approximation to the native English and Standard Indian English and also qualities of clear, effective and intelligible speech. It would, however, be better to aim at international intelligibility. (2013).

Problems and Solutions:

From the above comment it is clear that 'gross features of regional accent' under the influence of the mother tongue of the speaker is a central problem for the non-native speakers of English. In other words, *Mother Tongue Interference* (M. T. I) distorts pronunciation and comes in the way of learning pronunciation. It is very difficult to get rid of this influence. The reason is that we have a tendency to substitute the sounds of our own mother tongue for the actual sounds of English which may not be there in our own languages:

> By the time we are grown-up the habits of our own language are so strong that they are very difficult to break. In our own language we have a fairly small number of sound-units which we put together in many different combinations to form the words and sentences we use every day. And as we get older we are dominated by this small number of units. (O'Connor, 2008)

To overcome this difficulty O'Connor suggests "establishing new ways of hearing, new ways of using our speech organs, new speech habits" (p3) as solutions to break the M. T. I. For this, we have to learn the *points of articulation* of the actual sounds of English and their *manner of articulation* in addition to careful listening to Standard English CDs. At the same time we have to check whether the sounds in question are *voiced* or *voiceless*. If they are voiced we must make sure that the vocal cords vibrate during their articulation. In this way, we can produce the actual sounds of English RP and start using them in place of the sounds of our own language. Through careful practice we can thus overcome this difficulty.

A major problem faced by the non-native speakers of English is the inability to identify the right pronunciation of words since they are guided mostly by the 'one-letter-one-sound' formula, which is wrong in most cases when applied to English. There are 44 distinct speech sounds or phonemes in English when in fact there are only 26 letters. Good speech is possible only after mastering these 44 phonemes. Many erroneously confuse between letters and sounds and believe that particular letters have particular fixed pronunciation. But English displays a lot of disparity between sounds and letters. One particular letter may have more than one pronunciation in many different words. For instance the letter 'c' is pronounced /k/ in 'cat' and /s/ in 'city'. Good learners learn the variant realizations of the same letter in diverse situations or words. For this they need good guidance by language experts or they should know how to use an *English Pronouncing Dictionary* well, which, in turn, requires the mastery of the nuances of the phonemes in English and allophonic variations. In many cases, help should be sought from experts to avoid the misarticulating of sounds.

Another problem of good pronunciation is the inadequate working of our *voice apparatus* which is made up of four components, namely, *breathing, phonation, resonation,* and *articulation*. In the words of Cedric M. Kenny: "When one or more of these components are not put to use properly, or used defectively, the quality of speech suffers. A negative voice may sound raspy, squeaky, hoarse, weak or shrill. And, a positive voice may sound melodious, warm, modulated and cultured." (2006). As for improving 'breathing', it should be 'breathing from the diaphragm', and for better 'phonation' the sounds that are voiced by the vocal chords should be properly amplified through the resonators. In order to realize good resonation both *fixed resonators* and *flexible resonators* should be properly used and trained through appropriate exercises. Resonance 'amplifies and enriches sound by reflection and sympathetic vibration.'(p.11). A stream of sounds are generally required for articulation which in turn is moulded and shaped by the various organs of speech in the articulatory system. Articulation itself may be good or bad depending on how sounds are articulated through the articulating process. If there is *nasality, lack of resonance, indistinct articulation, haste and indifference,* articulation will be adversely affected. Andrew Radford *et al* aptly comment:

> At some stage in the production of speech the speaker has to formulate plans for moving the articulators in such a way as to produce the required sounds in the required order. This is far and away the most complex motor control problem faced by human beings. The number of

> different muscles involved is enormous and the fine tuning required to get even an approximation to human speech is extremely delicate. The complexity of the process is seen to be even greater when we realize that we can and do introduce extremely subtle changes into our normal speech, by altering its rhythm and loudness and especially our tone of voice (intonation) so as to achieve different nuances of meaning....Given the complexity of the problem, it is all the more remarkable that we speak with relatively few errors. (1999)

We must train, through appropriate practice, our organs of speech and voice apparatus for finer articulation and better voice quality which greatly improves our pronunciation.

An important issue in good pronunciation stems from the improper use of *volume, pitch,* and *speed,* while speaking. The *volume* should be adjusted depending on the situation, distance from the listeners, and the environmental noise. *Pitch* – the height or the depth of the tone – depends on the frequency of the vibration of the vocal chords. Effective and imaginative speakers resort to a variety of pitches between the highest and the lowest levels. Men of vivid imagination infuse passion into their speech and realize a wide range of pitch variations rendering their speech marvellously captivating. The *speed* of one's speech is conditioned by three things, namely, *the rate of speech, pauses made,* and *the lengthening or prolonging of a syllable.*

Yet another area of which poses great problems to ESL learners is related to *syllable* and *word accent* or *stress*. The ESL learners find it difficult identify the syllable structure of most words in English. Unless syllable structure is understood, correct accentuation becomes difficult and wrong. Again, the stress patterns of mono-syllabic, disyllabic, tri-syllabic and other polysyllabic words differ from one another. Since stress is both *free* and *fixed* in English, it has become highly problematic for the ESL learners. Even monosyllabic words have their own rules such as only *content words* are stressed and not *grammatical words* or *structural words*. But given a certain level of interest in this area, and some genuine practice, any ESL learner can learn word accent in a short period of time. Without practice this area will be only 'sour grapes' for most students. Sentence stress or accentuation in longer utterance, also have their own peculiar difficulties although word stress is maintained as such in longer utterances in most cases. To maintain the characteristic rhythm of the English language some modification is necessary including weakening of the function class words. All these weak forms have to be learned well for realizing the stress timed rhythm of English.

In addition to the above, there are problems related to assimilation and elision as well. Sounds are affected by their phonetic environments. *Assimilation* is nothing but alterations or modifications occurring to sounds under the influence of the neighbouring sounds. *Elision* implies the dropping of certain sounds in some words or phrases in rapid speech. Rhythm, sentence stress, intonation, assimilation, elision, etc., are features of *connected speech* or suprasegmental features. S. N. Arora makes this point clear when he says:

> Words constitute parts, not the whole of an utterance or speech. We may often speak words in isolation, and may, to some extent, be able to convey our meaning, as in 'Go', 'Right', 'Nonsense'. But in most cases, we convey our sense through a group or cluster of words or words in company, that constitute the whole or a part of a sentence. This use of words in groups - short or long - goes to make what is roughly and commonly known as connected speech. (2012)

Good pronunciation presupposes adequate knowledge and practice of all these supra-segmental features of which Indians and most ESL learners are ignorant, and have great difficulty.

Conclusion

In sum, we can conclude that pronunciation is of paramount significance in the globalized era of today. The complex problems caused by Mother Tongue Interference and other phonological features of English itself and the suprasegmental hurdles to the non-native speakers as also the issues emerging from Assimilation and Elision, etc., can all be overcome if the aspirants have genuine commitment to the cause of leaning and using English well. What is required is a little daily practice in pronunciation drills and the various nuances of cadences of the English language in the spoken form. Without adequate training no one can have an acceptable pronunciation. As far as possible, Phonetics should be included in the syllabus as a compulsory subject for all students of English, at least at the college level. EFLU and other authorized English Institutes established by the Central Government should give training to English teachers all over India to ward off the possibility of dearth of faculty to handle the subject. This will change the qualitative aspect of English teaching in India and prepare the students for the highly competitive international job market as well.

References

1. Arora, S. N. *Some Aspects of Linguistics, Phonetics and Modern English Grammar*, Bareilly: Student Store, (2012) p. 73.
2. Balasubramanian, T. *A Textbook of English Phonetics for Indian Students* (Second Edition), New Delhi: Trinity press, (2014).
3. Bansal, R. K., J. B. Harrison. *Spoken English: A Manual of Speech and Phonetics* (Fourth Edition), Hyderabad: Orient Blackswan Pvt. Ltd, (2013) pp. 3-4.
4. Kenny Cedric M. *Communication Skills: The Power of Spoken English – An Invaluable Guide to the Art of Oral Communication,* New Delhi: Sterling Publishers Pvt. Ltd, (2006) p.4.
5. O'Connor, J. D. *Better English Pronunciation* (Second Edition), United Kingdom: Cambridge University Press, (2008), p. 2.
6. Radford Andrew, Martin Atkinson, David Britain, Harald Clahsen, Andrew Spencer. *Linguistics: An Introduction*, U.K: Cambridge University Press, (1999), p. 125.
7. Sethi, J & P. V. Dhamija. *A Course in Phonetics and Spoken English* (Second Edition), New Delhi: PHI Learning Pvt Ltd (2012), p.vii.

13

A Critique of Innovative English Language Teaching- Learning Methods

Currently there is a craze for innovative English language teaching methods. But the application of these diverse methods has not substantially improved the teaching-learning outcomes as claimed by the advocates of these novel methods. It points to the fact that it is not the method that has to be changed but the teacher who applies these methods. The English language teacher has to undergo considerable quality changes to reflect those changes in the learners. His/ her entire approach should change from a non-planner to planner of his lessons and an unprepared one to a well-prepared one before s/he takes each period. His lectures should be lively, and throbbing with enthusiasm, vitality, as well as passion. He should evince genuine interest in what he teaches and understand the psychology of the learners. His changed approaches, attitude, and professional interest will make the students gravitate towards his classes. He has to play his roles to make the students feel or experience the language and the lexical, semantic, syntactic and other items should be daily drilled adequately to seep into them .The paper takes a critical look at the present frantic search for novel method and underscores the greater responsibility on the part of the teacher to change himself.

Introduction

Disappointed by the dismal teaching-learning outcomes, many educationists and academicians have been frantically raking up every nook and corner for novel methods of teaching learning for quite a while now. Numerous methods have been tried in vain and many more are being invented and earnestly applied though not without some tangible results. Currently it has become almost a craze to hunt for more innovative methods. Communicative methodology has been much praised, technology assisted language learning is also considerably recommended of late. There are many who oppose the traditional method of lecturing and come forward with some novel methods and several claims. Thus we have community language learning, co-operative language learning, task based language learning, e-learning, neuro-linguistic programming and many more.

There is nothing wrong with any of these methods and approaches. Everything contributes to the teaching learning process. "The quest for better methods was a preoccupation of many teachers and applied linguists throughout the twentieth century. Common to each method is the belief that the teaching practices it supports provide a more effective and theoretically sound basis for teaching than the methods that preceded it. " (Richards and Rogers, p.1) But, why is it that in spite of all these novel approaches and methods that tried their level-best to kill and bury the lecture method, there is always the hue and cry that the standard of English is going down steadily day after day? Why is it that these methods do not bring about drastic changes in the learning outcomes? A closer look at the problem will reveal that it is not the method but the teacher who is at fault. When a series of changes are brought about in the methodology and approaches, there is hardly any change taking place in he teacher. A good weapon is a good weapon, but only in the hands of a good fighter. Any method should be imbued with insight, zeal, and a relentless quest for commitment to the cause. Any weapon produces the desired effect only when used by the right persons.

It is not a series of innovations that will make learning more effective but the attractive application of the hitherto known method and approaches. For attractive application the teacher's role is pivotal. In both 'learner- centred' and 'learning centred' approaches teacher cannot be dispensed with. Any method has meaning only when properly used by teachers. Otherwise, it ceases to succeed. The presence of teachers brings an element of coercion which is a must for a good number of students, who otherwise idle away their precious time either reading the irrelevant or browsing the sensational and the lurid that pander to their fancy and low taste. The youthful days of the students goad them to hunt for things that titillate their senses and quench their curiosity. The new methodology advocates the internet use and the internet has such items in abundance, of which the new generation is keenly aware and has much expertise in locating since "they are born into the new technology". This often results in mental pollution and distraction. Further, such dillydallying does not result in learning that which is essential, but in developing and fostering the bad habit of 'mind wandering'. In the case of mature and responsible students, self learning leads to autonomy and considerable learning. But this is not the case with the majority who needs guidance, correction, and compulsion to fare well in their studies. For this purpose the teacher will continue to be a necessary co-traveller in the process of learning till the stage is set when the learner can stand on his own legs as an autonomous learner with developed metacognition. Half hearted and mechanical application of a method by the teacher is of little use. It is tantamount to sheer waste of time.

What is required is to train the teachers in using a particular method as best as possible provided the method is proved highly effective. Brilliant teachers develop their own methods to teach effectively, be it a traditional method or a modern 'technology assisted' one or a combination of both. On the contrary, if teachers are asked to keep on changing their methods and becoming innovative repeatedly, it may be quite disheartening and baffling to them. Rather than flitting from one method to another, merely for the sake of innovation or novelty, it would be better to stick to a method that has been proved quite effective. It is high time we questioned the relevance of this craze for the fashion of new methods or innovative methods for their own sake. Changes should come to remedy the defects, if any, and not for the sake of changes and innovation that may be a western craze which we do not need to imitate blindly.

In India we have our own way of handling classroom situations and maintaining the rapport with the students since teachers have been held in greater esteem here. Our cultural background demands a different mode of teaching from the one followed by the westerners. Too much exposure to the mass media and modern communication technology need not be healthy since there are many lurking dangers and in the quicksand of which if the students happen to get caught, they might be irredeemably lost, i.e., in the world of pornography and sexually tantalizing websites. If they naturally go on their own way, it is a different thing. But if the educationists sing rhapsodies of the modern technology and the students are lured to them on that score, the situation is deliberately created, which has serious consequences in the long run. For the damages caused to the current generation of students, then, the educationists turn answerable sooner of later.

Is there a way out of this situation? Does language learning become better through the technology dependence? Many are skeptical. We need time to study the effect of such approaches as the communicative approach to ascertain if they are fruitful for highly productive language experience. If the method proves to be a useful one, let us stick to it for a considerable period of time. If another method emerges with an upper hand, let us follow that to the exclusion of other methods. But, any one, or a combination of the good aspects of a few methods, would suffice the need. Our teaching span should not be a race after experimentations with numerous methods at a stretch, as if such a practice were to improve the quality of teaching.

English language learning calls for adequate knowledge in the areas of vocabulary, grammar and phonetics and considerable practice in the areas of language skills. All these require a certain length of time. Shortcuts to mug up a little and dismiss the rest and then claiming to know a language is but mockery. Language is to be learnt to be effectively used in both speaking and writing. These productive skills are the offshoots of the receptive skills-listening and reading.

Students need to be exposed to and given adequate practice in these areas to have mastery of the language. It takes time. As Lyons aptly points out, "There are, of course, considerable differences in the vocabularies of different languages. It may therefore be necessary to learn another language, or at least a specialized vocabulary, in order to study a particular subject or talk satisfactorily about it." (p.30) Students need time to memorize or internalize the meaning as well as grammatical rules. "The fact remains, however, not only that in all known languages it is the vocal-auditory channel that is used primarily and naturally for their transmission, but also that all known languages are of roughly equal complexity, a far as their grammatical structure is concerned" (Lyons.p.29) Escaping from grammar and vocabulary is escaping from language itself, for consciously or unconsciously the rules and meanings have to be internalized for language use. Otherwise, our expressions become highly limited and inadequate for rich and effective writing as also speaking. So every teacher should ensure that the students learn a few words and phrases everyday and some grammatical items. Occasionally, training in pronunciation should be given for elegant oral delivery. In Wrenn's opinion, "Two kinds of difficulty have been encountered by the advocates of English as a world language: - first its vast and complex vocabulary, and second, the lack of relationship between its spelling and its pronunciation." (p. 203).

Let the teacher apply any method to teach vocabulary, grammar, and pronunciation. The only condition is that these should go into the hearts and brains of the students in such a way that they come handy for easy and elegant written and spoken expressions. But unless considerable drilling is given, it is not easy to fix them in memory. Nurnberg and Rosenblum remark: "In vocabulary building, the problem is not so much finding new words or even finding out what they mean. The problem is to remember them, to fix them permanently in your mind. For, you can see that if you are merely introduced to words, you forget them as quickly as you forget the names of people you are casually introduced to at a crowded party – unless you meet them again or unless you spend some time with them." (p.16). Students should be given adequate practice in reading till they can read clearly and fast enough. They should also be given passages for silent reading to comprehend it. Both are equally needed for advanced learners to face social situations later. Students should be given training in listening to English talks, speeches, recorded matters on CDs, etc. Listening to English programmes on the radio or TV also will prove useful.

To do all these, the teachers have to plan their teaching and prepare well in advance before engaging every class. A passionate, fluent and clear lecture can never be forgotten by the students. There should be conviction and interest in what the teacher teaches. His/her teaching should arouse the curiosity, stimulate the emotions, provoke thinking and awaken the imagination of students. For lecture method to be effective, every lecturer should be a good orator as well. If he cannot become one, then the use of audio-visual aids such as the OHPs and power point presentations or interactive white boards could be the next best alternative to grab the attention of the students. Again, involving the students in activities may also prove useful. Stressing 'the philosophy underpinning the activities', McKay and Guse assert: "Even when children are practicing vocabulary, pronunciation or language structures, they do so in a meaningful way, in an activity where their own meanings are created, supported and exchanged with others". (p.3). Why a bad lecturer should resort to such practices is that a dull lecture is an insult to the imagination of the students and too trying an experience for students to be endured for long. When the number of such teachers is on the increase, students begin bunking the classes and turn chronically truants.

Teachers should have some knowledge of the student psychology to attract them to the classes. Their emotional needs have to be recognized; their fears and anxieties have to be duly perceived; their feelings of insecurity and uncertainty have to be duly noted; their need to love and to be loved has to be sensed; their desire for acceptance, recognition, and new experience should be understood, their lack of orientation or goal setting should be set aright. In short, their growing age with innumerable attendant problems come in the way of their learning process. The teacher must be a friend, a counselor, a facilitator, and a loving parent for them guiding them through the complex stage of their adolescent life in the higher educational institutions. Once many of these needs are fulfilled they will be drawn towards the class and the language learning experience. We should always bear in mind that we, as lecturers, are addressing a class of students who are like travellers on the desert having lost their way, but searching for someone to guide them, because the adolescents whom we teach are the ones who are 'baffled by the world that is growing within and without'. In short, when we approach the students as humans with all their attendant problems and age-specific needs, we shall be able to get into their hearts and they will be ready to listen to what we say. This will result in better students' performance and improved English language mastery.

Conclusion

To sum up, it is not the methods that need to be changed, but the teachers themselves and their attitude towards and preparation for the teaching profession. Methods in themselves cannot ameliorate the English language teaching-learning scenario, unless they are accompanied by attitudinal changes and commitment on the part of the teacher. Teachers should prepare well before engaging every period and plan their lessons in advance to make it most effective and attractive. Besides, they should have good rapport with the students and understand their psychology to help them genuinely so that they take to heart what the teachers teach. Let the teacher's main innovation be to change her/his 'self' and bring about an attitudinal change towards his/ her profession which calls for "life-long learning", commitment, and adequate preparation before each class is engaged. Let change come from 'within' if this serious profession of teaching is to benefit the nation and the world at large.

References

1. Lyons, John. *Language and Linguistics: An Introduction*, U. K: Cambridge University Press, 2007
2 McKay, Penny and Jenny Guse, *Five Minutes Activities for Young Learners*, New Delhi: Cambridge University Press India Pvt. Ltd, 2008.
3. Nurnberg, Maxwell and Morris Rosenblum, *All about Words: An Adult Approach to Vocabulary Building*, Delhi: W. R. Goyal Publishers & Distributors, 2011.
4. Richards, Jack C and Theodore S. Rogers, *Approaches and methods in Language Teaching*, U K: Cambridge University Press, 2007.
5. Wrenn, C. L. *The English Language*, New Delhi: Vikas Publishing House Pvt. Ltd, 2000.

14

Grammar: How Indispensible is it for Spoken English?

Grammar has traditionally been insisted on by most language teachers as a very important tool for language teaching-learning. Although it helps achieve excellent written mastery, it is not productive of the expected levels of spoken language proficiency. Too much insistence on grammatical rules and correctness turned out to be a handicap in easy and fluent spoken English. Fear of making grammar mistakes thwarted the easy expression of thoughts and feelings. It also produced inordinate self-consciousness while speaking. One always doubted whether one was speaking grammatically correct English. This doubt robbed one of the courage to speak confidently and without hesitation. Hence, in the minds of the speakers the focus shifted from matter to manner, from content to form. It caused a lot of difficulty in delivering with ease what one wanted to say. On account of this, there have been efforts by the detractors of grammar-focused teaching-learning to set aside grammatical concerns and develop communicative skills especially the spoken skill. This resulted in minimizing grammar topics from the syllabus. Nevertheless, the problem of fluency and language mastery still remains an enigma. No miracle has happened as yet even after eradicating the grammar phobia. This implies that one cannot speak well even in the absence of grammatical insights.

Dispensing with grammar is not the solution to achieving better speaking skills. Rather than cramming the syllabus with too many ill-chosen grammar topics, a careful selection has to be done of only those topics which boost the spoken skill. Internalization of grammar rules is a must for any form of language delivery whether written or oral, for grammar is a set of rules that governs the usage of a language both written and oral. What is required is to select and learn those essential grammar items without which both oiral and written forms are not possible in a non-native context as the one we have in India. It is not the question of 'grammar or no grammar', but the selection of the essential, practical and basic grammatical items in a syllabus to enable students to have both written and oral proficiency that is more important, because grammar - at least a good portion of it - is indispensible for good spoken English.

How is it possible for anyone to speak without any rules? It is simply impossible. In the native contexts, the learners learn the language mostly through imitation. They listen to the speech of the elders and through continuous listening imbibe the rules of the language and then after a certain period begin speaking. Here the grammatical rules have been internalized, though quite unconsciously. Constant language exposure and regular use enable them to speak fluently and in the accepted and appropriate style. But this is not the case in the non-native contexts. The listeners hardly get any opportunity to listen to English as is spoken, nor do they have sufficient opportunities to speak English and learn it through such practice. In such a situation, the next best alternative is to learn it in the way other subjects are studied following the rules and principles behind it. The study of grammar deliberately becomes an imperative need. True it takes some time to study and internalize the rules and it is not easy and absorbing at all. Yet grammar has to be studied. Even if we create situations, for want of minimum knowledge of grammar rules, students are unlikely to open their mouth. In English medium schools strict rule of language produces a near native situation and students do gain. But this is not the general situation prevailing outside the English speaking countries. So grammar must be taught as the next best alternative though fast fluency is not to be expected. But for the aspiring students it is not that difficult either, since it brings about clear understanding of the mechanism of the language. Viewed from this perspective, it is a scientific approach, through a systematic study.

Not all grammar topics are of relevance in Spoken English. One should be very judicious in selecting the appropriate topics that help fluency and felicity. A closer examination of the spoken version as is seen in any typical conversational passages reveals that spoken English makes liberal use of certain grammar items. It is these items or topics that have to be carefully chosen o develop Spoken English skill easy and well-grounded. Here one does not need to include in study such items as would exhibit hair-splitting differences between words, and grammatical concepts. One does not need to bother while speaking whether an '-ing form of the verb is needed after phrases like 'with a view to' and 'look forward to'. Such knowledge is of trifle consequence in Spoken English.

Here arises the pertinent question: What are the indispensible grammar topics for effective Spoken English, if at all grammar is an imperative element of Spoken English? My experience of having taught Spoken English for over a period of fifteen years has helped me identify some of these essential grammar items for Spoken English. They are more or less the following: 1. The Parts of Speech 2. The Sentence Patterns (SVO etc) 3. Subject-Verb Agreement 4. The Tense 5. The Verb: Its Elementary Forms; its Kinds 6. The Auxiliary Verbs (The Anomalous Finites) 7. Yes/No Questions 8. Wh-Questions 9. Tag Questions 10. Embedded Questions 11. Kinds of Sentences 12. The Voice 13. Transformation 14. Synthesis 15. Clauses 16. Direct and Indirect Narration.

Knowledge of this small number of topics and their practical applications will surely help the speakers to handle English well and speak with self-confidence and ease. Of all these topics the most useful one is 'The Anomalous Finites' (The Auxiliary verbs). When we speak we have to ask questions; to ask any kind of questions, we need the help of auxiliary verbs. For example, in the question, *'Do you know English?'* and *'What did she say?'*, the first Yes/No question and the second Wh-question are asked with the help of the auxiliary verbs 'do' and 'did' respectively. Even in Tag Questions and Embedded questions which are frequently used in Spoken English, the use of the auxiliary verbs is very important, as in *'You know him, don't you?' Can you tell me where she is going?* Further, short responses are characteristically used in Spoken English. In this case also we need the help of auxiliaries. For instance, auxiliaries are used in the following short responses to the questions asked: 1. *Will they come here? Yes, they will.* 2. *Do you read novels? Yes I do.* Whenever we want to make sentences negative, we have to take the help of the auxiliary verbs. In the following sentences, negatives are made with the help of auxiliaries. 1. *I like music. I don't like music.* 2. *She works hard. She doesn't work hard.* Except in a very few cases negatives cannot be made without the help of auxiliaries. A case in point is the use of *hardly* as in *'They hardly ate anything during the journey'*.

A few more such words to make negative sentences without the help of auxiliaries are: *too, scarcely, little, few, nothing, none, no one, nobody, never,* etc., but such words which do not require the use of auxiliaries to make sentences negative are very few. The large majority of negative expressions are made with the help of auxiliaries. Similarly, the different *Tenses* are formed with the help of auxiliaries. There cannot be a Passive Voice construction without an auxiliary verb. One form of the Primary Auxiliary – *'be'* – is a compulsory element in all passive constructions just as the past participle. When we make polite requests beginning with: *Could you please…? Can you please …? Would you please…? Will you please…? Dou you think you could …? Do you mind …?* etc., we begin them all with auxiliary verbs. How amazingly important all these expressions are in Spoken English! In fact, the grace of Spoken English comes from such expressions. All these point to the fact that a relatively ignored grammar topic like Anomalous Finites when applied properly to various situations can work wonders for those aspiring to master Spoken English.

Everything that is grammatical need not be appropriate to the context. We cannot tell a gentleman in the blunt manner; *Come here,* although it is grammatical. Only such expressions as are appropriate to the context and grammatical are acceptable. To be acceptable appropriateness and grammaticality are needed. Spoken English is highly conditioned by these three conditions of *grammaticality, appropriateness,* and *acceptability*. The problem is to identify the expressions which are suitable to the context and are equally acceptable. Such expressions have to be learned by the aspiring learners from the available resources such as standard Spoken English books, CDs, etc.

In Spoken English, grammar is not all. A strong vocabulary of commonly used words and a moderate vocabulary of contextualized words are also essential. Only this will help to use the right word in the right context while speaking. This enriches the beauty of the oral style as well. In addition, all those *formulaic expressions* conventionally used and *space fillers* should be mastered and used appropriately. *Linguistic conventions* specific to the conversational mode should be imbibed by any standard speaker. Yet, another important aspect of Spoken English is good pronunciation with the concomitants of *stress, rhythm,* and *intonation*. Considerable practice is needed in this area. Though we not need to sapeak English with the same accent as the English people do, yet a generally accepted and intelligible pronunciation is an asset to make our speech all the more appealing to the international community and to the educated class in our own country. Good articulation of the English phonemes is necessary for any clear delivery of speech. If phonemes are wrongly articulated the listeners will not be able to make out the meaning of words uttered because substitution of one phoneme for another brings about a meaning change in English. If we substitute the phonemes of our regional languages, then the listeners from other states are likely to get confused and may have to strain a lot to follow us properly. So the safeguard is to learn the correct sounds of the English language.

In conclusion, we can say that Grammar is one of the important ingredients of Spoken English. If not a sufficient condition, it is at least an essential condition for good Spoken English. For Spoken English to be sufficient, a good general vocabulary , adequate knowledge of grammar, mastery of context- conditioned expression and words, formulaic expression and slangs, informal expressions, abbreviations, elliptical expressions, good body language and all needed linguistic conventions specific to the conversational idioms are required. To realize this, one should expose oneself to the spoken mode of the language. Otherwise, one will have to take pains to learn the standard Spoken English books and listen keenly to the C.Ds available. Dispensing with grammar is not a wise step, nor is it something we can afford without incurring much loss. What is to be done is to select judiciously the easier and more useful grammar topics.

References

Wardhaugh, Ronald. *Understanding English Grammar – A Linguistic Approach*. Malden, U.S.A: Blackwell.2003.

Leather, Jonathan (Ed).*Phonological Issues in Language Learning*, Malden, U.S.A: Blackwell, 1999.

Nagraj,Geetha. *English Language Teaching – Approaches, Methods, Techniques*, Hyderabad: Orient Longman, 2004.

Fernandez, Martin, *Spoken English*. New Delhi: Commonwealth Publishers Pvt. Ltd, 2009.

Shockey, Linda. *Sound Patterns of Spoken English*, Malden, U.S.A: Blackwell, 2003

Gass Susan, M & Jacquelyn Schachter (Eds.), *Linguistic Perspectives on Second Language Acquisition*, U.K: Cambridge University Press, 1997.

Sharma, S.R & John Jacob, *Anthology of English Language and Communication Skills*, Jaipur: Mark Publishers 2007.

Thompson M.S.H & H. G. Wyatt, *Teaching of English Language*

15

An 'Integrative Skills-Knowledge-Kinesis-Approach' As the Holistic, Innovative Way to Mastering English Language

Joseph. T. C.

Introduction

Living in an era of specialization and super-specialization, we are deluded by a morbid tendency developed in us by our scientific fraternity to split and break everything into its fragments for closer examination and then study one or two aspects and ignore the rest. Then we rush to make generalizations based on these few aspects that caught our fancy and were subject to our analytical operation. Then, in no time, we apply that generalization (which is often superficial) to the 'whole' whose couple of parts we ventured to examine. Such superficial, hurried generalization are no less than dangerous, for the inferences we made were not based on an examination of all the relevant parts of that 'whole'. In approaching the English language also we generally make this mistake by going after one or two of its aspects and jumping to conclusions regarding and arriving at solutions for effective mastery of English. But such tendencies we have to be on the guard against because they are naïve and unrealistic. A rich language like English ('rich because it has the largest vocabulary in the world') has to be had good

SGM College, & Archana Lobo, CoE, Gondwana University

command of for at least two purposes good writing and effective speaking, both of which are productive skills. Mere speaking and minimal skill in writing will not gain us much. Both have to be duly taken care of for scaling the heights of achievement. The better the mastery of these skills, the better is the communicative skills that rule the roost in the current globalized market economy. In addition, and to foster these two, we must whet our receptive skills listening and reading. These two help us understand well, sharpen thinking skill, delve effectively into books/ magazines/ the internet for gleaning information, acquire knowledge for research and do further processing to enrich life itself. But for an integration of these language skills with the knowledge areas of the language, namely, vocabulary, grammar and phonetics, the former will be handicapped and will be an abortive attempt. Further, an effective body language (kinesis) is a strong pillar to the skills-knowledge edifice of the language. Hence, all these have to be integrated in any effective teaching-learning curriculum of English if the pedagogic linguistic dreams for the learners have to be fructified. Short-cuts have to be eschewed and work culture has to be cultivated in learners so that they will awake from their lassitude to metamorphose themselves into useful citizens of the country and the world at large. This paper attempts to proffer an integrative skills- knowledge-kinesis approach as a fruitful and holistic way to realize language in the real sense.

The Integrative Skills-Knowledge-Kinesis Approach

Our experience attests to the fact that people always appreciate those who speak English fluently. Yet our appreciation is greater for the ones who speak both fluently and with more of less a British accent. The charm of good pronunciation is an added advantage with good, stress, rhythm and intonation which turn English musical, giving it the typical English touch. If the English spoken is grammatically correct and appropriate the level of appreciation still rises. If the speakers' vocabulary is rich, a greater spell is cast in the listeners. At this stage the listeners' admiration borders on jealousy! Similarly, people generally have great regard for those write exceptionally well in beautiful English. These point to the linguistic possibilities open before the student to materialize. Radhakrishnan rightly observed, "For man, to live means, to give existence to the possible". The teachers can, if they try, bring about a holistic development in the students' English. What is required is to focus on all these areas while teaching the four language skills, listening, speaking, reading, and writing, and the three knowledge areas, namely, vocabulary, grammar and phonetics, as also the Body Language of the learners while doing speaking, listening or reading. The attention paid should be comprehensive and the areas covered vast for healthier language mastery. Neglecting any of these areas results in smatterings, and the consequence will be debility in expression. Hence, systematic training in all these is expected of the teacher to empower students in English. If teachers themselves are incapacitated by inadequacies in any of these areas, the students are doomed to suffer. However, devoted teachers overcome their deficiencies through life long learning process and come to the rescue of the learners. Much hard work and conscious effort on the part of the learners can lessen the actual time spent dilly -dallying about the issue. What the teachers can do is to help the learners in all these areas through actual practice.

At the very outset, the learners have to be motivated if they should take to salutary reflection and ponder over the necessity to master the language for a brighter future that lies in the womb of time. They should be convinced of the importance of English in the age of globalization despite English being implicated in many cultural or other issues. Teachers should demystify English of the prejudices that engirt it and baulk any easy approach to it. Preconceptions and prejudices are a great mental block in approaching any subject objectively. That learning English is a need of the hour and any degree of dislike towards it is not going to help us in facing the practical realities is to be accepted as a bitter reality. Then, they should be so guided as to have a yearning to speak well, listen well, and read well. The next step should be to give them listening practice. Here they can be exposed to English lectures, passages read out by the teacher or other students, speeches made by the teacher or other students, CDs/DVDs used in or displayed on the computers/ laptops, TV programmes, and radio programmes in English. Students should be given chance to listen to English debates, seminars, symposia, anchoring group discussions, and brain storming sessions, and so on. Time factor does not permit the teacher to include all these in his teaching paraphernalia in a single academic year. In such a case he can make judicious combination of a few items from these to suit needs. This practice will help learners develop listening skill in which process all their inner faculties will be brought to play and finally they understand the semantic content of the oral code.

The third step should be to encourage them speak whatever they can. Initially only the bright and the bold will volunteer to partake of the conversational practise. The teacher should encourage them and speak to them in such simple English and with such lighthearted approach that the shy and hesitant ones can be eventually cajoled in to the speaking activity. They themselves will begin to realize that it is a golden chance for them to speak a few words in English. Once ice-breaking is done, more fervent participation becomes easier. Then after a few days, students begin to speak better fashion. Correction at the initial level is unwise lest the learners should turn crestfallen. It should be taken up at a relatively later stage by which level their confidence must have been boosted. Such frequent speaking and interactive sessions are a part of the communicative language teaching which has been appreciated currently. Knowledge of grammar helps them speak correct English. Pronunciation is central to good speaking activity although communication can be done without good pronunciation. Yet, unintelligibility, strain on the part of the listeners to grasp the message, etc will mar good interaction and perception, in the absence of geed pronunciation. Therefore, it has to be emphasized at this point as a regular exercise. It takes some time to master good pronunciation. Not many teachers are good at pronunciation and so they have to improve themselves before correcting the students. In the same way, a good vocabulary enables one to speak well provided it is made 'active through constant practice'. 'Passive' vocabulary is of little help while speaking. An important aspect of spoken language is the use of kinesis of body language for appropriate expressions. Students should be so guided as to express well with the help c^ suitable facial expressions, gestures, body movements, postures, and deportment at this stage.

As the next step the learners must be given considerable reading practice. Loud reading is for improving the reading skill with the right articulation and silent reading for comprehension, for gleaning information, to acquire knowledge of all sorts, for pleasure, for instruction and so on. Loud reading sound good only if pronunciation is fine. So pronunciation has to be improved for reading and through reading. Books of different nature require different kinds of reading. Skimming, scanning predicting, etc, can be developed through right advice and guidance. Since much knowledge is to be obtained from books and periodicals, how to read with sustained attention and good concentration is to be demonstrated to students.

Then, writing skill should be focused on. Considerable writing activity can be given to students by way of class work and home work/assignment. Writing skill gas much value as if fosters critical thinking faculties. It also helps the learners to express themselves well, their emotions and thought, and observations and findings. It is a good exercise for the development of all their mental faculties. This process helps the learners to be good research scholars and famous writers. It is in writing that grammar has a pivotal role to play. In writing the feel for the matter written, thoughts about it, analytical, evaluative, interpretative, contrasting, reviewing, comparing, and such abilities have to be developed through adequate trainings. A good teacher is of immense help in this regard. Vocabulary, both active and passive, contributes to good writing. Similarly, a good style is to be developed eventually through constant reading and writing practice. Students should be helped to have a feel words.

Conclusion

Learning a language is to be done holistically. Focusing on one or two aspect and ignoring the others is detrimental to language mastery. Students be trained in all the language skills, knowledge areas, and body language skills so that all aspects of language are simultaneously developed enabling students to use it confidently, effectively and as an experience reaping for them rich dividends. Only an integrated skills-knowledge-kinesis approach can do this for the English learners whether of not they learn English as ESL/EFL.

References

1. Pretty Walter, Dorothy C. Petty, and Richard T. Salzer, *Experience in Language Tools and Techniques for Language Arts Methods,* Boston: Alley & Bacon, 1994
2. Leather Jonathan, (Ed.), *Phonological Issues in Language Learning.* Malden, USA; Blackwell, 1999
3. Fernandez, Martin, Spoken English, New Delhi: Commonwealth Publishers Pvt. Ltd. 2009
4. Shockey, Linda. *Sound Patterns of Spoken English,* Malden, USA: Blackwell, 2003.
5. Gass Susan, M and Jacquelyn Schachter (Eds.) *Linguistic Perspectives on Second language, Acquisition,* UK: Cambridge University Press, 1997
6. Thomson, M. S. H and H. G. Wyatt, *Teaching of English,* New Delhi: Sonali Publishers, 2006.
7. Kwal Gamble, Teri and Michael Gamble. *Communication Works.* New York: McGraw Hill, 2005.
8. Wardhaugh, Ronald. *Understanding English Grammar A Linguistic Approach.* Malden, USA: Blackwell, 2003.
9. Nagraj, Geetha. *English language Teaching Approaches, Methods, Techniques.* Hyderabad: Orient Longman, 2004.
10. Sharma, S. R and John Jacob, *Anthology of English Language and Communication Skills.* Jaipur: Mark Publishers, 2007.
11. Dr. S. Radhakrishnan, Recovery of Faith, New Delhi: Kalyani Publishers, 1982.

16

Globalization and Commodification of the English Language

Globalization has triggered an avalanche of change in the world community. The rate of change occurring in countries like China and India has really been at a staggering pace. Economic factor is at the epicentre of these changes. Nevertheless, tremors of changes have been felt in every walk of life. There are serious repercussions in the agricultural, industrial, service, and I.T. sectors of the economy. Economic factors have begun to dominate and govern all other aspects of life. The capitalistic market economy, with its demand and supply forces, has emerged invincible in the globalized world. Everything is now valued from the point of view of marketability. Education, which is in the service sector, is also viewed as a marketable commodity. The beneficiaries-the students-are regarded as customers. Practical utility, especially employability, is a major criterion to judge education now.

It is against this backdrop that the English language is now being approached. Being a world language and the most important literary language, English has great potentials in the employment market. When people of different nations interact, English comes handy for easy communication, especially at the place of work. Besides spoken communication, numerous occasions call for written communication, too. In short, the general communication skills of the students have to be developed for securing good jobs in numerous companies within the country abroad.

Sensing the need of the hour the English language is also re-modified for marketable purpose. Numerous books have begun to glut the markets with labels such as Communicative English, Spoken English, Functional English, Interactive English, Practical Grammar, Business English, etc. All such books lay claim to prepare the students with the necessary proficiency and fluency in English, which in turn enhance their employability. Claiming to be hob-oriented, as they inculcate the necessary language skills, they experiment a lot and dilute the English language. The degraded into a commodity to be bought and sold in the market, having tailored it to suit the customer needs. It has also begun to eclipse English literature. Several universities have now welcomed these changes. Literature is thought to serve no monetary benefits. Hence it is being relegated to the background and gradually getting eliminated from the syllabi. This is indeed an unhappy development.

User-friendly approach is being adopted in the design and presentation in most language books. This, in itself, is a good thing, but the content should not be diluted and over-simplified.

Commodification of the English Language:

As the major library language, computer language, language of science and technology, the world language etc. English continued to be valued despite hostile murmurs against it by the lovers of regional languages. Until Globalization ushered in a consumerist culture which views people as mere customers and every thing else as mere products, English language enjoyed a respectable position since it was closely wedded to its literature. Now that capitalistic culture, with its ulterior motive of profit, has come to overpower everything, the English language, too, is compelled to divorce itself from its great literature. Capitalists have shown the great market possibility of the English language in the changed circumstances and are convinced that being the major medium of international communication, it could be converted into an attractive commodity that can be profitably sold in the market. All business tricks are being applied to its increased sale. It is presented as though it were very easy to master it in a brief period of time. They dilute the language through oversimplification. In this attempt to commodify it, several attractive packages are offered at several levels and in beautiful paperbacks and cover design. Very often the quality and quantity of substance is too insufficient to have any considerable mastery of the language from grammatical, vocabulary and communication point of view. It is because no single book can ever capture all the nuances, diverse contextual vocabulary, grammatical, and phonetic depth, and complexity of the English language. Only high claims of mediocre books remain. The consumers (the current readers) do not get adequate satisfaction. If at all they learn something and believe that have the entire language in their mastery, they are in a fool's paradise.

Numerous publishers and scholars are involved in this Commodification activity, although some books and courses maintain good standard and are of any considerable quality. A good number of books which appear in the book stalls do not possess any genuine worth at all. Many are replete with errors and printing mistakes. They may be the result of either ignorance or careless hurry, or both. Many institutes which teach Spoken English and charge high fees do not do justice either to the language or to the students. They are just exploiting the ignorance of the people and making money out of it In the Commodification of the language even some reputed universities are also partners. They have come out with their different packages, certificate and diploma courses. They are vying with each other in capturing the market with their language products which they claim to be the outcome of much research. Many students who complete such courses when thrown into real life situations feel betrayed and ill-equipped. Then, they realize that much time has to be spent on language acquisition process and that there is no short cut to it, then, dawns upon them, that learning a complex language like English, with its peculiar spelling and phonetic systems, is a Herculean task requiring much longer periods than the short duration packages they have attended. Mastery is a matter of several years of toil and struggle.

In an attempt to commodify the English language, vile effort is now made to divest it of its rich literature. Teaching literature is thought to serve no practical purpose like securing a job. Hence, only language is being taught with its grammar, vocabulary, phonetics, and functional aspects. This may help students in learning the language and later getting a job. But lack of knowledge of literature is a great loss indeed. A job fetches money, but inner culture and sense of values is more important than money itself. Only literature and other humanities help a person develop a balanced view of life and enable him to encounter everyday attrition and challenges of life. Therefore, job-orientation should not be at the cost of literature, and diluting the language itself. Students can be guided to be voracious readers, and books are more eco-friendly and body- friendly than computers and mobile phones. Technology assisted language learning should be done only when necessary. Daily exposure to computer is harmful, so also the use of mobile phones. Tape-recorders and radios are quite harmless when compared with them. So, in a hurry to use the more modern technical devices, on account of their visual benefits and multi-media advantages, we should not destroy the brain neurons of the younger generation. Long-run benefits and harmful effects have to be analyzed before widespread installation and use of such most modern devices. All that is western need not be good for our culture. To swim with the current is easy, but perilous; to swim against the current is strenuous, but safe.

Conclusion

Since we have plunged into the whirlpool of globalization, we cannot possibly get out of it. What can be done now is to forge ahead very cautiously. Curricular changes are necessary but we should not part with humanities in the name of their non-career orientation. If we part with them, we are parting with culture itself only to welcome a 'death culture' of mere 'consumerism' emerging from excess money in the hands of people and falling victims to advertisements and 'demonstration effect'. Materialistic progress should not strangle spiritual and moral values which help the survival of man on this planet. Our cultural values foster enduring relationships which make life meaningful. We should be cautions of anything which debilitates our world famous culture. Running after career-orientation should not make us oblivious of this fact. As Will Durant aptly remarked in his 'Pleasures of Philosophy', "After all, it is better to be a Socrates dissatisfied than to be a pig satisfied. It is better to be Socrates in prison than to be Caliban on the throne". The cream of wisdom should not be skimmed from the milk of knowledge. Both should remain mixed for a healthy mental diet. Universities should take care to maintain a healthy proportion between language and literature to produce healthy and wise citizens in future.

Money matters, but it cannot solve all ills of our complex life. We must preserve the true spirit of language with all its complexities and encourage and convince the youngsters to master it despite the challenges it poses. We must desist from Commodification of the English language and view it as a part of culture and present it as such, although adaptation to the Indian context is quite sensible and justifiable, let us remember that what made India great was not its wealth, but its rich culture, deep philosophy, and profound spirituality. We have a duty to preserve the core of all these. Globalization should not lead to cultural impoverishment. Economic growth should not deprive us of our time-tested values. Viewing the dissemination of knowledge from mere commercial point of view led to the Commodification of the English language. This trend should not spoil the English language. We must discern between good and bad books, good C.Ds and mediocre ones. Awareness has to be created among students and the reading public to curb the unhealthy trend.

References

1. Thomas Friedman, *The World is Flat: A Brief History of the Globalized World in the 21st Century* (2005), New Delhi: Penguin Books India Pvt. Ltd
2. Brunton, Paul, *The Spiritual Crisis of Man* (1988), New Delhi: B. I. Publications Pvt. Ltd.
3. Clerk, Ian (1997), *Globalization and Fragmentation: International Relations in the Twentieth Century*, New York: Oxford University Press.
4. Tyrrell, Burgess, (ed.), (1986), *Education for Capability*, England: The NFER-NELSON Publishing Company Ltd.
5. Agrawal, Meenu (ed.) (2009), *Women Empowerment and Globalization*, New Delhi: Kanishka Publishers, Distributors.
6. Bhatt, Devendra Kumar & Aparna Raj (2006), *Quality Management Systems: Concepts, Strategies and Requirements*, New Delhi: Kanishka Publishers, Distributors.

17

Innovative Teaching-Learning Methods

Joseph. T.C & R.G. Munghate

In the clam sea of Indian educational system mountainous tides of changes were triggered off by the tempests of Information Communication Technology (ICT), Globalization, Privatization and Liberalization. These engulfing changes left no aspect of our educational system untouched. Teaching-learning methods were no exception. Traditional methods like the lecture method which was teacher-oriented, were excoriated and dubbed as old-fashioned. Numerous innovations in teaching learning methods are currently taking place changing the very countenance of our educational set-up. The twenty first century has, in short, become a century of great innovational efforts in every field of human activity. The innovative methods in teaching learning are expressive of the ardent desire to effect more fruitful teaching and facilitate the process of better learning.

The Need for Methods in Teaching

Methods are invaluable in teaching. According to Diane Larsen Freeman, a study of methods is essential for teachers for the following reasons:

1) Methods serve as a foil for reflection that can aid teachers in bringing to conscious awareness the thinking that underlies their actions.

SGM College, Kurkheda

2) By becoming clear on where they stand, teachers can chose to teach differently from the way they were taught.

3) Knowledge of methods is part of the knowledge base of teaching.

4) A professional discourse community may also challenge teachers' conceptions of how teaching leads to learning.

5) Knowledge of methods helps to expand a teacher's repertoire of teaching techniques. In Diane Larsen-Freeman's opinion, "study of methods can help teachers' attitude and perhaps transform their understanding to be teaching-learning process. Methods can serve as models of integration of the Theory (principles) and practice (techniques)". She views a method as "a coherent set of thought-in-action links."

Quest for Innovative Methods:

The flaws of traditional lecture method sparked off several innovative efforts. The lecture method was a one-sided phenomenon. Students had no chance for interactive learning and had to remain within the four walls of the classroom like dumb prisoners. It was a suffering experience for most students. This gave rise to serious deliberations as to the drawbacks of the lecture-method. The outcome was a series of novel supplementary methods to strengthen the lecture-method. Among these-discussions, assignments, symposia debates, group discussions, talks, seminars, computer aided learning (CAL), e-learning, interactive methods and multimedia aided learning etc, are prominent. These give students a chance for self-expression and so are more democratic.

It is quite absurd to insist pedantically on any one particular method and be dogmatic about it. No single method is foolproof. The approach should be to evoke methods which embody the good aspects all past methods yet remain pragmatic. Any good method should ultimately lead to self-learning. No good teacher will ever surrender his freedom to be enslaved by the 'terrific one-sidedness' of a single method. A wise teacher judiciously selects the methods which he finds effective in particular circumstances. A method should be 'adapted' and not 'adopted'.

There are several factors which affect the choice of materials, methods or techniques. Some of these factors are: 1) Objectives of teaching 2) The type of classroom 3) The age, ability and capacity of pupils 4) The ability and training of the teacher 5) The availability of aids 6) The size/ strength of the class, and 7) The location of the schools, or college rural or urban. It is the teacher who has to select for himself the best in each method according to his need. Teaching, after all approximates more to an art than to a science. Intuition or psychological insight of the teacher, his personal abilities and convictions play a significant role in teaching. The great qualities of a good teacher such as enthusiasm, intelligence, and love for students also account for his success.

Methods are desirable since they imply selection, gradation, presentation and repetition. A method also signifies a set of procedures and graded materials based on a given rationale. The problem before teachers, then, is how to reconcile working through prescribed course book routines with their creative instincts. A method-conscious teacher will effect reconciliation between the ideal of a supposedly perfect method and the reality of its imperfect application in the classroom. He will find a productive way of working which suits the context better than any inflexible, preconceived, methodic practice ever will. On account of the rapid pace of changes taking place in society a teacher's career is subject to these changes and so requires proper equipping with adaptability that only methods can bring to the classroom context. Otherwise, they will be stupefied by the bewildering changes and remain like fish out of water. There can be no ideal method. The existing methods have to be suitably altered and put to the best use. The modifications result in innovations.

Innovative Methods

Although teachers generally resort to repetition and reinforcements through contextualized practice to drive home their points. Of late, there is a market movement from teaching-oriented to learning-oriented methods, which are more scientific and more modern. It emphasize that it is the learner's own in built syllabus which determines the route of acquisition. In the best approaches, teacher-intervention is the minimum and learner's freedom is the maximum. So it is natural and rids the teacher of his anxiety to teach the portion.

The present century is known as the 'century of knowledge'. But knowledge entails innovation for its enhancement. The generation of new knowledge is done through innovation. It is innovation alone that converts knowledge into wealth and social good. Innovation has now become a way of life. Our teachers should be imbued with the spirit of innovation especially in devising new methods of teaching. Innovation think very differently compared with others. They succeed in converting aspiration into solutions and ideas into products. The birth of such innovators requires all pervasive attitudinal changes towards life and work. They need to move from a culture of lethargy to a culture of dynamism, from mere talk to deep thought and work. They need to learn from to greatest innovator Thomas Alva Edison. The secret of his creativity was open-mindedness and perseverance. He used to challenge the assumptions continuously and believed that nothing is final. So teachers also through unprejudiced mind, strive for the better. They should develop the powers of observation, analysis and synthesis. Innovations in teaching and learning will take place through application of a wide range of knowledge and experience. The recent innovative methods stress the following;

1) The Use of Multimedia

Of the innovative teaching methods, the use of multi-media is a significant one. Multimedia is an integration of sound, animation, still images, hypertext, and video through a computer programmer. A multimedia computer is very effective in providing dynamic environment for the instructors, students and others in the field of education. In order to make learning activity pleasant and enjoyable a wide variety; of media options can be packed together with the multimedia. These serve as efficient and highly fruitful means for enhancing the quality, delivery and presentation of educational and informational material. Multimedia systems, which are computer based tools for generating and displaying textual, graphic and pictorial materials, have diverse potential roles in the educational field. A good number of studies have clearly shown that interactive multimedia technologies are exceedingly useful tools for achieving instructional objectives. Studies have unambiguously proved that if one is stimulated with audio, one will have about 20% retention rate, audio-visual about 30% and in interactive multimedia presentations where one is really involved, the retention rate is as high as 60% (Jay Sandom, Einstein and Sandom). The main educational benefits of multimedia are critical thinking, individualized-learning and self-paced learning. It has been pointed out that multimedia storage and retrieval systems contain more information than any human training agent can possibly embrace and have more terminals through which students have access to information. As Smith says, "The time is ripe for a break-through in educational methods". In contrast to the single medium approach to instruction, an integrated multimedia system is one in which several different presentational chambers are used (either simultaneously or in sequence) in order to implement a particular instructional strategy. Multimedia teaching offers high potential for the production of very high bandwidth for information transfer. This is achieved through the use of a variety of communication channels-textual, sonic, graphic, tactile and so on. In a large class, the weak learner does not get individual attention and can not pace with the bright learners, and so feels neglected and helpless. But when the lesson is computerized, and when each learner can work at his own learning process using a computer, he is released from the anxious urgency to race through the process of learning along with the competent ones. The individual learner feels relaxed and the process of learning working, recalling, self-testing and re-doing are done at the pace allowed by his learning capacity. This is particularly useful in language learning. The learner can use multimedia mainly in self-access mode for reinforcement, reference, profit work, and remedial studies. In order to strengthen communicative skills there are a number of graphical-representations available. Graphics refers to human visual communication. It shares the quality of both an art and a craft. Picturesque communication captivates children rather than mere words in a textbook.

2) Syncopated Approach

In India there is a dearth of resources for academic innovations. Hence lavish use of educational technology may not be a practical idea. It is here the relevance of what is called-"Syncopated Approach" becomes evident. In musical terminology "Syncopated" implies making the strong-beat light and the light strong. Our traditional mode of teaching is highly teacher-centric and limited to the printed text. It is tediously lecture-based and form focused. It denies the learner sufficient freedom to put his mental faculty to any independent initiative. This method is not conducive to any meaningful activity in the classroom. It promotes and perpetuates only rote learning. Contrary to this method, the 'Syncopated Approach' shifts the focus to learner-centric methodology. It is function-based and technology-based. It will render learning quite enthralling and pleasurable. There are numerous web-sites, CDs audio-cassettes, T.V. programmes, etc, which can be profitably used to promote autonomous learning by the learners. This method is not intended to replace the teacher, but his role is limited to a facilitator with a different role as a guide and instructor. Nevertheless, the teacher's role is challenging, for he has to be endlessly imaginative, resourceful and must be always up-to-date with the latest developments in the field to perform his new role as facilitator.

The great advantage of syncopated method is that it minimizes teacher-interference and considerably increases learner-autonomy. The teacher's help is required only when the learner runs into some difficulty. So it aids self-study and self reliance. Learner's experience of learning becomes authentic and exciting. Another merit of this method is that besides learner-centric, it is interactive and technology-oriented teaching. It helps learners critically assess their needs and decide their own learning strategies. It makes allowance for the pace of learning suited to them an augments learner confidence.

3) Computer Assisted Learning (CAL)

The Information Communication Technology (ICT) is radically transforming our life style and work. The digital revolution has given mankind the ability to treat information with high precision, to transmit it at an equal level of accuracy and to manipulate it at will. Computers and Communication are fast becoming an integral part or our lives. They are changing the way we work. Their impact is now deeply felt in our education system, too. Computer Assisted Learning (CAL) is slowly replacing the traditional method of teaching .When it applied t language it is called CALL (Computer Assisted Language Learning)

CAL is a method of teaching a particular subject using the computer as a medium. CAL packages are available for people of all age-groups. CAL makes use of IT for illustrating what is being taught. It uses attractive pictures, animations, music and human voice in the back ground. These make teaching more effective and learning more lively. Students can easily study with single-mindedness.

4) The Use of Modern Educational Resources

The on-line revolution and the pervading of the internet into the daily lives of people have made a wide range of educational resources readily accessible t all. Up- dated materials are now a available to any teacher whether experience or in-experienced. These materials can be adapted for use in the classroom. The application of this method assures freedom and ease to students since they themselves have greater control over their learning and teacher assumers the role of a facilitator.

Teachers should make judicious use of such innovations. The teacher has to keep an eye on the on the learner when the latter decides to find own learning route on the computer. There is a potential danger of distraction from the profusion of links that they find on the screen. Again, students ate likely to be led astray and spoilt by the obscene web-sites easily available on the internet. The teacher has to step in and provide the learner with the necessary guidance and instruction to help the learner pursue his academic goal.

5) E-learning

E-learning is a new method of learning. Today's learning is not only Computer-Aided Instruction (CAI) or Computer Based Training (CBT), but also it comprises within its fold the use of CD-ROM, mobile phone and personal digital assistants. E-learning is a new kind of learning which makes use of a net-works for delivery, interaction and facilitation. It is also known as 'distributed-learning', 'distance-learning', 'technology-enabled learning' and 'on-line training'. E-learning can be categorized into two modes: l) Synchronous, and ii) Asynchronous. In a synchronous mode, classes are real time, which is instructional, and the students are connected through a chat-room. On the other hand, asynchronous e-learning is one in which a student can have access to pre-packaged training, based on his requirement and convenience. E-learning has:

a) Content Delivery Methods:

i) Live broadcasting.

ii) Video-on Demand (VOD) introduced via Cable Television (CATV), and

iii) Interactive communication with two approaches, namely, distance education and community approach.

All these three methods have two-way capabilities of the technology, reciprocal interaction is possible.

b) Authority tools/ software products to create content:

There are three basic types of software:

i) Software to convert documents, images and charts created on word processors, spreadsheets and presentation software into e-learning content

ii) Software that allows people without programming skills to create advance content such as simulations.

iii) Soft ware designed to synchronize audio and video materials with presentation content.

c) Learning Management Systems:

After the ushering in of the Computer Aided Instruction era, the most important component of e-learning system has been the Learning Management System (LMS). This system allows learners, managers and operators to check and assess individual progress and performance. E-learning has several advantages.

Some of them are:- a) Lower Costs b) Time saving c) Flexibility d) Faster response e) Greater effectiveness g) Better morale h) Greater competitiveness, etc.

On-line learning, virtual classrooms, virtual institutions, virtual universities are fast becoming a reality. Along with the growth of the integration of Information Technology inputs, we shall soon witness a sea-change in the teaching-learning methods and environment.

6) The Use of Proper Teaching Materials:—

In addition to the above innovative methods and modes of teaching-learning, and the conventional teaching aids, there should be innovations in the materials a teacher needs that can motivate and sustain the interests of the learners. Without these novel teaching materials, classes are likely to be boring. Therefore, teachers must make use of various items found in the news papers, magazines, books, and web-sites. Even cartoons have great value when used in teaching languages since they evoke fun and laughter lessening tedium. Pictures and graphic presentations have great visual effect and are worth a thousand words.

7) Group discussions, assignments, library works, seminars, workshops, interview, socialized classroom techniques; team teaching, brain-storming sessions, micro-macro teaching, the use of OHP, LCD, and other audio-visual aids, cassettes, tape-recorders, etc are comparatively new innovations in the teaching learning methodology and are widely used. Most of these are based on the interactive teaching learning method.

All these must be sensibly used depending upon the subject taught, the size of the class, time available and other aspects of the educational context. Teachers should participate in seminars, workshops, conferences, refresher courses, and involve in project works to keep abreast of the times. Above all, the pressing need is to be computer literates so as to have proper operational knowledge of various academic tools with the help of which a good number of innovations are taking place.

References

1. Jain, Rupal (2013), *How to Be a Good Teacher,* New Delhi: Pusthak Mahal.
2. Sharma, R. A. (2014), *Teaching of English,* Meerut: Vinay Rakheja c/o R. Lall Book Depot.
3. Ghormode, K. U. (2008), *Methodology of Teaching of English,* Nagpur: Shri. Pramod Munje Vidya Prakashan.
4. Richards, Jack C and Theodore S. Rogers, (2007) *Approaches and methods in Language Teaching,* U K: Cambridge University Press.
5. Baruah, T. C. (2009), *The English Teacher's Handbook,* New Delhi: Sterling Publishers Private Limited.
6. Morey, Lata Subhash (2008).*Methods & Techniques of English Teaching,* Nagpur: Piplapure & Co. Publishers.
7. Journal of English Language Teaching (JELT) (2006), Chennai: published by ELTA@I.

18

Teaching English Language to Under Graduate Students Hailing from Non-English Medium Classes

Teaching English language to under graduate students from non-English Medium classes is an intricate problem that has been vexing teachers for long. The seriousness of the problem varies from region to region and from states to states. Despite the variations in the nature of the problem it has been evading efficacious solutions everywhere. It is such a tangle that both the teacher and the taught are almost inextricably enmeshed in it. Nevertheless, a proper grasp of the problem is likely to help us divine some plausible solutions. English is a highly complex language with its notorious incongruity between the letters of the alphabet and their pronunciation. Added to it is the immensely rich vocabulary with its numerous language-specific idioms and phrases. It is a time and energy consuming process for the students to have mastery of these aspects and the teachers find it equally hard to drive home these difficult areas. If this is the realistic picture of any English language teaching learning process under normal circumstances, the case of the students who come to U.G classes from non-English medium backgrounds presents a really dismal picture when compared with the more fortunate ones from the English medium classes. Those from the non-English medium classes are generally quite poor in vocabulary grammar, pronunciation and stylistic aspects of the language. On the contrary, students from English medium schools have a fairly good mastery of the above areas of the language. Most of them are quite articulate and are in a position to fare well in their studies at the U.G or P.G levels.

The problem becomes really subtle when both these categories of students learn together at the U.G. level. One group is quite sluggish in their English learning process and the other quite quick. The slow-learners are obviously from the non-English medium back ground with comparatively poor schooling. They feel quite baffled and find English learning both boring and strenuous. It is quite natural that they bunk classes and at the time of examination resort to copying the answers as an easy shortcut and to realize the much needed pass in the exam. But this is really an unhealthy state of affairs. What is needed is real quality - good mastery of the language - and not mere marks on paper. For this purpose, the students have to be attracted to the classes and taught as effectively and charmingly as possible. Besides, the teaching of English at the school level has to be good enough, too. But, that must be ensured by the government and the educational authorities. Such a change at the grass root level with the appointment of quality teachers is a matter of time and concerted effort. The current reality must be tackled differently. There are several possibilities before the teacher and the students at the under graduate level. The students of such non-English medium background have to be made aware of what they could do to learn English with considerable speed and the teachers should systematically prepare a definite, pragmatic, result-oriented plan. However, the teacher's role is more important and crucial in successfully solving this enigmatic problem.

The Teacher's Role

As Goethe aptly remarked, "There is nothing worse than a teacher who knows no more than what the students ought to know". This implies that the teacher should have vast knowledge of his subject. A large number of teachers get into the teaching field without sufficient knowledge, proficiency and genuine interest in the teaching profession. Many of them lack teaching aptitude and a commendable mastery of the English language. What prompted them to opt for the teaching profession might be mere pecuniary motive or the notion that teaching is an easy job with plenty of non-working days affording them a lit of leisure, or their own feeling that they are misfits in their jobs. Such teachers spoil the entire teaching profession with their frivolous and flippant attitude. Their happy-go-lucky attitude dampens down the spirits of their more sincere colleagues, too. This vitiates the sublime teaching field and the upshot will be the poor standard of the students. There is some truth in the saying: "He who can does; he who can not teaches". Every teacher should realize that he has a serious task entrusted to him. For an English teacher the gravity of the situation is much more so. His/ her role is vital in raising the standard of the students, especially of those from the no-English medium backgrounds.

A good teacher comes to the class well prepared. His vocabulary is quite wonderful. This enables him to express with fluency, felicity and facility. He has a feel for words and can easily make out the fine nuances and subtle shades of meaning. This helps him make the students perceive the matter as it ought to be. He strengthens their vocabulary and thereby expands the horizon of their understanding. He realizes how necessary it is to teach the meaning of as many words as possible. Hence everyday he insists that the students learn the meanings of a few words. Once the students acquire the essential vocabulary learning English becomes more or less easy. It is not in just reading and telling the story, or in explaining the content and summarizing the important points of a given lesson that the real success of a teacher lies but in making the students learn the meanings of quite a large number of words. Students have to be motivated and encouraged to do this part remarkably well.

The next step and a necessary corollary to learning English vocabulary is teaching grammar well. No doubt, the teacher must be proficient in grammar. In non-English medium backgrounds the teacher should not straight start with the topics given in the syllabus to be followed. Rather, he must spend a few days and preferably a few weeks teaching them the basic or elementary lessons of grammar which these students are deplorably lacking knowledge of. This short period can thus be used as a bridge course. As soon as the proper grammatical foundation in laid, he can move on to the teaching of the prescribed topics. Mere lecturing does not suffice. A lot of oral drills and written work must accompany every grammar topic. Structural and grammatical items should be applied to develop communicative or conversational skills. Grammatical rules should be so used as to generate a large number of sentences of different types through which we ordinarily communicate. This kind of practical application of grammar to oral and written communication will stimulate the interest of the students. They will be delighted to realize that English can be learnt easily and will gradually attempt to speak and write and gain in confidence. This may be followed by Group Discussion for more interactive learning. But first the students should be able to answer to the teacher's questions and then ask the teacher a number of different types of questions. Their errors should be corrected without hurting their feelings. Initially, only serious errors should be corrected and minor mistakes can be overlooked. This will boost their courage and confidence.

A good teacher always makes the best of several methods. He tries to be up-to-date with the latest development in teaching techniques and be apprised of various approaches to language teaching. He is always on the look out for improving his own English language, both spoken and written, and attacks the language from several grammar, pronunciation, fluency, stylistic aspects, literary and functional aspects. He is a voracious reader always searching for more knowledge to sharpen the tools of his profession. He will delight in life-long learning process and takes into account the needs of the times, but never dismisses the enduring aspects of the language. His classes will be a joy for the students as well as a rewarding, memorable experience since they throb with vitality, enthusiasm and a judicious sprinkling of humour. A successful teacher develops good rapport with the students and stresses on interactive learning. He is more of a facilitator than a dictatorial lecturer. He displays great psychological insight and adopts a friendly stance. He tries to understand them and their peculiar cultural and familial backgrounds through continual interactions with them. This mutual understanding develops an intimacy between the teacher and the taught and the result will be a love of the subject taught. Then, English will no longer be viewed as a foreign language but one like theirs.

The teacher must occasionally conduct class tests to evaluate the progress of the students and the feed back must be timely. In prose lessons stress should be on vocabulary and content and in poetry more on the experience and beauty of the poetic expressions. In teaching drama, the teacher must act it out as far as possible to make it an exciting experience. Later, plot, characters, dialogue, them etc, should be discussed to increase the topical knowledge. In adopting the medium of instruction the acid test is that the students really understand what is taught in the class. For this purpose in U.G. classes with students of non English medium background, English can be taught through the mother tongue or any other language they understand. But at the same time, an English-to-English explanation must precede it to enable students to have adequate exposure to English.

In addition to speaking and writing practice to develop those language skills, the teacher should help them read well, too. After every lesson some time should be found to improve their reading skill since a considerable number of these students are not good at reading well, with sufficient speed and clarity. Repeated questions during teaching will make them alert and greatly contribute to the sharpening of their listening skill. Otherwise, they will be physically present, and mentally absent since most people are victims of the mind-wandering nuisance. Teacher should devise every strategy to bring them on the listening track with rapt attention or rather full concentration.

Occasional home assignments, seminars, quiz contests, elocution practice, interview training, debates, task-based activities, dividing the class into small groups to practise co-operative learning, use of audio-visual media, use of news papers, articles, pictures and such teaching aids, supplying them with content-rich materials from multi cultural sources, etc, will make English language learning an interesting and comparatively easy activity. Ultimately, the U.C. students should achieve a high level of metacognition by which process they self regulate their own studies and take to fine reading habits to become really advance students. Teacher should constantly advise and encourage them to make the best use of books, C.Ds, cassettes, and such learning resources from the library. Teacher's own example should inspire them to take to salutary reflections and spur them to consider study as a serious and pleasurable pursuit. Teacher's vigilant and judicious guidance goes a long way in making students' English language learning activity a steady and single-minded pursuit. Students should fall in love with English. A constantly hardworking teacher with ever-burning missionary zeal for his task alone can materialize this titanic task. Students are our raw materials and it is up to us to turn them into fine finished products.

Conclusion

In the peculiar situation of teaching English language to undergraduate students hailing from non-English medium classes, the teacher's role is pivotal and highly decisive. He must devise a judiciously pragmatic methodology of his own, imbibing the best from all available methods and ensure that these hapless students acquire knowledge of essential grammar, minimum required vocabulary for successful communication, generally acceptable pronunciation and acquire the four language skills to a fairly good level. Besides, classes should be so handled as to provoke their thinking process that will unleash their pent up language powers and make them highly creative in their written and spoken communication braced up with plenty of ideas to talk about and write about. Although students have to be co-operative and regular in classes for the success of tangible language learning outcomes, their failings have to be studied by the teacher against their backgrounds and strain every nerve to attract them to the classes through unforgettable teaching-learning experience offered by him. Necessary academic and psychological counseling should also be given to students. Bridge courses, remedial teaching, etc, can fill the gap these students have suffered on account of the discriminatory societal set up they are brought up in. Introducing value-addition certificate and diploma courses in Spoken English and Communicative English will also help them have a winning edge in today's competitive, globalized world.

References

1. Jesperson, Otto (2007), *Language: Its Nature, Development and Origin*, Delhi: Surjeet Publications.
2. Bansal, R. K., and J. B. Harrison (1994), *Spoken English: A Manual of Speech and Phonetics,* Hyderabad: Orient Blackswan Private Limited.
3. Thomson, A. J, & A. V. Martinet (1987), *A Practical English Grammar*, New Delhi: Oxford University Press.
4. Viney, Kirpal & Shridhar B. Gokhale (Eds.) (2011), *Unlock Their Future: A Skill-based Approach to Teaching and Learning English,* New Delhi: Sterling Publishers Pvt. Ltd.
5. Hands Penny (Ed.) (2009), *Collins Easy Learning Grammar & Punctuation*, Glasgow: Harper Collins Publishers.
6. Hands Penny (Ed.) (2011), *Collins Easy Learning English Vocabulary*, Glasgow: Harper Collins Publishers.
7. Mitra, Barun, K., (2007), *Effective Technical Communication: A Guide for Scientists and Engineers,* New Delhi: Oxford University Press.
8. Seely, John (2007), *Everyday Grammar*, New Delhi: Oxford University Press.

SECTION-D
ARTICLES ON GENERAL TOPICS

1

The Need for Communal Harmony in Nation-Building Process

Communal Harmony is a *sine qua non* for the unhampered and healthy development of any nation which comprises multi-religious, ethnic and cultural groups. Nation-building activities will be prematurely aborted if there are insidious activities involved in by the hostile communal factions in any country. The greater the degree of communal harmony prevailing over a long period of time in any given nation, the better is the prospect of economic prosperity, peace and stability. It is because there will be growing confidence in the investors that their capital will not be destroyed by the different communal groups, for they believe that there exist among them strong bonds of agreements especially of interests, opinions, and feelings. But in order to build such mutual agreements and trust, the different communal factions should develop deep knowledge, understanding and respect for one another's religious beliefs, ethnic variations and cultural differences. Mutual understanding born of tolerance, love and broad-minded nature begets true communal harmony.

The Need for Communal Harmony

Communal harmony is imperative from several perspectives. Society, which is a network of human relationships, can survive only if the individual members sacrifice several individual interests and practices so as to rise themselves to the demands of gregariousness. If the members belong to different religious, racial, and linguistic groups, they must be tolerant of one another and come together on the common platform where their general human interests converge. A common purpose unites them all. Thus, communal harmony paves the way for such solidarity stemming from good relationships.

Human beings are not mere wealth-getting and wealth-spending beings. Rather, they are personalities of immense complexity since they aspire after fulfilling numerous other needs such as spiritual, emotional, aesthetic, intellectual, psychological, moral, political, social, cultural, and so on. It is the nature of man to strive to transcend the limiting, narrower aspects of his human existence and keep yearning for nobler and broader planes of existence. Only communal harmony can elevate him to this level. Contrariwise, communal disharmony poisons the human psyche and plunges him to sub-human trivialities and dire depravity. Man becomes a victim of hatred, suspicion, unrest, jealousy, violence and even terrorism. Fanatic tendencies then loom large and make him blind to the good aspects of other people and their religions. A 'terrific one-sidedness' propels man in this situation. The only solution to escape from this ignominious state is nothing but communal harmony through collective good will.

There are also theological and metaphysical reasons why communal harmony is a prerequisite for any healthy society. Nearly all world religions view humans as created by one and the same God, whether or not they are the adherents of diverse creeds and cults. Hence, the sensible and educated people believe that all are brothers and sisters, being children of the one and the only God. We have no reason or justification, therefore, to hate others in the name of caste, creed, sex, language or any other aspect. No religion sanctions hating others, killing others, doing harm to others in thought, word, or deed. It is but the zealots who misinterpret and misuse religion. "Religion", as Dr S. Radhakrishnan said, "is not a theory of God, but it is a personal experience; it is something given to us in immediate experience" (2001).He also says: "God's revelation and man's contemplation seem to be two sides of one fact." (2000). Such an experience makes one jubilant, and exclaim in that state of exhilaration or rather, ecstatic delight: 'I am God', '*Aham Brahmasmi.*' This God-realization makes one humble, holy and purged of all hatred and ill feeling. Every religion offers opportunities for this. Our Indian *rishis* had this experience and many like Sant Tukadoji Maharaj, Shri Ramakrishna Paramahamsa, Vivekananda, Gandhiji, Pramahamsa Yogananda, etc, continued to have this transcendental experience. Shri. Buddha, Guru Nanak, Vardhamana Mahavira, Jesus Christ, Socrates, Mohammed Nabi, Kabirdas as well as a myriad of founders and saints of all religions had this God-internalization-enlightenment experience. All of them viewed mankind as one family – '*Vasudeivakudumbakam*', and not through a narrow perspective. It is the followers of different religions, who wanted to proselytize, viewed other religions disparagingly.

Arnold J. Toynbee writes that he would express his personal belief that the four higher religions that were alive in the age in which he was living were four variations on a single theme and that, if all the four components of this heavenly music of the spheres could be audible on each simultaneously, and with equal clarity to one pair of human ears, the happy hearer would find himself listening not to a discord, but to a harmony (1954). Thus, all religions profess basically the same ideas such as love, universal brotherhood, peace hope, joy, forgiveness, the belief in the existence of one supreme, all knowing, omnipresent, compassionate God, etc. What we need to do is to read and understand the holy books of all major religions and understand them so that we begin to respect the greatness in each religion. Once Gandhiji insisted, "I hold that it is the duty of every cultured man or woman to read sympathetically the scriptures of the world. A friendly study of the world's religions is a sacred duty".

Religions are storehouses of immeasurable spiritual wisdom and it is left to us to open them and take possession of the infinite wisdom and the invaluable riches. The secret to open these treasure houses is to meditate properly on the scriptures. Quarrels among religions are like quarrels among rich people – both the parties involved suffer losses. What is essential is co-operation and mutual support so that the followers learn to practise what they had been instructed by their own religions. Misuse of religion is our own fault, not that of religion itself. All religions aim at man's spiritual salvation and moral upliftment. But the attachment to one religion should not let us hate or disparage another religion. On the contrary, it should help us reach out in love to another one and hold it in high esteem. This and this alone, can avert the possibility of discord among religions and communities.

Similarly, people who belong to dissimilar cultural, linguistic and racial groups should be able to come out of the hard shell of their own culture, language or race and set their eyes steadily on the hitherto undiscovered magnificence of other cultures, languages and races. This will make everyone realize that there is none superior or inferior to any one else, and that every culture, race, or language is more or less equally great and blessed with diverse abilities and merits. This broadens the mind and helps them embrace mankind as the ultimate religion. Such cross-cultural, cross-linguistic, cross-racial perusals will avert the dreaded possibility of the rise of another Hitler or another Mussolini. This will avert the possibility of fanatics becoming terrorists and extremists, adopting homicide as a philosophy under one pretext or another. All can learn from one another's culture, religion, language and race certain lessons for self improvement without compromising anything of their own.

If we wish to achieve greater economic, political and social levels in our country noted for its diversity, we should fulfill certain preconditions. One such precondition is the so called communal harmony. Communal clashes adversely affect our economic activities and erode our national achievements. Communal riots will destabilize the political set up and lead to wanton violence and anarchy, relationships. Communal problems damage the entire social fabric which is built on social relationships Mistrust and antagonistic feelings vitiate the entire social ambience making life difficult, meaningless and agonizing. Hence communal harmony is a prerequisite for a healthy society whose economic, political and social aspects are expected to forge ahead untrammelled. In other words, every nation-building activity presupposes such a halcyon, harmonious, communal condition for its anticipated success.

Communal Harmony and Nation Building Process

Nation building is a secular process highly dependent on several variables. One major prerequisite is communal harmony. Again, nation building is highly complex, too. We need the simultaneous improvements in several variables such as economic, social, political, cultural, institutional, etc. Unless communal harmony is ensured whatever tangible progress we make in construction work, automobile industry, and other additions to capital stock, monuments, etc, may be destroyed, dragging us back to where we began. We have witnessed in India, soon after the partition, the maddening massacre, heartless destruction of houses, buildings and public property impoverishing our socio-economic condition. When communal factors further led to India's war with Pakistan three times, or so, our nation building process was terribly obstructed dragging into the morass of stagnation and deceleration. Further, the situation following the demolition of the 'Babari Masjid' at Ayodhya, poisoned our social and communal atmosphere triggering alienation, distrust, terrorism and such dreadful activities. Our politicians are to blame for fanning communal disharmony in India by appealing to the sensitive religious sentiments of the people to win their votes for political power. Nothing but secularism is capable of fostering communal harmony. Mingling religion with politics, or linguistic, racial, and regional factors with politics, leads to communal disharmony.

Only a peace-loving people can actively and wholeheartedly participate in the nation- building process which leads to rapid expansion in economic growth and development. Qualitative improvements in society constitute an essential accompaniment in economic development. But communal riots will not make such positive changes to seep in easily. Advancements in trade, commerce, transportation and communication, agriculture, industry, scientific and educational spheres, etc., can be made and sustained only if communal harmony is fostered. Communal riots, thus, pose grave threats to the growth of the economy and the security of the people. Communal disharmony causes serious mental derailments through violent emotional disturbances propelled by fear, hatred, vengeance and hostility. Healthy citizens are a great asset to the nation. India is presently one of the fastest developing countries in the world close at the heels of the Asian giant, China. No doubt, our nation building activities have been frequently affected by the recurrent communal problems. Hence we must strain every nerve to ensure communal harmony so as to facilitate our noble endeavour of building our nation into a more powerful and greater one.

Conclusion and Recommendations

In a country like India with its immense diversity, the absence of communal harmony makes peaceful co-existence and steady progress impossible. The key to our nationality - 'unity in diversity' - has to be maintained at any cost. For this purpose communal harmony is indispensable. All our nation-building activities will come to a standstill if problems stemming from communalism, parochialism, terrorism, cultural chauvinism, interstate disputes, linguistic prejudices, racialism, class differences, caste barriers, etc, are not judiciously solved. We must conduct as many useful programmes as possible to promote communal harmony. One major step would be to promote and encourage people to read the holy books of all religions. This will open the eyes of the public and help them realize that the underlying principles of all religions are more or less the same. Only the rites, rituals and ceremonies differ; and they are but the externals of each religion. We must also strive to establish, at national and international levels, certain organizations and platforms where inter religious meetings and recurrent discussions will prompt the representatives of all religions to come together and sort out the differences, and form deeper friendships. As Radhakrishnan wisely suggested many years ago, "If we can have a United Nations Organization, cannot we have a United Religions Organization?" (2001).We should also so modify our syllabi as to include topics on all major world religions, written without bias towards any one particular religion. We must also encourage, at college level, studies in 'Comparative Religion'. We must also bar our politician from forming any political party based on religions. Anyone who appeals to the religious sentiments through demagogy and rouses their passions against any other religion should be immediately put behind bars. Those destroying the places of worship of any religion should be meted out the harshest punishment. Similarly, commissions should be appointed to find out the root-causes of terrorism and then suggest feasible solutions for them. These solutions have to be implemented without any delay. In the same way, close watch should be kept over religious fundamentalists and their activities. No one should be allowed to ill-treat others in the name of religion, language, caste, class, sex and race.

Finally, let us remember the exhortation of Dr Paul Brunton for a lasting solution: "the way out of these afflictions is being desperately sought but seldom found...for it is being sought in the wrong direction. There is only one proper way out, and that is to correct the misunderstanding and to remove the misconception. This needs a dramatic change of moral attitude, a large renunciation of materialist outlook and a quick reversal of spiritual indifference. A change in thinking is the first way to ensure a change in the world's condition. In changing himself, man takes the first step to changing his environment and in changing his environment he takes the second step towards changing himself. For the first step of self-change, (it) must be a mental, not a physical one. Therefore, he will profit best in these difficult days by subduing pride and being perfectly frank with himself, even to the point of putting on mental sackcloth and emotional ashes. His mental attitude must effect an about-face. He must heed that inspired bidding, "Repent and be saved". This has been the divine message for all such times but it is especially applicable to the present time. He has lived a materialistic life which is but a half life.

The only cure for the newest chaos in which the whole world has fallen is also the oldest one. Those who wait for the announcement of miracle working prescriptions wait in vain. The truth that is around the corner is as old as mankind, only the face it shows is fresh and the clothes it wears are styled to the century itself. Some thousands of years ago India's sacred writing, the Bhagavad Gita, proclaimed that there is peace and prosperity on the earth for those who will learn and follow the laws of the inner life" (1988).

References

1. Radhakrishnan, S, *Spirit of Religion* (2001), New Delhi: Jaika Publications, p.2.
2. Radhakrishnan, S, *An Idealist View of Life* (2000), New Delhi: Harper Collins Publishers Pvt. Ltd, p.95.
3. Toynbee, J. Arnold, *A Study of History*, Vol. VII, (1954), p. 428.
4. Brunton, Paul, *The Spiritual Crisis of Man* (1988), New Delhi: B. I. Publications Pvt. Ltd, p. 64.

2

Progress: Myth and Reality

Introduction

Progress, a heavily hyped term, has long been the 'abracadabra' in the mouth of most politicians to entice the people and take on any course of action in its name to suit their expediency. The intellectuals were never niggardly in vociferously using this term either. Although most of them just float the idea of progress, hardly anyone delves deep into it to bare the layers of its meaning. Everyone, it seems, delights in merely skirting round the idea. Its repeated use in most discussions has divested it of much of its novelty and turned it a stereotype. Yet, ironically enough, it keeps exerting a queer 'charm' on the common man. This accounts for its being in untiring use for so long a period. Besides, it has an aura of vagueness, a nebulous halo that lures everyone into it. It is as though we could keep using this term so intriguingly and deceptively till doomsday.

Myth/the Fictitious Ideas/Fabricated Concepts about Progress

Progress is a highly subjective term since it does not mean the same to all. Contrariwise, it means many things to many people. Two predominantly antithetical views fabricated on progress, but complementary in certain respects, have occupied centre-stage on any discussion about it. One is a materialistic view and the other an idealistic one. There is a marked difference between the view a materialist holds of progress and an idealist does. But both envision a better society of the morrow though with different notions.

For the materialists, 'progress' signals an increased level of material well-being realized though rapid strides in science and technology. They also take it to be a condition of greater amenities of life, better education, freedom from superstition and ignorance, and a greater mastery over the physical world of nature. In their opinion, progress also includes the realization of man's potentialities. There might appear wry smiles on their faces if spiritual matters are brought within the ambit of the above list. They might grudge moral improvement provided morality is an offshoot of their materialistic ideology and not of religion. Nevertheless, the term is viewed to be expressive of a better state of affairs. Progress reveals itself in the lessening of pain and the augmentation of pleasure. It unfolds itself in the complete eradication of poverty, inequality, exploitation, and in the wiping out of all diseases. It offers us longer and better life. Such an enlarged list of diverse implications, may be, what constitutes the concept of progress for a materialist.

On the contrary, an idealist has a still more comprehensive view of it. He not only conforms to the above view, but supplements it with a few more items of much more import. For him progress also means the 'gradual unfoldment of the divine' and a greater approximation to the 'image of God' by the humans. S. Radhakrishnan, quoting from St. John's Gospel, affirms:

> The Kingdom of Heaven is the highest state attainable by man. 'It is within us.' 'He hath set eternity in the heart of man.' Man stands between the visible and the invisible worlds. Our ordinary level of consciousness is not the highest form or the sole mode of experience possible to man. To get at the inner experience, we must abstract from the outer. We must get away from the tumult of sense impressions, the riot of thoughts, the surging of emotions, the throbs of desires (*Indian Religions,* 13).

An idealist may conceive progress as a step forwards to moral perfection. It is also held to be the fuller realization of moral values. An idealist's perspective insists that progress make us more refined beings, more self-effacing, more civilized, more prudent, happier and more peaceful. Progress should enable us to experience the joy of living. It should rid our mind of all its fears, guilt, hatred, and inferiority feelings. Religion helps us advance in this direction. Real progress is conditional on God-experience. "One whose life is rooted in the experience of the Supreme spontaneously develops love for creation. He will be free from hatred for any man (*Indian Religions,* 14). Progress, the idealists hold, must harbinger psychological and spiritual freedom. It must usher in an era of social, political and economic freedom and a dawn of equality. Progress is expected to bring with it justice and brotherhood. It is hoped to liberate man from all shackles - visible and invisible. It is to be accompanied by a flowering of human personality. The latent talents should be actualized, as man progresses. He must learn, if he wants to progress, to be with his own self for a while each day, to plumb the depths of his inner world. Radhakrishnan who once said, "From solitariness spring forth masterpieces of literature", again underscores the idea: Genius has no place for team-work. Poets and prophets do not go into committees.... When the supreme light in us inspires the intellect, we have genius, when it stirs the will we have heroism, when it flows through the heart we have love, and when it transforms our being, the son of man becomes the son of God. Put the fire of spirit on any altar, it blazes up to heaven. Its powers are infinite, its dreams angelic, and its apprehension godlike (*An Idealist View of Life,* 200-201).

Such are the great notions of human progress for an idealist. These are very comprehensive and more fulfilling as far as human destiny is concerned and taking into account the spiritual possibility of man which has been cancelled out by the materialists.

The Reality/What has Actually Happened

Progress, thus, is a complex term with layers after layers of implications. We would naturally wish to actualize all the above associations that we attach to progress. But our efforts fall short of our wish. The reality is at variance with the myth – our notions – of progress. There is an incongruity between what we think of progress and what is realized as progress. So it is an ironic state. What passes for progress in the world today is 'mere corruption' (Rousseau). Somewhere, in our mad rush forwards, we have taken the wrong tracks which lead us farther and farther away from ideal progress. What we call progress today is but a distorted form of what ought to have been progress. It is mere advancement towards death and destruction. It leads us only to the horrid abyss of social and personal disintegration. In a way, it is only an impetuous move towards self-immolation. Progress today has degenerated itself as a feast to the beast in us. Life has become tensed up and strenuous. We are imploded by our own stress and strains. We have found for the current progress many sweet names – 'death culture', 'consumerism', 'scientific materialism' and so on. Dr. Paul Brunton's remarks are eye-openers in this context:

> Exposed to the agitations of our age as we are, it is harder to keep a serene mind than ever before. Discouraging news is heard too often and distracting fears have become too insidious to allow us to keep serenity without earning it the hard way. Without inward peace, without security, modern man, who for so long pitied his ancient and medieval fathers is now himself to be pitied. There are alarming features in the growth of his emotional disequilibrium and mental instability. There are neurotic excitements and pathological turmoil, vehement passions and dangerous indecisions in his mind and life (*The Spiritual Crisis of Man*, 7-8).

Victorian poet, Matthew Arnold's lines from *Dover Beach* reflect the dismal state of our progress:

> We are here as on a darkling plain,
> Swept with confused alarms of struggle and flight,
> Where ignorant armies clash by night (lines: 35-37).

How helplessly do we gape at the unleashing fury of evil forces which engulf us! How painful and stressful has become the accelerating rate of change and progress! Only the genius of an Alvin Toffler can fully perceive the immensity of massive changes and the consequent shock we sustain. His masterpiece the '*Future Shock*' is capable of opening our eyes to this less understood area of our experience of progress and the attendant evil of an avalanche of change. "Future shock is a time phenomenon, a product of the greatly accelerated rate of change in society. It arises from the superimposition of a new culture on an old one. It is culture shock in one's own society. But its impact is far worse" (*Future Shock*, 11). Such unbridled change bewilders and racks us. It may turn us neurotic! It upsets our 'durational expectancies' (42). It robs us of our peace and serenity. Our relationships with 'things, places, people, organizations, and ideas' 'become foreshortened, and telescoped in time' (45). A compressed 'transience' creeps in. (46) Happiness becomes alien to us, and love a mere pretence.

One of the worst offshoots of the current pattern of ill-planned progress is 'consumerism'. It is a morbid state in which nearly all people are crazy about consuming more and more luxurious and unnecessary items. Not even the monks nor the nuns of any religious sect seem to be liberated from this pernicious tendency. Man is enslaved by the glitter and irresistible charm exerted by novel commodities. Every virtue is sacrificed on the altar of enjoyment. Nothing matters but money and pleasurable articles. Toffler notes:

> The ocean of man-made physical objects that surrounds us is set within a larger ocean of natural objects. But increasingly, it is the technologically produced environment that matters for the individual. The texture of plastic or concrete, the iridescent glisten of an automobile under a streetlight, the staggering vision of a cityscape seen from the window of a jet – these are the intimate realities of his existence. Man-made things enter into and colour his consciousness. Their number is expanding with explosive force, both absolutely and relative to the natural environment (*Future Shock*, 51-52).

The tricky advertisements by the astute manufacturers ensnare every susceptible soul into it. Our clear thinking is blurred and reason held prisoner. Like asses we are led by the ears or in Russell's phrase, 'like a rabbit fascinated by a snake', along the path of unnecessary consumption. The repeated affirmations of blustering models in advertisements on the great merits of trite articles have a hypnotic effect on the minds of children and women who fall easy victims to their appeal to the emotion. This psychological manipulation, of the weak-willed and the ignorant members of our society, has far-reaching effects. Those preyed on are brain-washed. They soon lose their interest in the world of ideals, values and spirit, or rather in the transcendental world. The springs of an 'upward-rising urge' (Aristotle) and the impulse for a 'metaphysical quest' dry up all too soon. The result is the convergence of all the interests of these people to mere material things and the eventual loss of the moral and spiritual dimensions of their personalities. Consumerism tolls the knell of the human soul. Mobile phones have become potential weapons of evil and self-destruction. Speaking on the impact of mobile phones, Friedman warns: "There is plenty to worry about this in future, from kids being lured by online sexual predators through their cell phones, to employees spending too much time playing mindless phone games, to people using their phone cameras for all sorts of illicit activities" (*The World is Flat,* 170).

The current mode of progress makes us cheerless and disillusioned. It frays our nerves and makes us empty vessels. It adds gloss and lustre only to the outer surface, but leaves the inner world unattended and sickly. Consciously or unconsciously, we have become more callous and selfish. Progress has made life a never-ending pursuit of pleasure. Newly-wedded couples yearn to prolong as long as possible their honeymoon period in quenching their carnal appetites. If unexpected pregnancies knock at the door, the couples hate them, for they harbinger the end of their pleasure trip of life. The ensuing disillusionment does not embolden them welcome the births of their progeny. Such children turn psychologically 'unwanted' children. They are thought of as burdens and kill-joys. Often their births are welcomed not with jubilant smiles, but with bleak frowns. This attitude when questioned by their pricking conscience makes them relent and they strike a compromise. They are forced to introspect in the light of the traditional wisdom of humanity and rethink to accommodate the current reality. Hence they dam up the flow of hatred and slowly release the pent up emotion of love towards the children. This sudden change causes a split in their personality, and there might be a struggle between hatred and love for a while, a period of love followed by a period of hatred. In the case of some people hatred assumes greater power and the gentle love will be smothered. The outburst of hatred then turns destructive. It might claim the lives of children, and the frustration stemming from guilt feeling might lead them to self destruction as well. This could be one of the major reasons for the alarming rates of suicides and infanticides in our country even as we brag of progress. But there is another diabolic option - abortion. There are many in whose case this most inhuman act is resorted to with a smile. Not few are the doctors who fatten their purses from this horrid deed. It is high time we subjected ourselves and the prevailing type of progress to a thorough scrutiny. "An unexamined life is not worth living," avers Socrates. If we are lethargic and complacent, we shall be courting disaster, and we will be irredeemably lost. Why should we let this 'ugly and sinful shadow' (Diogenes) of the benighted but much-vaunted progress fall on us?

Having witnessed the monstrous dance of destruction by the child of scientific progress - atom bomb - at Hiroshima and Nagasaki, we still swagger about the more destructive ones -hydrogen bombs, neutron bombs, etc - but only with a shudder deep in our being. The sensitive ones realize that we are precariously perched atop a volcano which might burst at any moment from now. Scientific progress has strewn before us highly destructive weapons, as though they were great gifts. When we are fully bereft of reason we will use them on the global level and bring upon ourselves the retribution due to our own evil and folly. Radhakrishnan aptly observes; "Science, with its new prospect of a possible liquidation of the world by man's own wanton interference in nature, reminds us of the warning that the wages of sin is death" (*Recovery of Faith,* 1).

The looming menace of terrorism, with its growing tentacle-grip on the world and triggered by real or imaginary reasons, hanging overhead like the sword of Damocles, has become the worst bane on progress today. It has now added to the numerous existing woes in the globalized era. Through terrorism, any level of material progress achieved can be erased within seconds by an insidious, heavily armed attack. To attack is easy. Any imbecile can do it. But the true human merit and soul-force lie in refraining from it. Only the really great can desist from violence. Terrorism is a retrogressive step to our old crude, unfeeling and uncouth self from which we have over time progressed to a more refined self. It is the re-enactment of the Huns' invasion in modern times. It is recklessly impulsive and against the spirit of man. No God can ever watch their bloodshed and cruelty without wrath and reaction. The most treacherous form of terrorism, born of some out-dated religious cues and the insensible desire to re-establish some religious utopia of old, is far from the true spirit of any religion. It is merely sectarian, anti-human and merely a fiendish form of sadism. It is but a yearning to return to the outward trappings of some religion. This guarantees peace to none. All religions had their nostalgic beginnings, and if all people wanted the same condition to be recaptured and re-established, then, there will be no end to war and barbarity in the world. The world then becomes a cauldron of demoniac turmoil. We must forget and sacrifice many things of the past and try to develop common bonds of friendship with all to forge ahead as a well-knit human community. Only in this lies our hope for a better future for mankind. That will be real progress and humanity is at the heart every great religion.

Conclusion

We cannot run away from the current progress and its pace, but can modify it with our life-giving insights to elevate it onto a nobler plane, provided we are ready to put in the required level of concerted effort. True progress should consider all the dimensions of the human personality and develop them simultaneously and harmoniously. The material and the spiritual, the ideal and the pragmatic should be properly fused. No doubt, it should bring about material progress but spiritual matters should not be relegated to the background. Global peace and security should be ensured. Psychic and environmental pollution should be minimized. No wanton harm to nature should occur. Exploitation of all sorts and injustice should be fought against. Humanity should be upheld as the unifying principle. But, progress, as it is, now rears us like broiler chickens only to be slaughtered soon. Unless we apply the sudden brakes of prudence, with all our might, this bullet train of progress will either end us up with a terrible collision or get derailed mangling us to pieces. Should we wait smugly for such a nightmarish thing to happen, or hasten to avert the catastrophe? We must either act in time, or perish forever! The choice is ours, as to whether we should expedite the arrival of the Armageddon or strain every nerve to catapult it into a distant future!

References

1. Radhakrishnan S., *Indian Religions* (1988), New Delhi: Orient Paperbacks.
2. Radhakrishnan S., *An Idealist View of Life* (2000), New Delhi: Harper Collins Publishers India Pvt. Ltd.
3. Paul Brunton, *The Spiritual Crisis of Man* (1988), New Delhi: B. I. Publications Pvt. Ltd
3. Matthew Arnold, *Scholar Gypsy,* and *Dover Beach,* taken from 'Chaucer to Housman' (1990), (Ed.), C. T. Thomas, Madras: B. I. Publications Pvt. Ltd.
4. Bertrand Russell, *New Hopes for a Changing World,* (1975).
6. Alvin Toffler, *Future Shock* (1970), New York: Bantam Books.
7. Thomas Friedman, *The World is Flat: A Brief History of the Globalized World in the 21st Century* (2005), New Delhi: Penguin Books India Pvt. Ltd
8. Radhakrishnan. S, *Recovery of Faith* (1980), New Delhi: Jaika Books.